# DOROTHY STOPFORD PRICE

# DOROTHY STOPFORD PRICE

## *Rebel Doctor*

Anne Mac Lellan

IRISH ACADEMIC PRESS

First published in 2014 by Irish Academic Press
8 Chapel Lane,
Sallins,
Co. Kildare,
Ireland

This edition © 2014 Anne Mac Lellan

www.iap.ie

British Library Cataloguing in Publication Data
An entry can be found on request

ISBN 978 0 7165 3237 8 (paper)
ISBN 978 0 7165 3236 1 (cloth)
ISBN 978 0 7165 3240 8 (PDF)
ISBN 978 0 7165 3250 7 (Epub)
ISBN 978 0 7165 3251 4 (Mobi)

Library of Congress Cataloging-in-Publication Data
An entry can be found on request

Printed in Ireland by SPRINT-print Ltd

# CONTENTS

# ACKNOWLEDGEMENTS

In writing this biography, I have accumulated many debts. In particular, I would like to thank Dr Clara Cullen for reading drafts of this book and making many useful suggestions. Clara's work on Dorothy's cousin, Elsie Henry, has been an anchor as I tried to navigate my way through the various Stopford relations (and there were many of them!). Her elegant editing of Elsie's diaries, published as *The World Upturning: Elsie Henry's Wartime Diaries, 1913-1919* has been an inspiration.

Dorothy's great-niece, Sandra Lefroy, has patiently and generously answered many questions, welcomed me into her home, provided samples of Dorothy's handwriting and photographs and, along with her sister Penny, read drafts of the book.

Alice Mauger has read and commented on drafts of this book (and its endnotes!) with her customary meticulous precision. For her keen eye and her constant support, I say a heartfelt thanks.

I am very grateful to Greta Jones, Emerita Professor of Social and Intellectual History at the University of Ulster for reading this biography and writing the foreword.

Thanks to Dr Ida Milne for supplying a copy of the group photograph from which the image of Dorothy Stopford Price featured on the front cover was extracted. Her grand-uncle Dr Willie Elmes, a surgeon, is pictured in the original photograph which was taken in Meath Street Hospital, Dublin, in 1920.

I owe an enormous debt of gratitude to the Centre for the History of Medicine in Ireland in University College Dublin's School of History and Archives. I would especially like to thank Dr Catherine Cox, Dr Lindsey Earner-Byrne and Dr Susannah Riordan for their help and support over the years. I would like to take this opportunity to thank the Wellcome Trust for funding some of the research which underpins this book. In UCD's School of Medicine and Medical Sciences, Conor Ward, Professor Emeritus of Paediatrics and Brendan Kelly, Associate Clinical Professor of Psychiatry, were encouraging readers of drafts of this book.

My first introduction to the work of Dorothy Stopford Price was through an essay written by Dr Margaret Ó hÓgartaigh about Dorothy's work in the 1930s. Margaret's enthusiasm for this project is gratefully acknowledged.

I would like to thank all my friends and colleagues who contributed to the *Growing Pains: Childhood Illness in Ireland 1750-1950* collection and who have been so encouraging about this project – Alice Mauger (my co-editor), Conor Ward, Gaye Ashford, Ian Miller, Ida Milne, Jean Walker, June Cooper, Phil Gorey, Laura Kelly and Susan Kelly.

Other friends and family have persevered with reading drafts – thanks to Joan, Sinead, Pat, Peter, Peggy and Fiona.

At Irish Academic Press, I would like to express my gratitude (once again!) to a wonderful team: Lisa Hyde, Conor Graham, Colin Eustace and their hardworking copy editor.

This book could not have been written without the expert assistance of numerous archivists and librarians: I am most grateful to the staff of the Bodleian Library in Oxford, Dublin Diocesan Archives, Irish Military Archives, Irish Red Cross, National Library of Ireland, National Archives of Ireland, Royal College of Physicians of Ireland Heritage Centre, Royal College of Surgeons in Ireland, Trinity College Dublin Manuscripts Room, University College Dublin Library and the Wellcome Trust Archives, London.

I must also acknowledge my debt to four books in particular: *Protestant Nationalists in Revolutionary Ireland: The Stopford Connection* by Leon Ó Broin; *Dorothy Price. An Account of Twenty Years' Fight against Tuberculosis in Ireland* by Liam Price; *The Price Notebooks* edited by Christiaan Corlett and Mairead Weaver and *Kathleen Lynn: Irishwoman, Patriot, Doctor* by Margaret Ó hÓgartaigh. Thanks to Gillian Leonard who generously gave me a precious copy of Liam's book.

A big thank you to all those – named and unnamed – who helped me research Dorothy's life and work.

Anne Mac Lellan, February 2014

# LIST OF PLATES

1. Dorothy Stopford's diary, 8 December 1910. Courtesy of Sandra Lefroy.

2. Dorothy Stopford, clinical clerk at Meath Street Hospital, Dublin, January 1920. Courtesy of Ida Milne.

3. Dorothy Stopford's graduation, Trinity College Dublin, April 1921. Reproduced by kind permission of the Board of Trinity College Dublin.

4. Christmas card (exterior) from Liam Deasy, Mountjoy Gaol, Dublin, to Dr Stopford, 1923. Courtesy of the National Library of Ireland.

5. Christmas card (interior) from Liam Deasy, Mountjoy Gaol, Dublin, to Dr Stopford, 1923. Courtesy of the National Library of Ireland.

6. First Research Licence granted to import BCG vaccine into Ireland, December 1936. Reproduced by kind permission of the Board of Trinity College Dublin.

7. Dorothy Price, undated. Courtesy of the National Library of Ireland.

8. Liam Price, undated. Courtesy of the National Library of Ireland.

9. Exterior of Dorothy Price's former home, 10 Fitzwilliam Place, Dublin.
   Courtesy of the Irish Medical Organisation. Photograph by Fiona Byrne, 2013.

10. Interior of Dorothy Price's former home, 10 Fitzwilliam Place, Dublin.
    Courtesy of the Irish Medical Organisation. Photograph by Fiona Byrne, 2013.

11. Drs Dorothy Price and Kathleen Lynn, St Ultan's Hospital, Dublin, April 1949.
    Reproduced by kind permission of the Royal College of Physicians of Ireland.

12. Tuberculin testing in a teacher training college. National BCG Committee annual report 1955 (SU/2/6). Reproduced by kind permission of the Royal College of Physicians of Ireland.

13. Student nurses are given BCG vaccine. National BCG Committee annual report 1958 (SU/2/9). Reproduced by kind permission of the Royal College of Physicians of Ireland.

# FOREWORD

*By Emerita Professor Greta Jones, Professor of Social & Intellectual History, University of Ulster*

This is the first full-length study of an important figure in the history of twentieth century Irish social and medical history. Dorothy Stopford Price was distinguished in many ways. A Protestant who became a fervent Irish nationalist and who took part in the struggles for Irish independence in the 1920s at the same time, she was a leading figure in the Irish medical community. She was one of the first generation of Irish women who made names for themselves in medicine. She became a key figure in the development of paediatrics in Ireland working in St Ultan's Children's Hospital. She was also an important contributor to the debate on the eradication of tuberculosis and is to be credited with being the key figure in promoting the use of BCG in the 1940s and 1950s, a measure for which she was , for a long time, the leading advocate in Ireland.

Her path was not always smooth. She came up against the pressures to expand Catholic influence in Irish medicine after independence and, because of that, and because there were limits to the advance of women in medicine in twentieth-century Ireland, Price experienced frustration in achieving her objectives. Nonetheless, she significantly changed the landscape of Irish medicine and public health.

Price can therefore be looked upon from many perspectives; as a first-wave feminist for whom networks of female friends and colleagues were crucial; as an innovative and combative controversialist in medicine whose interventions, though not always welcome, were significant; and as a patriot of the newly-independent state of Ireland who honestly and doggedly tried to improve social conditions.

Anne Mac Lellan is one of a new generation of Irish social and medical historians. This biography will prove to be one of the building blocks of an expanding discipline.

# PREFACE

My grandmother's younger sister was Dorothy Stopford Price. My sister Penny and I knew her as a loving and funny great-aunt, having then no understanding of the huge importance of her work or the skill and courage it involved. She never 'talked down' to children, treating us as equals, and consequently we trusted her implicitly – this trait was probably a huge factor in her success as a children's doctor. Although she used to tease us unmercifully, she was our great champion and (rightly or wrongly) always went out of her way to protect us if we had done something dreadful and were in trouble with the family 'authorities'.

Her husband, our great-uncle Liam, was extremely supportive and proud of Dorothy in her BCG campaign and pioneering work, at a time when female doctors had to fight to establish their position. She and her fellow female colleagues were really an extraordinary group of women, and their work in St Ultan's and elsewhere undoubtedly broke the mould and enabled others to follow in their footsteps. Liam's biography of Dorothy, written for private circulation, is a testament to the esteem in which he held her.

Noël Browne certainly got much of the credit for the implementation of the national programme against tuberculosis. I don't think Dorothy would have had a problem with this – her only motivation was to get the job done, and it didn't matter who did it as long as it was done properly. It is probably true to say that no-one of Dorothy's gender or persuasion would ever have been allowed credit or responsibility for anything on Archbishop McQuaid's watch, anyway.

It has been a privilege and a pleasure to liaise with Anne Mac Lellan in her careful research and preparation of this biography, and to see her developing such a sympathetic rapport with Dorothy as the work progressed. My sister and I are grateful to Anne for her courtesy and attention to detail, as well as for her obvious understanding of our remarkable great-aunt.

Sandra Lefroy, Killaloe

# PART I

# THE
# STOPFORD YEARS

CHAPTER ONE

# OF GOD AND ASCLEPIUS: THE STOPFORD AND KENNEDY CLANS (1890–1916)

*We never mention Ireland*
*Oh that we never do*
*And thus the subjects left to us*
*Are most select and few*

Why attempt to stitch together the pieces of a life, long ended, into a garment that can still be read? Lengths of material are missing and the resulting patchwork will be a construct of available scraps, some of these of dubious veracity. The missing parts will tug at the edges of the stitching and the final shape will never resemble the original. But, the reason for making this attempt to resurrect the life of Dorothy Stopford Price is, simply, the richness of the available material. Sometimes luminous, shining with mischief, laughter, courage and eccentricity, sometimes of a duller worthier hue, the extant pieces of her life tell a tale of unexpected variety.

Dorothy lived through two world wars, the Spanish influenza pandemic, the 1916 Rising in Ireland, and the foundation of a new Irish state. She was brought up as a child of the British Empire, living in Dublin and, later, London. Her family were loyal to the British crown. The aftermath of the

Easter Rising led Dorothy to question her allegiances and she became a committed Irish nationalist, later a Republican. She was actively engaged in the War of Independence and the subsequent civil war in Ireland. The foundation of the Irish Free State, and its separation from Northern Ireland, was a huge disappointment to her and Dorothy subsequently ploughed her energies into medicine.

She became a paediatrician: her views were radical, her voice was often loud, and her work was occasionally mired in controversy. Nonetheless, she made a substantial contribution to the ending of the tuberculosis epidemic in Ireland. She is best known for her role in the introduction of the preventive *Bacille Calmette Guérin* (BCG) vaccine into Ireland. However, her championship of the diagnostic tuberculin test was equally, if not more, important. She crossed swords with the Catholic Archbishop of Dublin, John Charles McQuaid and lost: he put a stop to her attempt to found a national Anti-Tuberculosis league. Another controversial figure, Dr Noël Browne, is also entangled in her story. Often formidable in her determination, Dorothy was a loyal friend, and during her turbulent professional journey she merged the professional and the personal, becoming lifelong friends with many Irish paediatricians, physicians and surgeons as well as international medical experts, such as the Swedish Professor Arvid Wallgren and the German Jewish doctor and medical historian Walter Pagel.

Dorothy married Liam Price, a talented antiquarian as well as a district justice. Hill walking brought them together and climbing the 'Lug' – Lugnaquilla, the highest peak in Leinster – was a rite of passage for visitors to their country house in Wicklow. Their main residence was a spacious Georgian house in Dublin's Fitzwilliam Place but the poverty that marred the lives of so many of the citizens of the Irish capital was never far from Dorothy's mind.

To go back to the beginning: Eleanor Dorothy Stopford was born in Dublin, Ireland, on 9 September 1890. She was introduced to the world as Dorothy.[2] With time, other affectionate names attached themselves: Dodo, Deora and Doctereen. Later, she took the surname of her husband, Liam Price, and throughout her professional life, was known as Dorothy Price.

Her background was conservative with an occasional streak of eccentricity enlivening the family tree. Dorothy's father, Jemmett, came from a long line of Church of Ireland clerics. His father was the Archdeacon of Meath, his grandfather had been Bishop of Meath. The family lived outside the monastic town of Kells in beautiful green rolling countryside largely populated by Catholics. In the town itself, a round tower, high crosses, and the remains of an early stone church all bear witness to a settlement probably founded in the sixth century by St Columba. The famous *Book of Kells* described in the Annals of Ulster as the 'chief treasure of the western world' may have been partly compiled there.[3] Living in this landscape, with its iconic Catholic associations, did not deter the gallant Archdeacon from attempting to convert his neighbours to the Protestant faith with its overtones of conquest and colonialism. Pragmatically, he combined an opportunity to proselytise with an opportunity to further the religious education of his nine children by inducing them to write out religious texts on pieces of card and scatter them by the road in the hopes of converting any passing Catholics.[4] The success or failure of this naive enterprise is not recorded. Conversions are unlikely to have accrued. Moreover, its effect on the children was of dubious merit. Although Jemmett, Dorothy's father, remained a regular 'church-goer' throughout his life, he did not become a 'convinced churchman, or even a religious man at all'.[5]

Dorothy's mother, Constance Kennedy, was also a Protestant. Her father was Dr Evory Kennedy, a Master of the Rotunda Lying-in Hospital, Dublin, from 1833 to 1840. He was an active and outspoken Master, opening the first gynaecological unit in the hospital for the 'humane and beneficial purposes of alleviating the suffering of patients labouring under the diseases peculiar to women'.[6] He also founded the Dublin Obstetrical Society. Later, as a past Master, he did not endear himself to the board of the hospital when he claimed that the Rotunda Hospital – and, by extension all maternity hospitals – by its very nature was dangerous to women's health. Dr Kennedy elaborated somewhat drily that as Bartholomew Mosse, the founder of the hospital, had not possessed the 'power of divination' he could not have foreseen that the 'congregation of a number of lying-in women under the same roof engenders and spreads among them a disease [puerperal fever], *sui generis*, and of the most fatal character'.[7] His plain speaking on matters medical was to be inherited by his grand-daughter Dorothy.

There were other genetically- or culturally-engendered traits that Dorothy would also inherit, and later, reject. Both Constance and Jemmett were of Anglo-Irish stock. This was a strange chimerical 'clan', often perceived in England as Irish and, in Ireland, as English. The descendants of English settlers in Ireland, their allegiance was to the British crown and they usually looked to London rather than Dublin as their social and cultural capital. The Anglo-Irish spawned a disproportionate number of playwrights, poets, satirists, scientists, soldiers, doctors, and landowners.[8] The Protestant clergy in Ireland was peopled by them. The Anglo-Irish were usually middle or upper class, educated and well-to-do. Dorothy's Stopford ancestors had come to Ireland with the Cromwellian armies and settled on confiscated lands. They had prospered and could boast an Admiral of the British Navy and members of the British peerage as well as senior clergy among their ranks. Her Kennedy ancestors had settled in Ulster, having come over from Scotland in the reign of King James I. Some of the family moved to the south of Ireland, including clergy, land agents and doctors among their number.

A few of the Anglo-Irish inclined towards Home Rule in Ireland and a very few were interested in establishing an independent Irish state. Within Dorothy's family, there was a diversity of political opinion, with the majority tending to believe that Ireland would be best served if it was ruled by England. There were two notable exceptions: Jemmett's historian sister Alice (Aunt Alice to Dorothy and her siblings and cousins) embodied a mixture of high-minded cultural nationalism and high-flown rhetoric, along with a penchant for pamphleteering. Jemmett's brother, Edward (Uncle Ned) was, along with Aunt Alice, an ardent proponent of Home Rule. Ned might even have contested an Irish constituency if his health had not failed. However, Dorothy's parents, Jemmett and Constance, were content with the political *status quo*. Constance's mother's family never veered towards Irish nationalism. The Kennedys 'saw no reason for trying to change the fundamentals of their society, just adorning with their looks and their wit that state of life to which it had pleased God to call them'.[9]

Dorothy's older sister Edie described herself and her siblings as 'Irish Protestant Ascendancy with both parents coming from sound settler stock'. Edie's insightful unpublished memoir which is to be found in the National Library of Ireland, in Dublin, provides a unique glimpse of the life of Jemmett and Constance and their four children: Alice (b.1888), Edith, known as Edie (b.1889), Dorothy (b.1890) and Robert (b.1895).[10] Jemmett was a senior civil servant, an accountant in the Church Temporalities Association and with the Irish Land Commission and a 'firm supporter of the British connection'. They lived in Wyvern, Bushy Park, Dublin. Edie later suggested that her father possibly 'had some share in that latent streak of unconventionality which has cropped up from time to time in our branch of the Stopfords'.[11]

Constance read family prayers and saw to the children's religious education. Dorothy and her siblings were brought up in the 'true Irish Protestant social and cultural tradition'.[12] They attended Church regularly with their governess or parents. They 'consorted only with other little Protestants, the children of our parent's friends'.[13] There were worries that the Stopford children would pick up the Irish brogue, so their governesses came from England and their 'children's maids' were French-speaking Swiss girls. The Stopfords learned English rather than Irish history and grew up as 'devoted little West Britons'.[14]

Dorothy's earliest memories include walking slowly down a straight flight of stairs on summer holidays in a house hired in Howth, a seaside suburb of Dublin. Her heart failed her and she sat down until she was found and 'borne in triumph' into the sitting room to be admired. It was the first time she had worn long stockings – black ribbed ones – 'an awe-inspiring moment' aged about four. She also remembered, at the age of five, being spanked twice solemnly by her father. The fact remained although the offence was forgotten, she recalled, while musing that she had no doubt that it was a just punishment. She wrote that she and her siblings were never afraid to tell the truth although they didn't always do so. The little Stopfords were afraid only of the possibility of robbers lurking under the bed – a fear Dorothy attributed to stories told by the maids.[15]

As the British Empire began to enter its final death throes, the young Dorothy and her siblings were made aware of events abroad. During the Boer War (1899–1902), Dorothy and her sisters and brother wore buttons in the lapels of their coats, sporting pictures of their favourite generals – Lord Frederick Roberts, Lord Horatio Kitchener and Sir Archibald Hunter. They built a fortress in their garden and called it 'Ladysmith' while their neighbours built 'Mafeking'. The Stopford children celebrated the relief of the real Mafeking by dancing and cheering around a bonfire in their neighbour's garden. The background booing of the local population barely impinged, according to Edie, who, nonetheless, recalled this detail years later. In London, Aunt Alice's perspective on the war differed from that of Jemmett and Constance. According to historian R.B. McDowell, she approached colonial problems with the 'preconceptions of an English radical and an Irish nationalist'.[16]

When Queen Victoria died in 1901, the three sisters, aged eleven, twelve and thirteen, were put into 'black mourning coats and skirts' on the day of her funeral while the blinds were drawn in their home. Edie wryly notes that she was 'moved' to compose an elegy which began 'Our hope, our strength has passed away. Oh England, weep for her'. Dorothy and her brother and sisters were unaware of any 'Irish problem' – as far as they knew, English rule in Ireland was 'perfect'. The young Stopfords were class conscious, aware of their position in society, believing that Protestants were naturally upper class and Catholics lower class. Edie recalls her astonishment, at about the age of 10 years, when she visited London and learned that the ragged barefoot women and children walking the streets and sitting in doorways were Protestant. It seemed to her 'almost to contradict a law of nature'. The Stopford children, were 'in spite of snobbery', devoted to their three Roman Catholic maids and to their gardener, all of whom were with the family for many years.[17]

In 1902, the foundations of their privileged early life were shaken when their father, Jemmett, died suddenly of typhoid. Edie suggested that over-work contributed to his death: 'My father's work for the Land Commission in an era of great land reforms meant that he bore an unusually heavy official burden, was grossly overworked, and died prematurely … at the age of fifty-three.'[18] Jemmett had also enjoyed life and had lived up to his means with the result that there was little money left. Constance had to sell Wyvern, the family home. She moved, with the children, to England where she had two sisters and a brother-in-law. Jemmett's sister, Aunt Alice, lived there also. Constance enjoyed a very strong bond with all of her children, who seemed to have adored her and confided in her. She was '…in politics, as in all else, completely loyal to those near and dear to her, whatever their principles'.[19] In London, 12-year-old Dorothy, 13-year-old Edie and 7-year-old Robert attended St Paul's School in Hammersmith on foundation scholarships. A governess was employed for the oldest daughter, Alice, who, at 14 years of age, was considered almost grown up and was destined for domesticity.[20] At school, the Stopford children were conventional – 'neither politically minded nor politically educated, receiving with equal boredom our Aunt Alice's expositions of Irish nationalism and our teachers' occasional outbursts on Women's Suffrage, then becoming a burning question'.[21]

Dorothy prospered in the progressive St Paul's School. The High Mistress, Frances Gray, retained a 'very high opinion of her'. She noted that Dorothy 'from her family connections' had 'received an education more valuable than any she could have gained at school, and it has given her a wider outlook and a variety of interest which have helped in the development of her mental powers'. Even allowing for the fact that Ms Gray was writing a reference for Dorothy, her praise was unequivocal: 'I know very few young women of her age who are gifted with such good judgement as Miss Stopford invariably shows.'[22]

Dorothy's sister Edie was academically brilliant. In October 1908, Edie went to Newnham College in Cambridge, where she ceased to attend Church which 'at home had been compulsory and a trial' to her. She revelled in new friendships and interests such as women's suffrage. But at heart she was still conservative and she dismissed socialism as a fad, mainly because its exponents at Cambridge tended to wear 'arty and crafty clothes'.[23] Edie went on to earn a double first in English and a triple blue at games (hockey, tennis and cricket). Meanwhile, during Christmas 1909, the 19-year-old Dorothy put up her hair, later writing in her diary of how this symbol of womanhood inspired her with 'great ideas of dignity, of womanhood and behaviour'.[24]

Alice fulfilled her domestic destiny by getting engaged to Christopher Wordsworth. Christopher was the son of the Rector of St Peter's, Marlborough and a grand-nephew of the poet William Wordsworth. Christopher worked with his uncle Reginald Reeves, managing mines in India. Dorothy was delighted for Alice as Christopher was 'so nice and good and she and he love one another so very much and they are going to be married in November and go out to Bombay and be ever so happy together'. The romance, and the trip to India, also demanded delightful shopping excursions. Dorothy and Alice bought an entire wardrobe, including twenty-five pairs of gloves, twenty-four pairs of stockings, two pairs of boots and two pairs of shoes.[25] Although she was thrilled for Alice, Dorothy noted that there was a downside as the marriage was the 'first break in our family life'.

In 1910, Alice, now living in Bombay, became pregnant. It was decided that Dorothy and Christopher's sister, Susan Wordsworth, would sail to

7

India to support Alice. The voyage itself may have offered possibilities of marriage for the two young girls, according to Leon Ó Broin, who was of the opinion that marriage was never far from Dorothy's mind at this time. Certainly, she wrote in her diary that 'a perfect, almost mysterious and holy love must exist between the persons united, otherwise how could they be helpmeets to each other?'[26]

Dorothy and Susan had fun on board the ship, socialising and getting to know their fellow passengers. When the captain opened up the interior of the ship to the passengers, they were pleased to find the storerooms, pantry and kitchens 'clean and quite inviting'. Dorothy was interested, too, to see the Marconi (wireless) operator at work.[27] As for socialising, she worried about her appearance, deciding she looked best at night when her hair was down and she was in her night gown and that simple clothes suited her best.

> My upper lip is a source of annoyance to me. It starts from the tip of my nose, and goes in a rounded curve until it meets my lower one; but it does not meet it fairly. It protrudes and give me a small-chinned air. My nose is also very weak and rather cocked out. It is so small and, though straight, the nostrils are uninteresting and flat, joining my cheeks at the side in a flat insensitive way. My hair is wavy and pretty enough in its way, but the colour is not remarkable, and I don't do it very well, I know. My eyes are the only good feature I have, but I hide behind glasses.[28]

These frivolous concerns faded into triviality when, en route to India, a devastating cable informed Dorothy and Susan that Christopher had died of enteric fever, while another cable brought more welcome news: Alice had safely given birth to a daughter, Mary. Dorothy and Susan spent the next day, Thursday, 8 December 1910, quietly on the deck, writing and avoiding people.[29] Married at 21 years of age, Alice was widowed at 22. Christopher's brother, Gordon, met Dorothy and Susan at the quay in Bombay. He reassured them that Alice was well and they went directly to her flat. Their new niece was a 'jolly little thing, rather long and thin with an awfully nice face. She is very like Christopher'. Ten days later, Dorothy bathed Mary and began to fancy herself a dab hand at handling babies.[30] Dorothy and Susan stayed for a month in India and helped Alice bring baby Mary back to England. Later, Dorothy, who was addicted to pranks and jokes and didn't know when to call a halt, used to tease her niece Mary that she was born black, in India, and that they had had to tie her to the back of the ship and haul her through the water for the colour to wash off.[31] This was one of a number of running jokes that continued to resurface until Mary was in her early teens.

Back in England, Alice had to make a life for herself and little Mary, while Dorothy had to make decisions about her own future. Perhaps surprisingly, Dorothy did not follow Edie to college. Instead, Dorothy was pulled between two careers: social work and art. She passed the entrance exams into Regent Street Polytechnic and into the Royal College of Art. She spent long days in museums and galleries, sketching and studying but, in the end, she settled for social work. She went to work with the Charitable Organisation Society in the hopes of becoming an almoner (the forerunner of today's social workers) in a London hospital. Aunt Alice helped by inviting important social workers to dinner to meet her.[32] Meanwhile, Edie left college and got a job in the Labour Department of the Board of Trade (later the Ministry of Labour), living until 1914 with her family and then, for two years with Aunt Alice. Edie's new friends were progressive, particularly about Home Rule.

Aunt Alice, too, had come to support Home Rule. In 1877, she had married the historian John Richard Green and begun to help him with his work. After his death in 1883, she continued to edit his work and to write histories. She was left financially secure and moved to Kensington Square in London where she employed a cook, butler and maid and began to cultivate a wide circle of acquaintance. Aunt Alice was a 'woman of vitality and charm ... an intelligent woman, during most of her life devoted to intellectual pursuits, she was also a woman of strong feeling'.[33] During the thirty-four years she lived in London, Aunt Alice got up at 5 a.m., to research, study and write. 'Then the door opened to parties, and intellectual exchange with scholars, writers, politicians and social reformers', according to Máire Comerford, who later became Aunt Alice's secretary in Ireland.[34]

Guests at Aunt Alice's home included the lawyer John Francis Taylor, the Protestant nationalist Douglas Hyde, a founder of the Gaelic League, who later became the first president of Ireland, and the civil servant Eoin MacNeill, another Gaelic League founder and a leader of the Irish Volunteers. Aunt Alice began to write Irish history including *The Making of*

*Ireland and its Undoing* in 1908. She was also interested in the colonial situation in Africa and was friends with Edward Morel and Roger Casement of the Congo Reform Association. Aunt Alice collaborated with Casement, who was a nationalist, on various Irish projects.[35] Edie recalls meeting Roger Casement, Robert Barton, Robert Lynd, the poet Padraig Colum, Lord Monteagle and his daughter Mary Spring Rice, and Allesbrook Simon at social gatherings in Aunt Alice's home. The writer George Russell (AE) was also a friend of Aunt Alice's, as was Robert Barton's cousin, Erskine Childers.[36]

In her diary, Dorothy commented on suffrage and the unemployed rather than the intricacies of Irish politics. She was disapproving of the more extreme suffragette initiatives, condemning shouting in parliament as 'foolish and undignified'.[37] She seems to have got on well with Aunt Alice who could occasionally be moody. Aunt Alice gave dances for her nieces and chaperoned them to social events. She also gave them presents such as a clasp for an evening gown and a dress which Dorothy described as a 'great excitement'. It was a grey *crepe-de-chine* empire gown with a long train. Dorothy adorned it with bright red ribbon and Aunt Alice bought her some red carnations. In turn, Dorothy would help her aunt with her coiffure, 'rubbing and massing her hair so as to make it nice and curly'. Dorothy's interest in clothes continued: she was delighted with a pink Liberty silk dress sent to her by her cousin Violet Kennedy.[38] These early rhapsodies about clothes would have surprised those who knew Dorothy in later years when, in her enthusiasm about her medical work, she lost interest in her appearance and had to be reminded to wear a hat or adorn an outfit.

Extended family was extremely important to Dorothy – cousins, aunts and uncles formed a comforting backdrop, a network of connections that spanned the Irish Sea. She was particularly close to her Aunt Alice and Uncle Ned and to her cousin Elsie Henry.[39] When he visited London, Dorothy liked to 'jabber' with her cousin Charlie Dickinson at Aunt Alice's. Dorothy and Edie continued to visit Ireland from time to time and they attended Irish dancing classes at Mary Spring Rice's.[40]

Although Dorothy had little interest, Aunt Alice and other high nationalists were encouraged about England's plans for Ireland's future. In 1912, it seemed that Home Rule for Ireland was inevitable. Ulster Unionists were, however, formidable opponents of the proposition and a separatist solution was posited. The Irish Volunteer movement, a nationalist response to the Ulster Volunteer movement, was founded in November 1913 by Aunt Alice's associates Eoin MacNeill, Bulmer Hobson and Michael Rahilly (known as the O'Rahilly).[41] The Ulster Volunteers began to arm themselves, and, in response, the Irish Volunteers began to discuss the possibility of acquiring arms. Edie became aware of a subscription list for buying arms for the latter group. She also remembers a number of suspicious wooden packing cases stowed in a back room of Aunt Alice's house in London which may have contained arms.[42]

Events became even more exciting in the spring and summer of 1914 when Aunt Alice helped to plan the running of guns into Ireland. At this time, Dorothy's brother Robert, who was in his final term at St Paul's school, was staying with Aunt Alice in her house at 36 Grosvenor Road, Westminster. All of the young Stopfords, including Dorothy, must have known what was afoot. It was not just Aunt Alice who was involved – Dorothy's friend Mary Spring Rice was also one of the group of plotters. Roger Casement was a frequent visitor to Aunt Alice's house and 'impressive with his beard and sparking eyes'. Dorothy's brother Robert had become keenly interested in the Home Rule question and the 'formation of the volunteers as a counter measure to the Ulster Volunteers. In fact, I asked my Aunt how I could best give my treasured air-gun to the Volunteers to help with their training.' At his aunt's urging, he presented Casement with the gun.[43] Robert noted how Aunt Alice played a real part in keeping Irish developments to the fore with English liberal politicians such as Lord Haldane, Herbert Samuel and Sir Edward Grey.

Robert went to live with his mother, Constance, who had evidently been away but had returned to London and taken a flat in South Kensington. Then, on 21 March 1914, he was summoned to an 'interesting' dinner party in Aunt Alice's house. The party included 'a certain Professor Schiemann, who was known to be one of the Kaiser's personal advisers on foreign affairs and to have been sent by him to London and Belfast to report on the effect which the Ulster situation would have on the British Government in the event of war breaking out'. Lord Haldane and about eight people, including Wickham Steed, the foreign editor of *The Times* and Madame Rose, the Vienna correspondent of the *Morning Post*, were there. Aunt Alice had invited more men than women, something she often did, Robert noted. The general opinion was that the Liberal Government would not be able to persevere with the Home Rule Bill. Wickham Steed remarked to Aunt Alice that she might be sure that a full report of the evening would be going to Berlin by the next German diplomatic bag.[44]

Germany, with its anti-British stance, was the most likely place for the Irish to seek succour. Roger Casement was alive to the possibilities. In July 1914, Aunt Alice encouraged and part-funded a gun-running expedition which sourced the guns in Germany. The group who organised the gun-running were, by and large, 'Anglo-Irish, liberal Protestant, Home Rulers, and of the upper and professional classes. Mrs Stopford Green [Aunt Alice] was the chairman of the Anglo-Irish centre in London.'[45] This group also included another Stopford connection – Alice Young. It has been suggested that the committee saw the gun-running as a symbolic gesture rather than an attempt to procure arms for use.[46] Erskine Childers offered the use of his yacht, the *Asgard*, to bring the arms back to Ireland. He wrote to Geoffrey Young, a Stopford cousin (Alice Young's son), to ask him if he would like to join the venture but was turned down.[47] In the end, the *Asgard* was crewed by Erskine, his wife Molly, Mary Spring Rice,[48] Gordon Shephard and two fishermen who had not been informed of the purpose of the trip. Aunt Alice suggested to 19-year-old Robert that he might wish to join the party on the *Asgard*, stipulating that he must not tell his mother. Robert turned down the invitation and later recalled that, with one exception, he never had to make such a 'heart-rending' decision:

> Apart from my Irish enthusiasm, what boy would not have been thrilled at the prospect of gun-running on the high seas! But I was leaving for Germany in a few days and could not face the prospect of my mother's consternation if I failed to turn up there and – to all intents and purposes – disappeared off the face of the earth for two or three weeks.[49]

Robert dutifully went to stay with a family in Heidelberg in order to learn German. He left Germany on 25 July 1914 when 'everything was still quiet, though my host (the headmaster of the Oberrealschule there) had shaken his head very much when we got the news of the Sarajevo murders and expressed his fears of the repercussions'.[50]

Dorothy's erstwhile dancing companion, Mary Spring Rice, sent a postcard to her. Posted on the Isle of Wight, Mary confided in Dorothy that they were having 'quite a good time' with the exception of the first day and a half when she felt 'extremely seasick.' She continued: 'Then a grand turn up from Land's End to the needles with the wind behind us and every stitch of canvas set. We sail on today eastwards perhaps to the Dutch coast. I expect you are having a very interesting time in Belfast.'[51]

In all, some 1,500 rifles and 45,000 rounds of ammunition were landed safely at Howth, on 26 July 1914, and, later in August, at Kilcoole, County Wicklow.[52] Erskine Childer's yacht, the *Asgard*, brought the consignment that was landed at Howth and Aunt Alice went to Dublin to greet the gun-runners. Although Aunt Alice and others in the group may have seen the gesture as symbolic, the guns were the harbinger of real violence. Later that day, British soldiers killed three civilians and wounded others on Bachelor's Walk, in Dublin.[53]

The following month, Aunt Alice and Dorothy stayed with Aunt Alice's friend F.J. Bigger[54] in Belfast, Northern Ireland, and watched the Twelfth of July celebrations. Dorothy recorded that the procession was 'most orderly and the big drums are grand'.[55] Meanwhile, world events began to overshadow the Irish situation. Robert's German host had been correct in his gloomy assumptions of the effect of the assassination of Archduke Ferdinand, of the Austro-Hungarian Empire, in June 1914, for, by August, the world was at war. British priorities immediately shifted – Home Rule for Ireland was no longer of primary importance. The war was all. The Irish Volunteers split, with the majority supporting John Redmond's call to support the war and a minority, led by Eoin MacNeill, opposing it.

The war brought little change to Dorothy's routine; she continued to work for the Charitable Organisation Society, while Edie also continued to work. Alice and Constance looked after Mary. However, there was an immediate impact of the outbreak of hostilities on the only male member of the family. Dorothy's brother Robert had been due to go to Cambridge University to study economics. Instead, on 11 November 1914, he left Charing Cross at 7.50 p.m. to join an Anglo-Belgian (Quaker) ambulance unit. Their immediate destination was Dunkirk where they established field dressing stations. Robert worked as an orderly tending to the large number of wounded who arrived on long trains of cattle trucks. The wounds were horrific – often gangrenous.[56] Constance, Dorothy, Elsie Henry, Aunt Alice and Lady Alice Young saw him off. Elsie Henry wrote poignantly in her diary about 'The dark station and the crowds in uniform with Red X, the kit and stretchers like the dim confusion of a dream.'[57] By Christmas,

Robert was well established, enjoying a 'Royal feast' on Christmas day with two huge turkeys, plum puddings, beers, wine, chocolates and preserved fruit. He thanked Dorothy and Constance and all the family for the gifts of chocolates, socks, hankies and the mittens which Constance had sent and which he loved to wear all day long as 'they alone save me from frost bite this bitter cold weather'.[58] In 1915, he was transferred to Ypres where he helped moved sick and injured people from the town to the hospital.[59] In 1916, he would join the army and serve with the Army Service Corps in Salonika and Egypt. Other cousins of Dorothy's joined the war effort: Edward Brunton (Ted), a newly-qualified doctor, joined the Royal Army Medical Corps; Henry Stopford Brunton 'Top' was in a Canadian regiment which later went to France; George Jemmett Stopford was in the Royal Flying Corps. Another cousin, Bob Venables, who was in Germany with his family when war broke out, was interned in a camp near Berlin until late 1917. An uncle, Colonel James Stopford (father of George) was in the Duke of Cornwall's light infantry. Elsie Henry became quartermaster of the Sphagnum Moss Depot in the Royal College of Science in Dublin.[60]

Although Aunt Alice's group had sourced guns in Germany, she was distressed at the 'pro-German tendency' in Ireland. According to Elsie Henry, Aunt Alice's 'line is perfectly clear, she has always worked for Home Rule in Ireland, but from the very first she has said "foreign intervention would be disastrous"'.[61] Aunt Alice was somewhat encouraged by the appointment of Sir Matthew Nathan to the position of Under-Secretary to Ireland in 1914. She knew Sir Matthew, who was a former colonial governor, through her membership of the African Society. At the time of Sir Matthew's appointment to Ireland, government in Ireland essentially comprised a three-person Executive: a Lord Lieutenant, John Hamilton-Gordon, Marquis of Aberdeen and Temair, his Chief Secretary, Augustine Birrell, and the Under-Secretary. The Lord Lieutenant and the Chief Secretary were politicians, while the Under-Secretary was a civil servant. The role of the Lord Lieutenant was largely ceremonial. The Chief Secretary was in Cabinet and largely based in London, leaving Sir Matthew Nathan as 'the man at the wheel'.[62]

Aunt Alice introduced Sir Matthew to Dorothy, perhaps in the hopes of kindling in Dorothy some political interest in the fate of Ireland. While the introduction did not immediately have that effect, it did spark an intense relationship between Dorothy and Sir Matthew that endured for several years and which is partially captured in letters held in the Bodleian Library, Oxford, England and the National Library of Ireland. Who was this man who played such a significant role in Dorothy's life? Sir Matthew was born on 3 January 1862, in London. He studied engineering with the British military and served in Sierra Leone, Egypt, India and Burma. He rose to the rank of Lieutenant Colonel. In 1899, he was appointed acting governor of Sierra Leone, becoming governor of the Gold Coast (1900–4), Hong Kong (1904–7) and Natal (1907–9). Nathan Road, the main thoroughfare in Kowloon, Hong Kong, is named after him. In Hong Kong, he played a major role in improving transportation by rail.[63] He became secretary of the British Post Office in 1909, and of the Board of Inland Revenue in 1911.[64]

Sir Matthew's parents were Jewish. It has been suggested that Sir Matthew 'toyed briefly with the Anglican faith, only to reject it in favour of a professing but not particularly pious adherence to Judaism'.[65] In Ireland, he appeared to forge some links with the Irish Jewish community, and in late September 1915, he said: 'They of the Jewish faith lived in these islands in complete freedom, in the enjoyment of equal advantages with other fellow-countrymen'. He believed that 'a Jew born in Dublin was just as good an Irishman as any Catholic and Irishman'.[66]

Sir Matthew was a civil servant and he followed the lead set by the chief secretary Augustine Birrell in getting to know the Irish people and their concerns. He read extensively about Ireland and began to socialise with thinkers such as George Russell and Aunt Alice. Augustine Birrell was not an admirer of Aunt Alice, suggesting that she and Roger Casement suffered from the 'hierarchy of treason' but Sir Matthew was not deterred and often invited Aunt Alice to stay.[67] Sir Matthew was attractive to women: rakish, flirtatious and unattached. The British Prime Minister's daughter-in-law Cynthia succinctly described him as 'the famous charmer'.[68]

In 1915, Aunt Alice brought Dorothy with her to stay at the Under-Secretary's Lodge, in the Phoenix Park, Dublin, as guests of Sir Matthew. Dorothy jokingly wrote some doggerel entitled 'The Ballade of the Ogre'. The second verse ran:

In an official dwelling
Neath the eye of the police
Where dwelt a fearful ogre
Came a lady and her niece

Dorothy followed this up by suggesting that she and Aunt Alice were cowed by the 'ogre':

> They spoke in awed whispers
> They kept the law like fun
> But never did they venture
> To the den of the dread one
>
> But lo at last came a day
> When eager prying led
> These elves to the forbidden den
> Fearing they'd come out dead
>
> But he greeted them most kindly
> They'd scarce believe twas him
> Who was the stern-eyed governor
> Of Africa and Pekin
>
> They sat upon the table
> They climbed upon the chairs
> They bit at monster apples
> And discussed liberal peers
>
> We never mention Ireland
> Oh that we never do
> And thus the subjects left to us
> Are most select and few…
>
> Thus from the Castle-yard released
> How false the ogre's name
> In his coat decked by contrite hands
> Resplendent sword and flame
>
> The ogre's den did thus become
> The favourite spot of everyone.[69]

As the Ogre thawed, Dorothy got up to more mischief. She wrote a letter to her cousin Elsie while 'masquerading in Sir Matthew's best clothes': 'a privy councillor's coat, a Lieutenant Colonel's trousers, an insignia and cloak around my neck of the Grand Cross of St Michael and St George'.[70] It seemed that she and the famous charmer were getting along wonderfully well. There was a touch of hero worship in Dorothy's response to his charms – she was awed by his achievements and erudition as well as beguiled by his willingness to play along with her sillier whims.

All the while, even as she was dressing up, playing pranks and indulging in tomboy pursuits such as scaling a high wall in the Phoenix Park, Dorothy was thinking about enrolling as a medical student. Sir Matthew, twenty-eight years her senior, had a long and distinguished career as a soldier and administrator to his credit. Dorothy may not have been aware of Sir Matthew's reputation as a charming rogue when, inspired by high-minded sentiment, she expressed her youthful admiration of him in verse:

> Two spirits wandering o'er this goodly earth
> Met, and the better for meeting were
> Mingled in comradeship of joy and mirth
> For a brief moment mid the weight of war
>
> He wise and just and set in high estate
> She who has written this had nothing ever done
> But always could wholeheartedly admire,
> And share the great desire to be sincere.[71]

These latter verses were written in the Under-Secretary's Lodge and dated September 1915. She clearly gave them to Sir Matthew as they are among his papers in the Bodleian Library. In October, Dorothy wrote to him from London. She had spent most of the day typing up a 'eulogy' about him for the African Journal.[72] She teased him that she wanted to put in a few words about his work in West Khoker but wasn't allowed – presumably Aunt Alice forbade it – as he seemed to keep up 'the ogre side' there. The prospects of her coming over to Dublin again soon were 'remote', she said, finishing the letter to the backdrop of a short air-raid, with 'nothing to be seen, only the sound of the guns booming'.

Meanwhile, in Ireland, throughout 1915 and early 1916, Sir Matthew's chief Augustine Birrell was of the opinion that any attempt to suppress Sinn Féin would be reckless and foolish. Sir Matthew accepted his conviction that the only danger lay in isolated terrorist attack rather than a full-scale uprising.[73] Although work was worrying, with the possibilities of an uprising seeming to wax and wane, Sir Matthew found time to enjoy the company of another young woman, Mrs Constance Heppel-Marr. (Constance Heppel-Marr was the daughter of an assistant secretary at the Department of Agriculture and Technical Instruction, George Fletcher. In later years, she was Constance Spry, florist and author.) It seems the relationship was not platonic.[74] Dorothy was apparently oblivious. She continued to confide in Sir Matthew as she made up her mind to study medicine in Dublin.

NOTES

1. D. Stopford to Sir M. Nathan, 1916 (University of Oxford, Bodleian, Nathan papers, MS 204, folio 179). Doggerel written by D. Stopford.

2. Birth certificate, Eleanor Dorothy Stopford (TCD, Price papers, MS 7534 (1)).

3. http://www.tcd.ie/library/manuscripts/book-of-kells.php, (accessed 14 October 2013).

4. L. Ó Broin, *Protestant Nationalists in Revolutionary Ireland: The Stopford Connection* (Dublin: Gill & Macmillan, 1985), p.2.

5. E. Stopford unpublished memoirs, p.1 (NLI, MS 11,426 (1)).

6. For an account of Kennedy's Mastership, see O'D.T.D. Browne, *The Rotunda Hospital 1745–1945* (Edinburgh: E. & S. Livingstone, 1947).

7. T.P.C. Kirkpatrick and H. Jellet, *The Book of the Rotunda Hospital: an Illustrated History of the Dublin Lying-In Hospital* (London: Adlard and Son, Bartholomew Press, 1913), pp.170–1.

8. R. Huntford, *Shackleton* (London: Hodder & Stoughton, 1996), pp.4–5. The explorer Ernest Schackleton was Anglo-Irish.

9. E. Stopford unpublished memoirs, p.3 (NLI, MS 11,426 (1)).

10. Ibid., pp.1-4.

11. Ibid. She points to the role played by her grandfather, the Archdeacon, in the dis-establishment of the Irish Church. He was the only supporter of this measure among the Irish clergy. Aunt Alice was also unconventional turning 'her political coat completely'.

12. E. Stopford unpublished memoirs, p.3 (NLI, MS 11,426 (1)).

13. Ibid.

14. Ibid.

15. Silhouettes, hand-written notes by D. Stopford (NLI, MS 15341).

16. R.B. McDowell, *Alice Stopford Green: A Passionate Historian* (Dublin: Allen Figgis, 1967), p.62.

17. E. Stopford unpublished memoirs, p.4 (NLI, MS 11,426 (1)).

18. Ibid., p.2.

19. Ibid., p.3.

20. Interview, Sanda Lefroy, daughter of Mary Wordsworth and grand-niece of Dorothy, Edie and Robert. Dorothy's sister Alice (Stopford) Wordsworth was Sandra's grandmother.

21. E. Stopford unpublished memoirs, p.4 (NLI, MS 11,426 (1)).

22. Testimonial, 25 April 1911, Frances R. Gray, High Mistress, St Paul's Girls' School, Brook Green, Hammersmith, London (NLI, MS 15343).

23. E. Stopford unpublished memoirs, p.5 (NLI, MS 11,426 (1)).

24. Ó Broin, *Protestant Nationalists*, p.19.

25. Quotation from D. Stopford's 1910 diary, cited in Ó Broin, *Protestant Nationalists*, pp.50-3.

26. Ibid.

27. D. Stopford diary, 8 December 1910. Courtesy Sandra Lefroy.

28. Ó Broin, *Protestant Nationalists*, p.54.

29. D. Stopford diary, 8 December 1910. Courtesy Sandra Lefroy.

30. Ó Broin, *Protestant Nationalists*, p.54.

31. Interview with Sandra Lefroy.

32. Ó Broin, *Protestant Nationalists*, pp.19–20.

33. McDowell, *Alice Stopford Green*, preface.

34. F.X. Martin, *The Howth Gun-Running and the Kilcoole Gun-Running 1914: Recollection and Documents* (Dublin: Browne and Nolan, 1964), p.21. Máire Comerford was secretary to Alice Stopford Green from 1919 to 1922.

35. Sir Roger Casement (1864–1916) travelled to the Congo as British Consul. In 1904, he condemned the colonial policies of the Belgians. In 1913, he retired from the Foreign Office. He joined the Irish Volunteers and travelled to the US and Berlin seeking aid.

36. M.A. Hopkinson, 'Erskine Robert Childers', *Dictionary of Irish Biography* online, (accessed 29 September 2012). Robert Erskine Childers (1870–1922) served in the British army, later becoming a civil servant. He converted to Irish nationalism, at the instigation of his cousin Robert Barton (who became a close friend of Dorothy's). Childers was a successful novelist, having written *The Riddle of the Sands*, a spy thriller. Childer's yacht, the *Asgard*, was used in the 1914 gun running. In 1919, he relocated from London to Dublin.

37. Ó Broin, *Protestant Nationalists*, p.49.

38. Ibid., pp.20–53.

39. C. Cullen (ed.), *The World Upturning: Elsie Henry's Irish Wartime Diaries, 1913–1919* (Dublin: Irish Academic Press, 2013), p.235. Edward Adderly Stopford (Uncle Ned) lived in Dublin with his wife Mary Elizabeth (Aunt Lily). He was a tea merchant and worked with Sir Horace Plunkett in the Irish Agricultural Organisation Society.

40. E. Stopford unpublished memoirs, pp.10–11 (NLI, MS 11,426 (1)).

41. A. Jackson, *Ireland: 1798–1998* (Oxford: Blackwell, 1999), pp.162-9; C. Townshend, *Easter 1916: The Irish Rebellion* (London: Allen Lane, 2005), pp.410–1. Bulmer Hobson (1883–1969) was a Quaker and a member of the Gaelic League. He was vice-president of Sinn Féin 1907–10 and a member of the Supreme Council of the Irish Republican Brotherhood. Eoin MacNeill (1867–1945) was co-founder of the Irish League, founder and first Chief of Staff, Irish Volunteers 1913 and Professor of early Irish history at UCD; Michael Rahilly (1875–1916) was a member of the national executive of the Gaelic League, co-founder of the Irish Volunteers, joined the GPO garrison in Easter 1916 and was killed in Moore Street, Dublin on 28 April 1916.

42. E. Stopford unpublished memoirs, pp.1–4 (NLI, MS 11,426 (1)).

43. R. Stopford, Irish Affairs 1914, unpublished recollections (NLI, MS 21205 (2)).

44. Ibid.

45. Martin, *The Howth Gun-Running*, p.xix.

46. L. Piper, *The Tragedy of Erskine Childers: Dangerous Waters* (London: Hambledon and London, 2003), p.123.

47. R. Stopford, Irish Affairs 1914, unpublished recollections (NLI, MS 21205 (2)).

48. Mary Spring Rice (1880–1924) was the daughter of Thomas Spring Rice, the baron of Monteagle and a founder of the agricultural co-operative movement. They lived at Mount Trenchard in Foynes, County Limerick.

49. R. Stopford, Irish Affairs 1914, unpublished recollections (NLI, MS 21205 (2)).

50. Ibid.

51. M. Spring Rice to D. Stopford c/o Mrs Green, Ard Righ, Belfast, postcard, 11 July 1914, Isle of Wight (NLI, MS15131).

52. A second boat, the *Kelpie*, which landed at Kilcoole, County Wicklow, was crewed by Conor O'Brien and Diarmid Coffey among others.

53. Jackson, *Ireland*, p.168.

54. Francis Joseph Bigger (1863–1926) was an antiquarian and supporter of the Celtic Revival. He lived in Jordan's Castle, in Ardglass, County Down. Jordan's Castle was not a family seat: he purchased it in 1911 and renamed it Castle Shane. His city home was in Belfast.

55. D. Stopford to E. Henry, 14 July 1914, cited in Cullen, *The World Upturning*, p.41.

56. R. Stopford to L. Brunton, 15 November 1914, cited in Cullen, *The World Upturning*, pp.78–94.

57. Elsie Henry's diary, Wednesday, 11 November 1914, cited in Cullen, *The World Upturning*, p.77.

58. R. Stopford to C. Stopford (his mother), 26 December 1916, cited in Cullen, *The World Upturning*, pp.86–9.

59. R. Stopford to C. Stopford, 1 March 1915, cited in Cullen, *The World Upturning*, p.101.

60. Cullen, *The World Upturning*, p.1. Thomas Lauder Brunton, 1844–1916, and his wife Louisa Jane Stopford (d.1909) had four children: Alice Helen (Elsie), 1881–1956, James Stopford (Top), 1884–1944, Anne (Nance), 1888–1956, and Edward (Ted), 1890–1915. Bob Venables was the son of Gilbert Venables and Elizabeth Stopford.

61. Cullen, *The World Upturning*, p.84. Elsie Henry Diary, 14 December 1914.

62. L. Ó Broin, *Dublin Castle and the 1916 Rising* (Dublin: Helicon, 1966), pp.19–20. John Hamilton-Gordon, Marquis of Aberdeen and Temair, was Lord Lieutenant from 1905–1915; Ivor Churchill, Baron of Wimborne, was Lord Lieutenant from 1915 to 1918 (he was re-instated after being forced to resign following the 1916 Rising); Birrell was Chief Secretary from 1907–1916 while Nathan was Under-Secretary from 1914–1916. Birrell and Nathan resigned after the Rising.

63. Anon, 'Sir Matthew Nathan: Hong Kong's Jewish Governor', *Jewish Times* (Dec. 2009–Jan. 2010), http://www.jewishtimesasia.org/contributed-articles-topmenu-39/374-2010-10/1527-sir-matthew-nathan-hong-kongs-jewish-governor, (accessed 6 September 2013).

64. P.D. Wilson, 'Nathan, Sir Matthew (1862-1939)', *Australian Dictionary of Biography*, Volume 10, (Manchester: Manchester University Press, 1986); http://adb.anu.edu.au/biography/nathan-sir-matthew-7728, (accessed 6 September 2013).

65. A.P. Haydon, 'Sir Matthew Nathan: Ireland and Before', *Studia Hibernica* 15 (1975), p.164.

66. D. Keogh, *Jews in Twentieth-Century Ireland: Refugees, Anti-Semitism and the Holocaust* (Cork: Cork University Press, 1998), p.69.

67. Ó Broin, *Protestant Nationalists*, pp.65–6.

68. Ibid., p.128.

69. D. Stopford correspondence (University of Oxford, Bodleian, Nathan papers, MS 204, folio 177–8).

70. D. Stopford to E. Henry, 19 September 1915, cited in Cullen, *The World Upturning*, p.122.

71. D. Stopford, Under-Secretary's Lodge, Phoenix Park, Dublin, 19 September 1915 (University of Oxford, Bodleian, Nathan papers, MS 204, folio 179).

72. D. Stopford to Sir M. Nathan, 13 October 1915 (University of Oxford, Boldeian, Ms 204, folio 164).

73. C. Townshend, *Easter 1916: The Irish Rebellion* (London: Allen Lane, 2005), pp.144–5.

74. Ó Broin, *Protestant Nationalists*, p.70.

CHAPTER TWO

# 'Doing the Formula': The TCD Years (1916–1917)

*He is the same dear ogre. Yet he's been through scorching flame*
*And, more good to him accruing, He's nicer than the same.*[1]

In January 1916, at the age of 25, Dorothy plunged into the unknown: the work of a medical student would be emotionally and physically demanding as well as intellectually rigorous. The list of contagious killing diseases was long: gastro-enteritis, pneumonia, tuberculosis, diphtheria, polio, measles, influenza. The list of crippling diseases was equally long. Medical students might learn about palliation and prevention, (although effective vaccines had still not been developed for many diseases) but they would not be imbued with the ability to cure many of the conditions they would see. Germ theory had brought an understanding of the causes of infectious illnesses but antibiotics would not be available until Dorothy's career as a doctor was coming to an end. Hormones and vitamins were not fully elucidated. When she was a student, and for much of her professional life, syringes were made of glass or metal and had to be sterilised between uses. X-ray equipment was scarce in Ireland. Medicine was still scrabbling towards modernity.

There were other considerations. This was an unusual career for a woman. Women's entry into the academic world *per se* was still seen as a novelty and, occasionally, as a nuisance. However, a collective biography of more than 700 women who studied medicine in six colleges in Ireland from the 1880s to the 1920s has shown that the medical authorities, in general, accorded fair treatment to this first tranche of female students. Women attended the same lectures and sat the same examinations but, in some respects, they occupied a separate world to the male students, with separate dissecting rooms, ladies' rooms and their own societies.[2] In her chosen college, Trinity College Dublin (TCD), Dorothy would have to abide by different rules to the men, leaving the campus when the clock struck 6 p.m. Female students were looked after by a woman registrar, while female academic staff were a rarity. They, too, had to manoeuvre within a narrower world than their male peers – female academics were not admitted to the staff Common Room or allowed to dine in Commons. Women's social activities largely took place in House No. 6 where female staff ate with female students. Some societies in TCD remained male preserves during Dorothy's TCD years, and this would provide Dorothy with an opportunity to test her mettle and attempt to alter the *status quo*.

However, in 1916, Dorothy was just happy to gain a place in the college. She was admitted to the School of Physic in TCD with 'flying colours in oral Euclid [classical geometry] and a squeak in algebra'. In a letter to her mother in London she reviewed her entrance exam marks which ranged from a disgracefully low 3 in algebra and 3.5 in Latin composition to a 9 in oral Euclid and 10 in her essay. Dorothy was rueful: 'Not at all brilliant, you see how weak I am in maths. I enjoyed the orals this morning though I am very disgusted I didn't get a better French mark [6 out of 10]; I did it all without a single mistake, it must have been my accent.'[3] Constance may have felt, with some justification, that the money spent on importing French-speaking Swiss maids for her children had been wasted. But she must also have been proud of her daughter's achievement in gaining admission to TCD's School of Physic.

In choosing TCD, Dorothy was following a family tradition as her grandfather (Constance's father) Evory Kennedy had attended the School in the 1820s.[4] TCD was tardy in its admission of women, finally admitting them in 1904. Other medical schools in Ireland first admitted women in the 1880s. Of the Irish colleges, it has been suggested that TCD was the most expensive option but its degrees were thought to be prestigious.[5] Religion as well as family tradition would have dictated Dorothy's choice of college.

Students from a Catholic background tended to opt for universities with a Catholic ethos and those from a Protestant background naturally chose TCD.[6] While TCD was open to students of all denominations, by 1920 only one fifth of TCD's students were Catholics.

TCD's School of Physic is one of the oldest medical schools in Europe with a long proud tradition of association with the 'great men' of Irish medicine, including William Stokes and Robert Graves. The School celebrated its bicentenary in 1912 with great pomp and ceremony, four years before Dorothy entered its walls.[7] The compact college campus was and remains a beautiful space, circumscribed by high grey cut-stone walls, and located in the centre of the bustling city of Dublin. The arched main entrance leads to green squares of lawn and specimen trees, surrounded by cobblestone walkways and flanked with impressive stone buildings.

The early twentieth century was a time of turbulence for TCD – in addition to taking the momentous decision to admit women students, it lost many of its lecturers, graduates and students temporarily, and some permanently, to the Great War. There were more than 3,000 men on the TCD War List. Almost one third of these were members of the School of Physic. Of the twenty-eight women on the list, the majority were young doctors who had qualified during or before the War.[8] In all, there were 454 deaths among those who left TCD to serve in the armed forces. Female medical students helped fill the void left by those who had gone to war. These students were usually confident women from middle-class backgrounds, with sufficient educational and cultural capital as well as money to equip them with the aspirations and skills to commence their studies. Dorothy was no exception.

For her, the TCD years (1916–1921) were to prove a personal watershed – she spent five heady years at the college and its associated hospitals. By the time she graduated, she had turned her back on her Anglo-Irish heritage with its unionist leanings, campaigned for a nationalist Sinn Féin parliamentary candidate, joined an Irish nationalist organisation for women, Cumann na mBan,[9] and had lectured on first aid to the 'lads' of the West Cork Irish Republican Army. She was also involved in an unsuccessful attempt to induce one of TCD's most venerable societies, the Dublin University Biological Association, to allow women to participate in its activities.

At times, external events were so exciting, absorbing and disturbing that Dorothy found it difficult to concentrate on her medical studies. The

Easter Rising (1916), the Great War (1914–18), and the Spanish influenza pandemic (1918–19), were to infuse her introduction to medicine with drama, difficulties and opportunities. However, she started off with great determination tempered by some trepidation.

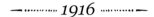

— ·········· *1916* ·········· —

Constance raised no objection to her daughter's 'plan of medicine' and, indeed, Dorothy expected that her mother would accompany her and live with her in Dublin. Unconventional Aunt Alice was also 'most awfully good' about it.[10] It is likely that she funded Dorothy's medical education – at least in part. Constance elected to stay in London and Dorothy's widowed sister Alice Wordsworth and Alice's six-year-old daughter Mary came to Dublin. Alice kept house for Dorothy and Mary, first at 32 Hollybank Avenue, Ranelagh, and later at 53 Leinster Road, Rathmines. Keeping house for three was surely more expensive than taking up residence in Trinity Hall, the college's residence for female students. However, having family close by was very important to Dorothy. She and Alice helped pay the bills by taking in students as boarders.[11]

The remarkable series of letters written by Dorothy to Sir Matthew Nathan provide insights into her feelings and actions during the TCD years. Dorothy's brother, Robert, who donated Sir Matthew's responses to the National Library, in Dublin, wrote, in 1966, that he thought that she was 'rather flattered by Sir Matthew's interest and anxious to help a man who was down on his luck!'[12] The correspondence belies this rather cold reading. The tone of Dorothy's letters is light, laced with irony and enlivened by occasional pieces of doggerel with Sir Matthew as their subject. Dorothy's signatures would seem to trace the arc of a relationship that deepened from 'Yours sincerely' to 'Yours with love' and, five years later, waned to 'Yours affectionately'. The content of the correspondence is largely personal with an occasional gesture towards politics. While not overtly flirtatious, Dorothy's letters are not those of a young woman writing to an older mentor. Fewer of Sir Matthew's letters survive and their tone is affectionate but measured. Perhaps, it was a friendship with possibilities that were not to be realised.

As the first examinations loomed, Dorothy told Sir Matthew that he would be amused to see how hard she was working. She was on a trial period in TCD until March, she wrote, and might have to give it up then.

It's not clear if this was a condition laid down by the college, her family or herself. In any event, Dorothy got through the first exams 'without discredit and no worse than anyone else though for the type of exam my marks were far from brilliant'.[13]

To celebrate, Dorothy asked Sir Matthew to 'waste' his Saturday afternoon with her at the Abbey Theatre. The play was one of William Boyle's, 'The Mineral Workers', followed by one by Lady Gregory. Dorothy and Sir Matthew would not be alone as she had already invited her cousin Elsie Henry and 'one of the children'. She told him it would be very good for him and that the Abbey was 'educative not dissipative'.[14] They met for lunch prior to the play with Dorothy calling to Dublin Castle to collect Sir Matthew – these lunches became a regular feature of Dorothy's TCD years and were laughingly referred to by Dorothy and Sir Matthew as 'doing the formula'.

On a more serious note, Dorothy wished Sir Matthew would coach her in mathematics as he seemed to be 'rather a nut'. This was hardly surprising as he had trained as an engineer.[15] However, when Sir Matthew and George Webb,[16] a fellow of TCD and the husband of Dr Ella Webb, helped Dorothy she was less than grateful for their efforts. In fact she admonished Sir Matthew that she was 'rather bored at the way you and Mr Webb bullied me last night, because I had quite good lines to go on'. She complained that her tutor had advised her differently and it was no good mixing up one's advisers.[17] Dorothy was also explicit about how difficult her studies were: 'because I pretend it's quite easy and no need to take trouble doesn't mean I don't realise what a big thing I am up against. Every night I decide to give it up but feel more courageous with the morning, so you can guess how glad I am of your encouragement.'[18]

In March 1916, Aunt Alice spent a few days with Sir Matthew. As they walked together in the Phoenix Park, he told her that his great fear was 'that some action of the anti-British in Ireland during the war would set back the growing English sympathy with your country'. She reassured him that no such isolated outrage was likely to occur.[19] On 10 April, Sir Matthew told General Macready at the War Office that although the Volunteers had been 'active of late', he did not believe that their leaders meant insurrection, or that they had sufficient arms to make it 'formidable' if they did intend it.[20]

Dorothy had just begun to grapple with mathematics and chemistry (which clogged her brain) when the unthinkable happened and Dublin city centre was briefly taken over by rebels. The question of Home Rule for Ireland had been overshadowed in Britain by the Great War. Aunt Alice was a proponent of Home Rule and Dorothy was mildly inclined in this direction. The short-lived Rising, which took place during Easter 1916, was an attempt by Irish nationalists (all dubbed Sinn Féiners by the British establishment although many were not members of Sinn Féin) to bypass the Home Rule solution and establish an independent Ireland.[21] The brutal bloody aftermath of the Rising where the leaders, including the injured founder of the Irish Citizen Army, James Connolly, were executed, was to change the views of many.

Dorothy had promised to spend Easter with Sir Matthew at his residence, the British Under-Secretary's Lodge in the Phoenix Park. This was her second stay at this bastion of the British administration. As we know, on her first visit, she had been accompanied by Aunt Alice. Once again this would be a very correct visit, in that Dorothy would be chaperoned by Sir Matthew's sister-in-law, Estelle Nathan whom she refers to in her diary, and later correspondence, as Mrs Nathan.[22] Estelle's children, Maude and Pamela, aged 16 and 10 years old, would also be there. Sir Matthew enjoyed discreet liaisons with a number of women throughout his life but his relationship with Dorothy seems to have been a very open friendship with the Nathan and Stopford families aware and approving. Indeed, a marriage between Dorothy and Sir Matthew, who was some twenty-eight years older than Dorothy, would not have been unexpected, at least by the Stopfords.

Dorothy was looking forward to spending time relaxing and having fun with Sir Matthew and his family. She had been home to London and would arrive back in Ireland by boat, landing at Dublin's North Wall at 7.30 a.m. She asked Sir Matthew to put on 'all his robes and stars' and greet her there. His 'beloved London' had become 'unbearable'.[23]

While we don't know if Sir Matthew complied with Dorothy's request for sartorial splendour, she obviously arrived safely on Maundy Thursday as her diary of Easter 1916 opens on Friday 21 April with the mundane note that she bicycled to church in the morning.[24] Sir Matthew was at home all day working in his study and they only saw him for a brief half hour at lunch. Dorothy and the children put up a tent in the garden and played around. When Sir Matthew did not emerge from his study at 7 o'clock after the last post had left, Dorothy and the children 'raided him in his study, fetching him out: Leap-frog we played, he joined in a universal race in which he beat us easily. Maude came down to dinner and we had quite a gay little party.' After dinner, Sir Matthew read *El Dorado* out loud and they talked of 'getting things done' and 'one's conscience'.

The next morning, Sir Matthew departed for his office in Dublin Castle where his conscience and the need to get things done were very soon to be severely tested. He had received news that a ship, the *Aud*, had been stopped off the coast of Kerry. It had been carrying arms for the Rising. Unbeknownst to Dorothy, Aunt Alice's great friend Roger Casement had accompanied the arms, landed from a German submarine on Banna Strand and had been arrested. A discreet Sir Matthew, who was well aware of the facts, did not disclose any details of this incident to Dorothy.[25] There were other portents of trouble brewing. Sir Matthew was aware that the Irish Volunteers were planning a march on Easter Sunday but he did not think that a rising was imminent. He diverted himself by playing patience with Dorothy and telling her of some of the people he admired. She was astounded that he included people younger than himself on the list. She was trenchant that she could never admire anyone younger than herself. Mrs Nathan had been out visiting and joined them at about 11 p.m. Dorothy recorded: 'They did not talk much about Ireland – a feeling about that everything is not quite right, trouble somewhere.'

On Sunday, Dorothy bicycled to early service and hastily scanned the papers. The announcement by Eoin MacNeill in the *Sunday Independent* countermanding the planned marches seemed to confirm Sir Matthew's belief that a rising was not imminent. Nonetheless, Sir Matthew spent most of the day at the Castle, returning late for dinner and to watch a play put on by the children before heading out to the Viceregal Lodge, the residence of the Lord Lieutenant.[26]

On Monday, Sir Matthew once again went to the Castle but asked Dorothy and his sister-in-law not to use the car as he might need it. Dorothy, Mrs Nathan and the children walked to the Furry Glen in the Phoenix Park and spent the morning sitting there in the sun. Just as they were turning in at the gate, at 1.15 p.m., they heard '3 loud booms'. Dorothy recalled: 'All stopped and we conjectured what it was. I guessed the salute to the LL [Lord Lieutenant] who was starting by the 2.30 train for Belfast. We did not pay much attention but walked on up to the Lodge for lunch.' Dorothy had read, in the *Freeman's Journal*: '...a few censored remarks about some gun-running in Tralee, in which two prominent local Sinn Féiners were implicated and had been arrested – also a man of foreign nationality also arrested and brought to Dublin under strong guard of police. I thought this was the clue to the situation.'[27]

The Nathans and Dorothy, *sans* Sir Matthew, were sitting at lunch when a telephone call from Captain Maitland at the Viceregal Lodge brought the news that the 'Sinn Féiners' were out. It seemed the Castle was surrounded but the police 'managed to shut the gates in time'. Captain Maitland reassured them that Sir Matthew was 'quite safe'. Later, Dorothy heard that the policeman at the Castle gates 'had fallen riddled with bullets and there had been heavy loss of life, mostly on the side of the military'. She was of the opinion that the Sinn Féiners seemed to be 'no wild mob but an organised army, well-armed and munitioned'.

There was one comic incident to brighten the day. Dorothy saw a volunteer dressed in green with something white in his hand, advancing across the fields about 300 yards away. Every now and again he knelt down, taking cover, then got up, ran a few paces and dropped down again. She watched petrified for a few moments thinking every moment he was going to fire. She told Sir Matthew's nice Maude and they fetched her opera glasses. 'One glance through was enough. It was a child in a green frock picking cowslips!'[28]

Later, as the Nathans and Dorothy sat on the veranda after tea, a sudden and much louder volley of rifle fire made them all jump. They closed the shutters and went into the bedrooms. Sir Matthew rang to say he would spend the night in the Castle and to enquire whether Dorothy, Mrs Nathan and the children would like to spend the night at the Viceregal Lodge. They refused and spent the evening talking of 'Sir Matthew and his career and his policy in Ireland and the whole tragedy'.

On Tuesday, there was still no post or papers but an early phone call from Sir Matthew, at the Castle, said that things 'were a bit better'. Dorothy got up, intending to go to TCD to attend the botany laboratory at 10 a.m. but was prevented by Mrs Nathan. Dorothy was irritated: she deemed this 'very fussy' but felt she had to give in out of politeness. After lunch, she and Maude went for a walk and posted some letters at the Castleknock Gate. Another comic incident unfolded when they thought they saw five men on the road signalling with a white flag. Using glasses, they found their five Sinn Féiners were 'aged road-menders wielding their tools and spades and picks and talking to a young lady holding a bicycle and wearing a white jersey'. They were 'much chaffed' for their imaginative vision.[29]

News about more serious incidents began to emerge. Dorothy heard that there was a machine gun on top of the Rotunda Hospital sweeping Sackville Street,[30] and that the Shelbourne (a hotel) and the Archbishop's house were taken. The rebels were entrenched in Stephen's Green and the soldiers at the Curragh camp in County Kildare had been brought to Dublin. In the Lodge, Dorothy and the Nathans were almost in the dark as night came on and the gas pressure was lowered. They had to use candles and endured 'a rather jumpy night, wild rumours of Germans landing'.[31]

On Wednesday, still without post or newspapers, Sir Matthew's replies to Mrs Nathan's telephone calls were terse. He warned them not to go into town but said that they might go into the park on the north side. The children cooked for amusement, Dorothy worked, Mrs Nathan drew and the servants shopped in nearby Parkgate Street. Plans were made to get away by the Lucan gate of the Phoenix Park if necessary. That evening there was a tremendous bang when a shell exploded. Twenty lancers were sitting in the ditch at the back of the house and Dorothy for the first time began to feel 'very exhilarated'. At 8 p.m., it was confirmed that the bang was a shrapnel shell of the military's which was badly aimed and landed in the Viceregal garden but did not do any harm. In the midst of her worries about Sir Matthew, Dorothy also thought of the 'the poor misguided Sinn Féiners. They were given every chance for their lives but I fear many have been lost now. Such a glorious spring day and bright sun…'.

Two hours later, Sir Matthew rang up to convey the understatement that 'things were troublesome', that it was a kind of 'Sidney Street business' with each house having to be emptied of its occupants and that they had 'had to turn the guns on'.[32] He told Mrs Nathan that there was no need to be anxious on their own account as they were well-guarded and that fresh troops were arriving from England. He himself hoped to get to bed that night, he had only lain down for a short while the previous night. It looked, to him, like a 'long and terrible' business. He had got through to Mrs Nathan's husband at the War Office each day and would see if the wire Dorothy sent to her mother in London had got through.

Dorothy was, by now, tired of being 'mewed up' but, admitted to herself, that even if she had been allowed to leave, she might not have got anywhere. On Thursday, there was still no post. A telephone call from Sir Matthew to his sister-in-law informed them that the Chief Secretary, Augustine Birrell had arrived by a torpedo boat and was now in the Castle. Dorothy had no option but to stay *in situ* in the Lodge and play with the children for diversion. She told her mother that they were 'apparently safe and secure here and are allowed to exercise daily in the park where all is quiet'. However, she said the sounds were worse than the zeppelin raids in London. She complained that she had not got any useful books to read and was not able to go to any lectures. It was 'a great impediment to passing my next exam but I hope everyone else will do as badly'.[33] Writing to Edie, Dorothy confided that it was all very 'thrilling'. It has been an 'utter surprise and the Sinn Féiners just walked in everywhere, tremendously organised and armed and munitioned and took possession before anyone knew what was happening...They are all very English here but very nice...it's very safe but most exciting at the same time and simply awful for the whole of Dublin. I can't think of anything more disastrous.'[34]

Food was becoming a problem and meals were 'simpler' with a fire in the drawing room only. However, Dorothy was relieved to be able to send a letter to her mother and sister Edie with a Mrs Bell Irvine who was going to England. Some gossip got through to the Nathans and Dorothy via the servants. For instance, Dorothy heard from the under-housemaid that there were women 'Sinn Féiners' about with guns.[35] These included Dr Kathleen Lynn and Madeleine ffrench Mullen, both of whom would later become colleagues of Dorothy's.

On Friday, Sir Matthew had a very bad cold and wanted some belongings taken to the Castle. According to him, the fighting was now 'mostly sniping and very difficult for the military'. Dorothy saw almost twenty-five soldiers marching across to the Castleknock Gate[36] but, other than that, she had to divert herself by playing with a snail for some hours, making it jump over a gap in the seat. Sir Matthew told Mrs Nathan of a zeppelin raid on England and how the German naval fleet was turned back *en route* to England. Dorothy's wire to her mother failed to get through. Sir Matthew was apologetic about his cavalier abandonment of his guests. Dorothy told him they missed him 'most awfully' and was glad to hear that he seemed more cheerful.

Unexpected titled guests dropped in. Lady Freddy Coyningham and her mother arrived suddenly from Meath, telling of trouble in their county.[37] They were making their way to England and wanted to stay the night at the

Lodge. They had 'thrilling and horrid tales of their experiences – Castle Slane is safe however'. Dorothy had a very bad night as the guns were firing very heavily until 3 a.m. Nonetheless, she was amused by the Viceregal cook who had 'struck and refused to cook food while his wife and children were starving in Dublin, threw the saucepan at Murray Graham and went off. Our chauffeur is very nervous, is sure he is a marked man'. On Saturday, Lady Freddie and her mother made plans to go to England by the night boat. Sir Matthew's cold was improving and he advised Dorothy to go to Foxrock, where she had family living. Then, word came through – they were all to leave:

> the others for England and I to be dropped at Foxrock…I'm glad the children are going, they are getting jumpy and no wonder. Mrs Nathan is a perfect brick but it is getting rather a strain for her. I wouldn't mind staying where I am but can't when she goes. Anyhow, it will be rather nice to get away from all this elaborate plain-clothes police protection.[38]

Dorothy busied herself trying to stuff the 'necessities of life into suitcases and handbags'. Before she left, she wrote to Sir Matthew to tell him that Mrs Nathan was 'simply splendid'. However, she was glad that they had gone as it was 'rather jumpy for the children'. She thanked him for being so 'awfully nice and careful' of them in the midst of his own 'overwhelming anxieties' and finished off by saying she was 'glad every minute' she thought of him 'in charge of Ireland now'.[39] A Viceregal Lodge chauffeur was assigned to drive their car as their own chauffeur, Clements was well known and still a 'trifle nervous'. The only difficulty they encountered on their journey was a tyre blowout.

On 29 April, Constance wrote to Sir Matthew to thank him for sending a telegram to say Dorothy was all right. Constance had been anxious as she was unsure of Dorothy's whereabouts. She also told Sir Matthew that she was grateful for all his kindness to her daughter since Dorothy had returned to Dublin.[40]

From Foxrock, Dorothy went to Ranelagh to spend some time with her cousin Elsie Henry. Elsie had helped to establish the innovative Sphagnum Moss Depot at the Royal College of Science for Ireland. The absorbent moss was used for wound dressings and was much in demand by the War

Office and more immediately was needed in the Dublin hospitals during the Easter Rising. Elsie was later awarded an OBE for her work with the depot.[41] For now, Dorothy and Elsie greedily exchanged news and Elsie invited Dorothy to stay with her. Dorothy was reluctant on account of the shortage of food but Elsie told her she could go out foraging. A relieved Dorothy stayed with Elsie and made bandages.

Dorothy biked into Trinity Hall where Miss Cunningham – presumably Elizabeth Margaret Cunningham, the warden of TCD's women's residence Trinity Hall – told her that the college should re-open the following week. She also said that 'old Tommies [slang for a common soldier] and officers belonging to nowhere had dropped in, Dorothy's cousin Cyril [Dickinson] amongst them, and a garrison was formed which did splendid work, and TCD was all right'. The campus, with its strong associations with the British establishment, had come under attack during the Easter 1916 Rising. It survived unscathed. Its few gates made it relatively easy to defend. With these gates closed, it was defended by the College Officers Training Corps.[42] One of the best officers, was, apparently, Captain Alton, 'a quiet little middle-aged man' who had supervised Dorothy's last Latin exam. He 'had the heart of a lion and took command splendidly'.[43] British officers were billeted in the college and it was used as a safe haven for military horses.

On 3 May, a relative, Charlie Dickinson, told Dorothy that the pacifist Francis Sheehy Skeffington had been court martialled and shot. She recorded in her diary: 'In the *Final Buff* – the only evening paper now published except the *Irish Times*, we see that the three who signed the Proclamation of the Republic, Pearse, MacDonagh and Daly have been sentenced to death by court martial, and the sentence was carried out this morning.' She got the order of executions wrong: Padraic Pearse, Thomas Clarke and Thomas MacDonagh were the first to be shot. Edward Daly was, indeed, executed but his death came after these three.

As well as hearsay and newspaper reports, Dorothy found that the Rising had left the city severely damaged. In Rathmines, she walked alleys and side paths barricaded by branches of trees and with barbed wire entanglements, 'realistic evidence of heavy fighting which took place in that neighbourhood'. The next day, letters were delivered for the first time but there were none for Dorothy. She was comforted, though, by her first sight of a baker's cart. The food supply was returning to normal with 'heaps of meat and butter coming in again'. Dorothy noted that Sir Matthew had resigned and that there were

34

four more executions, including Joseph Plunkett, and many penal servitude sentences. She wrote: 'The Countess Plunkett is going about Dublin like a demented creature, mourning him [her son], they say.'[44]

On 6 May, the weather was miserable – cold and wet. Nonetheless, Dorothy determined to go out to the Under-Secretary's Lodge and fetch away her luggage. At the Lodge she found the maids 'all nearly in tears at Sir M's departure. He went to England last night. He doesn't care a rap about losing office but is very much cut up at the rebellion. He will be back soon to wind up his affairs'. She remarked that everything looked very desolate: bullet holes on the Quays and the windows of the Four Courts smashed although she did not see the library strewn on the road as rumour had said. When she went to visit her uncle, Edward Stopford, in Frankfort Avenue, Rathgar, she heard that a 'vigorous search' had been carried out the previous day by military armed with bayonets and Royal Irish Constabulary (RIC). Their house, although the property of Madam Markievicz, was not searched, as it was now nearly empty but the military 'thrust their bayonets, *en passant*, into the sacking in the van at the door. It's too pouring to go down and look at town as I meant'.

On Sunday, Dorothy was anxious to find out if her letters had been censored as she wanted to send the remainder of her diary to her mother. This would be the last day on which she would write a diary about events as she told Constance:

> things are almost normal. Such is life! One almost forgets in the calm what has taken place – at least I never shall forget those days at the Lodge, just two or three until we knew where we were. One learnt to listen all day and look all day all without being frightened but awfully alert with your heart ready to spring into your mouth at the first sound.[45]

She had been 'quite sure they were going to shoot Sir Matthew' but she was glad TCD was opening the following day and there would not be much time for thought.[46]

Dorothy and Elsie cheered each other up and on 8 May the Spaghnum Moss Depot re-opened. TCD also re-opened on that day although the normal confident calm of this intellectual oasis had still not returned and the campus was 'teeming' with soldiers when Dorothy resumed her studies 'in earnest'. It looked more like a barracks than a college, as Dorothy informed her brother Robert in a letter to him in Salonika, where he was stationed with the British army. He had left the Ambulance Corps to serve with the army proper in Salonika and Egypt. In the Officers' Mess, he was regarded with horror for declaring he was a Home Ruler.[47] Dorothy was in poor spirits. She told Robert: 'The outlook here is not exactly cheering. I began Trinity in earnest yesterday.' She was concerned that the 'physical force minority' were 'very small and violent and heaven knows they may have wrecked Home Rule'. She reassured Robert that she herself had spent the Rising in 'the dullest jumpiest safest place' and that now, on account of her gender, she was invisible to the authorities. However, it had been a beastly time. I thought there was going to be much more of a general rising but it was very well dealt with from the start. Military law is very funny, you have to be home by 7.30 but it practically ignores women...Women can go anywhere almost unchallenged and could ride in trams long before men! We felt rather insignificant.'[48]

Dorothy continued: 'the British had already shot twelve rebels' and put in place 'heaps of penal servitudes. It looks as if they were going to do more than necessary and enjoy revenge'.[49]She told him that his cousins Cyril and Charlie had 'both been out', Cyril helping to defend TCD and Charlie defending Beggar's Bush Barracks. In typical sisterly fashion, she told him she loved his photograph 'all except the smile which is rather asinine'.

On 11 May, Augustine Birrell resigned as Chief Secretary and, on 12 May, the last of the executions in Ireland – Seán MacDermott and James Connolly – took place. James Connolly, who was wounded, had to be tied to a chair in front of the firing squad.[50]

Dorothy was not the only TCD woman to keep a diary of her experiences during the Rising. Her ignorance of events was equalled by that of another diarist Elsie Mahaffy, the Provost's eldest daughter. Elsie recorded her experiences of being effectively trapped in their home, the Provost's house on the grounds of TCD, with very little knowledge of what was happening outside the walls of the college.[51]

Meanwhile, Sir Matthew confided to Dorothy that he would not go back to Ireland. He did not wish to 'see again the land I had hoped and failed to help' but he hoped to see her when she is in England at the next vacation.[52] In July 1916, Dorothy visited London. Sir Matthew was now living there and they arranged to meet for lunch. Dorothy was delighted to 'do the formula' but reminded Sir Matthew that London was bigger than Dublin and she didn't know Odone's, the restaurant he suggested for lunch, so she would need a postcard with further details.

Later that summer, Dorothy and her family gathered in West Lulworth, Dorset, beside the sea for a holiday. Dorothy and Constance stayed in a thatched cottage belonging to a fisherman who, to their eyes, looked like St Peter. Alice and her daughter Mary and a 'huge family' ranging from 4 to 18 years old were close by. All the 'big ones' swam with 4- or 5-year-olds on their backs. There were long swims out to lobster pots where the fun was trying to climb on to them and they lobbed and pitched so they ended up head first or tail first in the sea. Dorothy gave up reading Charles Darwin's *The Origin* in favour of *Beelore* and she commented ironically that 'they really are the only civilized people ... the women do all the work and the men look on and all so well regulated!!'. She was happy to be lazy after her studies and the trauma of the Rising. Sir Matthew was ill in a nursing home and she sent him a bunch of flowers plucked from the cliffs. It was 'simply perfect' in Dorset, she somewhat heartlessly informed him.[53]

In London, Roger Casement was arrested and charged with treason. On the day of the preliminary court hearing, Edie battled her way through a hostile mob to lunch with Aunt Alice and the writer Robert Lynd in a Lyons teashop. Both Alice and Robert were very distressed – they had not been able to speak to Roger Casement but he had seen them in court and smiled at them.[54] Prior to his trial, he was held in the Tower. Aunt Alice was profoundly upset by the conditions in which Roger Casement found himself. She spoke to the Afrikaner General Louis Botha pleading for sympathy for Sir Roger who had been 'kept for three weeks in the Tower [of London] behind barbed wire in a damp gloomy and airless cell with the window boarded up except for one pane...'. He had no change of clothes and 'suffered much from vermin and cold' because his great coat was taken from him.[55] Aunt Alice also wrote to her friend, Prime Minister Henry Asquith.[56] As a result, Roger Casement was provided with a change of clothes, allowed books and newspapers, to see visitors and to receive letters.[57] Later, Aunt Alice attended the trial and watched, helplessly, as her controversial friend was sentenced to death. He appreciated Aunt Alice's support and thanked her in his final writings from his cell.[58] In August 1916, Roger Casement was hanged for treason. There is no record of Dorothy's reaction to the execution – she and her sisters had met him in Aunt Alice's house but he had taken little interest in them and was either silent or prone to long tirades on his pet subjects.[59] Whatever about her feelings with respect to Casement, her aunt's distress must have impinged on Dorothy.

Back in Ireland again, with her blissful summer over, Dorothy found it was strangely quiet on the surface but she intuited that there was a lot of bad feeling underneath this seeming calm. She contrasted it to the visit to the Under-Secretary's Lodge in September of the previous year where they enjoyed 'great revels'. She was worried about the prospect of conscription being extended to Ireland. Aunt Alice visited but returned to London for the funeral of her brother-in-law, Sir Lauder Brunton who died on 16 September 1916.[60] Brunton, who was a 'highly successful doctor' and a lecturer in *Materia Medica* and Pharmacology at St Bartholomew's Hospital, London, was married to Louisa Jane Stopford, and was the father of Dorothy's cousin Elsie Henry.

Meanwhile, Dorothy's medical studies reclaimed her attention: a mechanics exam was looming – a 'black nightmare'. She had become so enthralled with rationalist literature that she had forgotten to get to grips with the 'dull figures'. It would be a 'great squeak' to get through. She told Sir Matthew that his 'stern and relentless influence' was greatly missed. Sir Matthew was unimpressed: He adjured her to apply herself to her studies and 'not be reading irrelevant matter however momentarily attractive when you should be absorbing the laws of motion…I am prepared to be really cross with you if it shows you to have played the little fool and thrown away your chance'.[61] He told her that he would be thinking of her on 9 October, the date of the exam.

Dorothy passed the mechanics exam and she exulted that she was now finished with maths and mechanics 'for ever more'. She alternated her studies with outdoor pursuits such as sailing around Dublin bay with her friends, the Hannarys. There was more open air fun with 'alfresco sleepovers' on a heather-covered hill behind a hostel in Wicklow. She missed Sir Matthew and said the British were 'mad fools' to let him go when good people were wanted. Dorothy asked him to 'accept much love'.[62] When Edie visited Dublin in October, Dorothy introduced her sister to 'soulful Dublin' in the shape of writers AE (George Russell) and James Stephens and essayist and poet Susan Mitchell, along with a 'few sound brains' among the TCD professors. Later, Dorothy sent Sir Matthew a copy of James Stephen's newly-published book *Insurrection in Dublin*,[63] a vivid account of the Rising written just six months after it happened. Stephens had observed the fighting at St Stephen's Green. Dorothy was in agreement with his account of the week but criticised some of his remarks. She also read Darrell Figgis's study of AE published in 1916. It may have made for occasionally uncomfortable reading as Figgis suggests that Dublin was a humane, friendly city with a 'dignity that is easy, and in which all, save those that cluster around the ominous Castle, share with an accepted comradeliness'.[64] Dorothy's sojourns in the Under-Secretary's Lodge in 1915 and 1916 and her intimacy with Sir Matthew surely fell within Figgis's 'cluster'.

She then buckled down to work for the rest of the autumn – everything was 'going swimmingly' with lectures every morning at 9 o'clock. She reminded herself that she would have to buy a lamp for her bicycle to light the way on winter mornings. On Sundays she went for 'great tramps' on the tops of the Dublin mountains where she enjoyed the red bracken and squelshy bog and gales blowing...' She told Sir Matthew that she had dreamt about him: '...you turned up on a visit here with two wives and six grown-up daughters, in a motor car! I have been having a series of strange vivid dreams. They say it's a peculiarity of medical students'. The only other 'dissipation' was a trip to the Abbey Theatre to see 'John Bull's Other Island', George Bernard Shaw's only full-length play that included a 'sustained consideration' of the Irish issue.[65] A new Under-Secretary for Ireland, Sir William P. Byrne, was appointed and Sir Matthew approved: 'an Irishman and a Catholic – which is the right direction...I hope the new man is given a fair chance'.[66]

By the end of November, Dorothy declared herself as doing nothing but work and she was 'accordingly stupid'. Her doctor and tutor were coming to tea. 'Don't they sound grand like that – perhaps you don't recognize them in the Webbs?', she asked Sir Matthew. Then, disaster stuck as Dorothy's recurring enemy – asthma – took hold. She missed an exam, thereby losing her chance of honours, but bore up in the expectation of going to London and dining with Sir Matthew. But, it was not to be. Dr Ella Webb forbade the crossing with a whispered threat of pneumonia on the icy journey. Dorothy was distraught: 'She says I am to say it is her fault but I think the Gods have a spite against me and she is only their tool'. She consoled herself that Sir Matthew would be equally sorry and miss her as much as she would miss him. In a rare burst of self-pity, Dorothy admitted she was 'sitting literally on the point of tears'.[67] It all ended happily as Sir Matthew sent her a gift of 'most cheering' wine and Dorothy joined him later in the week. She also breakfasted with him on the occasion of his fifty-fifth birthday. He was now secretary of the Pensions Ministry based in Albany in London. The pomp that surrounded him prompted a wicked response from Dorothy. She sent him the following verses:

> His den is now in grandeur decked
> A princely hermit he,
> For he's ensconced like any swell
> In stately Albanie

> Gold hangings, leathern sofas
> The simple mind overwhelm;
> For he is Lord of Pensions,
> The stricken of our realm.

She concluded 'The Ballade, part 11' with a more kindly verse:

> He is the same dear ogre
> Yet he's been through scorching flame
> And, more good to him accruing,
> He's nicer than the same.[68]

— ········· *1917* ········· —

Dorothy told Sir Matthew that there were 'one or two exciting antidotes' to work: Dorothy had just started smoking and was caught by the authorities in TCD. Her friend, Theo Hannary, headed a deputation to the Provost asking that female students be allowed to smoke in their society rooms. However, permission was not forthcoming but Dorothy was sanguine: 'he was quite nice about it… and said he would like to receive a deputation from the girls every week'. A parliamentary election in February 1917 also provided some amusement. Arthur Warren Samuels and Sir Robert Henry Woods were up for election. The medical school favoured Woods. There were girls at the polling booths for the first time and Dorothy wished she had been more senior as she might have participated. However, it was 'more fun outside in some ways'. The men made 'an effigy of Samuels in his pink law gown and pulled it around town, then burnt it on the steps of the dining hall'.[69]

In the classroom, Dorothy continued to find the basic sciences somewhat difficult. Electricity was 'bewildering' and her brain was 'like a suet pudding'. All of the students thought the Christmas holidays were too short. The 'eternal topic' was food production with 'everyone using up every spare inch (and no-one using the spare acres)'. However, Dorothy and Alice were fine – they rationed conscientiously but still managed to have plenty to eat.[70]

A great storm was brewing; it was snowing in February and Dorothy dreamed of being torpedoed. She didn't think she would go to London at Easter. She busied herself by conjuring up projects for social reform and counting the days until she finished her degree. She was deeply concerned at the plight of the poor in Dublin, housed in appalling slum conditions in the city centre. 'At present the more energetic of us feel as if we're cumbering the earth, awful parasites.' She read Dostoevsky's *Crime and Punishment* which was not suited to the 'small hours of the morning' as it was very 'blood-curdling' in parts.[71] In the end, Dorothy decided to brave the boat home to her mother in London at Easter. Three ships were torpedoed in the Irish channel the morning of her departure. According to her cousin Elsie Henry: 'They came on a sailing vessel and 2 boats tied together with 30 men from a torpedoed collier.' The mail boat stopped and offered to take the men aboard but they said it was not safe to stop and they could reach port. The mail boat 'went ahead with great speed and arrived safely alright'.[72]

In May, Dorothy picked up her pen to write to Sir Matthew when she should have been studying and mischievously delighted in using notepaper headed 'Medical School, TCD' as it would be sure to annoy him that she was writing when she should have been studying. In her letter, she wrote that she would stay with Theo Hannary the following weekend and they would sail in the Hannary's small boat in Kingstown Harbour.[73] The boat belonged to Theo but her father, Canon Hannary was very fussy and would probably insist on sailing with them. Trinity term promised to be lighter and she hoped to achieve better marks than she had got to date.

In early summer, Dorothy met Dr Kathleen Lynn at an evening at Susan Mitchell's and was misled by her appearance into dismissing her as a 'very charming lady of an old-fashioned type, if you can image the exact reverse of Dr Webb' who was more of the Sinn Féin sort.[74] While Dorothy was aware that Kathleen Lynn had spent some time in Kilmainham Gaol following the 1916 Rising, she thought that nothing could be proved against

41

her other than 'doctoring and bandaging Sinn Féiners'. In fact, Kathleen Lynn was one of the most radical Republican women in Ireland at that time.[75]

The summer of 1917 was relaxing for Dorothy. She went to stay at Lord Monteagle's estate, at Mount Trenchard, County Limerick, as a 'sort of farm labourer'. Thomas Spring Rice, Second Baron Mounteagle and the father of Dorothy's friend, Mary, was a patron of Sir Horace Plunkett's co-operative movement and on his own farm there were a variety of societies from poultry to credit to wheat-growing as well as a branch of the Gaelic League. There was another family connection: Dorothy's cousin Anne Brunton who had done a course in Rural Science for Teachers had spent some of the war years working there.[76] The war had divested many of the large estates of labour and women were replacing them on the land. In the end, Dorothy did odd jobs such as cheese making and fruit bottling. It was peaceful, looking out over the River Shannon and hearing of nothing but crops. The tempo increased when she sailed over to Clare Castle for the East Clare elections which were contended by Sinn Féin candidate, Éamon de Valera and Irish Party candidate, Patrick Lynch. Election literature mocked Lynch for 'dwelling in shoneen circles, where Castle gold abounds' while de Valera 'lay in prison for the sake of County Clare'.[77] Although not yet convinced by the Irish nationalist cause, de Valera, who won the by-election, struck Dorothy as a 'very fine man and I think might be able to lead with a clear head and not get carried away'.[78] Throughout her life, Dorothy was to be unswerving in her loyalty to de Valera even though most of her own family with an interest in the Irish question eventually plumped for his opponents, the Free Staters.

Later that summer, Dorothy joined her mother on a visit to Wookey Vicarage in Wells, Somerset, England. There, they lived in a 'swirl of bishops, deans and canons' but with 'three noisy cousins and the Bishop's two daughters' they were cheerful. The Stopford and Nathan families deepened their acquaintance when Sir Matthew's sister-in-law, Mrs Nathan, and his niece, Pam, did a 'marvellous bike ride' to join them. From Wells, Dorothy and her mother progressed to Pippin Cot, Everton, England. They stayed in a tiny thatched cottage and, at night, Dorothy slept in a camp bed in the orchard where pippins literally dropped on her. They lived mainly *al fresco* and largely by their own efforts. However, after struggling unsuccessfully for two hours in the early morning to light the kitchen fire, they engaged a farmhand. Dorothy proudly cooked a three course dinner – celery soup, cold ham, stewed blackberries and Devonshire cream.

On her return to Dublin, Dorothy deplored the fact that Sinn Féin support was on the increase. She thought that the Thomas Ashe 'fiasco' had provided the Sinn Féiners, who were 'only too eager for a handle' with a grievance, and the opportunity to make capital from the funeral. It was all too 'awful'. Ashe (1885–1917), a member of the Irish Volunteers who had taken part in the Rising in Ashbourne, County Meath, had died on 25 September following force feeding while on hunger strike. Dorothy now 'loathed' politics and flew to 'solider things – hospitals and concrete facts'. In addition to her medical studies, she was working as a parlour maid in a VAD (Voluntary Aid Detachment) Hospital several times a week 'under the eye of Rachel Mahaffy', another daughter of the Provost of TCD. Presumably this work was done at the Dublin University VAD Hospital for the wounded, in Mountjoy Square, Dublin.[79] Dorothy teased Sir Matthew that he would rather she did this than attend the East Clare elections.[80]

In September, Dorothy celebrated her twenty-seventh birthday with the Barton family. Among others, Aunt Alice had introduced Robert Barton and his cousin Erskine Childers to Dorothy. Robert Barton came from a wealthy background with an enormous estate at Glendalough in County Wicklow where he enjoyed putting his ideas as an agricultural improver into practice. In 1908, on a tour of Irish co-operatives with Erskine Childers, both men became committed to Home Rule. In 1914, Robert Barton accepted a commission in the British Army and was sent to Dublin during the 1916 Rising. The treatment of the rebels in the aftermath of the Rising caused him to resign from the British Army and join the Republican Movement. During Dorothy's sojourn with the Bartons, the emphasis was on rural delights such as mushroom picking and blackberry dumplings. There was 'great betting' on a roof climb that Dorothy had determined on. She didn't think it would be more difficult than one of her previous feats – scaling a high wall in the Phoenix Park.[81]

Dorothy continued to socialise with the Hannarys who got 'nicer and nicer'. She remained annoyed with the Sinn Féiners who were, in her opinion, wrecking the Peace Convention (July 1917 to May 1918) which was an attempt to come to some resolution about Home Rule. More local tensions also affected Dorothy. Although, as we know, Irish medical schools treated women fairly during their medical education – students being separated on gender grounds for anatomy classes only; there was a separate ladies' dissecting room – there were tensions among the TCD students themselves and some inequalities remained.[82] Dorothy wondered 'was there ever anyone so narrow and prejudiced as so-called educated young men?' In November 1917, TCD and the Royal College of Surgeons in Ireland (RCSI) announced that they would hold a 'medical retreat' open to medical students of both institutions. This would be chaperoned and addressed by a couple of doctors, including Dr Ella Webb. Dorothy thought it might be useful to 'make a good atmosphere between the men and girls and medical students generally' if it was kept 'intellectual rather than goody'. In the end, she found the medical retreat 'rather fun'.

This term also marked the beginning of clinical work for Dorothy, an opportunity that she relished. Irish teaching hospitals were generally welcoming to women and, according to historian Laura Kelly, possessed an 'egalitarianism lacking in their British counterparts'.[83] For Dorothy, it was 'very nice to get in touch with human beings again after so long an acquaintance with dry bones'. She undertook her clinical work in the Meath Hospital, in Dublin, where she quickly found that she knew or had links with most of the staff. Oliver St John Gogarty, playwright and doctor, 'turned out a trump', while the hospital itself was 'very nice' with everyone 'natural and friendly and the tone is very good'. She eulogised that nothing in the world mattered except to 'drink in all you get of those miraculous human beings, physicians and surgeons who (the good ones) seem to know everything (there is nothing more detestable than a bad surgeon)'.[84]

Meanwhile, the Great War continued apace. Dorothy's brother Robert was *en route* to Jerusalem for Christmas. He was reportedly very happy working nineteen hours out of every twenty-four. Dorothy bemoaned that, for her part, 'life is a terrible distraction to work'. She worked a 'paltry' eight-hour day, Saturday included, with about two to three hours on Sunday. She found it difficult to concentrate on any one thing when life was so distracting, even though her sailing companion, Theo, had left for London. Oliver St John Gogarty's play 'Blight' which focussed attention on the Dublin slums, was the talk of the town but Dorothy thought it was 'so brilliant and witty that the audience seemed to miss the propaganda part somewhat'. Dorothy's interest in the plight of the poor prompted her to accompany Dr Ella Webb to her 'slum dispensary' on Tuesday evenings.[85]

Dorothy didn't go home for Christmas of 1917 as the holidays were too short and the journey 'difficult and expensive'. So, this festive season, she did not suffer a 'thinking attack', something that often came on after she met Sir Matthew with her friends accusing her of adopting a 'most supercilious frame of mind'.[86]

## NOTES

1.  D.Stopford to Sir M. Nathan, 1916 (University of Oxford, Bodleian, Nathan papers, MS 204, folio 219).

2.  For a comprehensive history of early female medical education in Ireland, see L. Kelly, *Irish Women in Medicine, c.1880s–1920s: Origins, Education and Careers* (Manchester: Manchester University Press, 2013). Of the 759 women who matriculated in medicine in Ireland, 452 succeeded in qualifying. This may somewhat underestimate the number of female medical graduates as, for instance, Dorothy Stopford is not included.

3.  D. Stopford to C. Stopford (Dorothy's mother), undated letter, 1916 (NLI, MS 21205 (4)); also cited in M. Ó hÓgartaigh, 'Dorothy Stopford-Price and the Elimination of Childhood Tuberculosis', in M. Ó hÓgartaigh (ed.), *Quiet Revolutionaries. Irish Women in Education, Medicine and Sport, 1861–1964* (Dublin: The History Press Ireland, 2011), p.107.

4.  O'D. Browne, *The Rotunda Hospital, 1745–1945* (Edinburgh: E. &S. Livingstone, 1945), p.267.

5.  Kelly, *Irish Women in Medicine*, p.62.

6.  S.M. Parkes, 'Higher Education, 1793–1908', in W.E. Vaughan (ed.), *A New History of Ireland VI: Ireland under the Union, 1870–1921* (Oxford: Oxford University Press, 2010), p.569.

7.  P. Gatenby, *The School of Physic, Trinity College Dublin: A Retrospective View* (Dublin: Trinity College, 1994), pp.9–10. In the early 1700s, the School of Physic was situated in 'The Anatomy House' where the Berkeley Library now stands. In the nineteenth century it moved to the east end of the campus.

8.  S.M. Parkes, 'The "Steamboat Ladies", the First World War and After', in S.M. Parkes (ed.), *A Danger to the Men? A History of Women in Trinity College Dublin, 1904–2004* (Dublin: The Lilliput Press, 2004), p.91; Gatenby, *The School of Physic*, p.20.

9.  C. McCarthy, *Cumann na mBan and the Irish Revolution* (Cork: The Collins Press, 2005), p.1. Cumann na mBan (Women's Association) was a nationalist group whose membership was entirely female. In 1919, the British establishment outlawed the organisation.

10. D. Stopford to Sir Matthew Nathan (University of Oxford, Bodleian Library, Nathan MS 204 folio 166). The letters of Dorothy Stopford to Sir Matthew Nathan (MS. Nathan 204, fols.164–291) are held in the Bodleian library in Oxford, England (many are undated so the chronology of the letters is not always clear).

11. L. Ó Broin, *Protestant Nationalists in Revolutionary Ireland: The Stopford Connection* (Dublin: Gill & Macmillan, 1985), p.147.

12. R. Stopford, Introductory Note, (NLI MS 15341 (1)).

13. D. Stopford to Sir M. Nathan, 25 January, year not given (University of Oxford, Bodleian, Nathan papers, MS 204, folio 256).

14. Ibid.

15. M. Millerick, 'Nathan, Sir Matthew', in *Dictionary of Irish Biography* online, (accessed 12 October 2013); P. Wilson, 'Nathan, Sir Matthew (1862–1939)', in *Australian Dictionary of Biography*, National Centre of Biography, Australian National University, http://adb.anu.edu.au/biography/nathan-sir-matthew-7728/text13539, (accessed 19 June 2013).

16. M. Ó hÓgartaigh, *Kathleen Lynn. Irishwoman, Patriot, Doctor* (Dublin and Portland: Irish Academic Press, 2006), p.71.

17. D. Stopford to Sir M. Nathan, February 1916 (University of Oxford, Bodleian, Nathan papers, MS 204, folio 180, 183).

18. Ibid.

19. R.B. McDowell, *Alice Stopford Green: A Passionate Historian* (Dublin: Allen Figgis, 1967), p.102.

20. C. Townshend, *Easter 1916: The Irish Rebellion* (London: Allen Lane, 2005), p.146.

21. The insurgents were members of the Irish Volunteers, the Irish Republican Brotherhood and the Irish Citizen Army. The Rising, which did not have a popular mandate, was largely confined to Dublin.

22. Estelle Nathan was married to Sir George Nathan, who worked at the British War Office.

23. D. Stopford to Sir M. Nathan, 12 April 1916 (University of Oxford, Bodleian, Nathan papers, MS 204, folio 188).

24. D. Price, 1916 Diary (NLI, MS 16063).

25. L. Ó Broin, *Dublin Castle and the 1916 Rising: the Story of Sir Matthew Nathan* (Dublin: Helicon, 1966), pp.7–8.

26. D. Price, 1916 Diary (NLI, MS 16063).

27. Ibid.

28. Ibid.

29. Ibid.

30. Now named O'Connell Street, Dublin.

31. D. Price, 1916 Diary (NLI, MS 16063).

32. On 2 January 1911, Sidney Street, London was besieged by police searching for members

of a gang of thieves. The Home Secretary, Winston Churchill brought in the Scots Guards as reinforcements for the police. Churchill himself attended the scene which was captured on newsreel. http://content.met.police.uk/Article/The-Siege-of-Sidney-Street/1400015482933/historicalcases (accessed 14 January 2014).

33. D. Stopford to C. Stopford, undated (NLI, MS 21205 (4)).

34. D. Stopford to E. Stopford, undated, Wednesday (NLI, MS 21205 (4)).

35. D. Price, 1916 Diary (NLI, MS 16063).

36. Castleknock is a suburb to the west of Dublin city, separated from the city by the Phoenix Park.

37. Slane Castle, Slane, County Meath.

38. D. Price, 1916 Diary (NLI, MS 16063).

39. D. Stopford to Sir M. Nathan, Saturday, undated (University of Oxford, Bodleian, Nathan papers, MS 204, folio 189).

40. C. Stopford to Sir M. Nathan, 29 April 1916 (University of Oxford, Bodleian, Nathan papers, MS 204, folio 190).

41. For a full account of Elsie Henry's life and work during this period, see C. Cullen (ed), *The World Upturning: Elsie Henry's Irish Wartime Diaries, 1913–1919* (Dublin: Irish Academic Press, 2013).

42. Parkes, 'The "Steamboat Ladies"', pp.91–5.

43. D. Price, 1916 Diary (NLI, MS 16063).

44. Ibid.

45. D. Stopford to R. Stopford, 9 May 1916 (NLI, MS 21205 (4)).

46. D. Stopford to C. Stopford, Sunday, undated (NLI, MS 21205 (4)).

47. Ó Broin, *Protestant Nationalists*, p.65.

48. D. Stopford to R. Stopford, 9 May 1916 (NLI, MS 21205 (4)).

49. Ibid.

50. Sixteen people were executed following the Rising, including the seven signatories of the Proclamation and Roger Casement who was hanged in London. Ninety-seven others were also sentenced to death, but had their sentences commuted to various terms of imprisonment.

51. Parkes, 'The "Steamboat Ladies"', pp.92–4.

52. M. Nathan to D. Stopford, 13 May 1916, Sir Matthew Nathan letters (NLI, MS 15341 (1)).

53. D. Stopford to Sir M. Nathan, 4 August (University of Oxford, Bodleian, Nathan papers, MS 204, folio 196–201).

54. Ó Broin, *Protestant Nationalists*, p.134.

55. A.S. Green to General Botha, 26 June 1916 (Bureau of Military History Contemporary Document Collection (1913-21), BMH CD 45/2/2). Copy of letter.

56. A.S. Green to H. Asquith, 17 May 1916 (BMH, CD 45/2/22). Copy of letter.

57. Ó Broin, *Protestant Nationalists*, p.133.

58. R. Casement to Nina, 25 July 1916 (BMH, CD45/2/24). He requested Nina to thank various individuals, including 'Mrs Green, my loving friend, you can never thank her enough for all she has been to me...'; A.S. Green to L. Botha, 26 June 1916 (BMH, CD 45/2/23); A.S. Green to H. Asquith, 17 May 1916 (BMH, CD 45/2/22).

59. E. Stopford, unpublished memoirs, p.16 (NLI, MS 11,426).

60. Sir Thomas Lauder Brunton, Obituary, *BMJ*, 2, 2908 (1916), pp.440–2.

61. Sir M. Nathan to D. Stopford, 25 Sept 1916 (NLI, MS15341).

62. D. Stopford to Sir M. Nathan (University of Oxford, Bodleian, Nathan papers, MS 204, folios 205-7).

63. J. Stephens, *Insurrection in Dublin* (Dublin and London: Maunsell, 1916).

64. D. Figgis, *AE (George W. Russell): A Study of a Man and a Nation* (New York: Dodd, Meade and Company, 1916), p.15.

65. L. Ramert, 'Lessons from the Land: Shaw's John Bull's Other Island, *New Hibernia Review*, 16, 3 (Autumn 2012), pp.43-59.

66. M. Nathan to D. Stopford, 23 October 1916, Sir Matthew Nathan letters (NLI, MS 15341/1).

67. D. Stopford to Sir M. Nathan, 1916 (University of Oxford, Bodleian, Nathan papers, MS 204, folio 219–22).

68. D. Stopford to Sir M. Nathan, 1916 (University of Oxford, Bodleian, Nathan papers, MS 204, folio 219). Doggerel written by D. Stopford.

69. D. Stopford to Sir M. Nathan, 1916 (University of Oxford, Bodleian, Nathan papers, MS 204, folio 221).

70. D. Stopford to Sir M. Nathan, 1916 (University of Oxford, Bodleian, Nathan papers, MS 204, folio 219).

71. D. Stopford to Sir M. Nathan, 1916 (University of Oxford, Bodleian, Nathan papers, MS 204, folio 222-3).

72. C. Cullen, *The World Upturning*, p.182.

73. Now Dun Laoghaire, County Dublin.

74. D. Stopford to Sir M. Nathan, 1916 (University of Oxford, Bodleian, Nathan papers, MS 204, folio 226).

75. For a full assessment of Lynn's career, see M. Ó hÓgartaigh, *Kathleen Lynn: Irishwoman, Patriot, Doctor* (Dublin: Irish Academic Press, 2006).

76. C. Cullen, *The World Upturning*, p.234.

77. Anonymous, *Ballad of East Clare*, 1917. Literature for the East Clare by-election, 1917, can be viewed at http://freepages.genealogy.rootsweb.ancestry.com/~bwickham/elections.htm (accessed 17 August 2013).

78. D. Stopford to Sir M. Nathan, 1916 (University of Oxford, Bodleian, Nathan papers, MS 204, folio 233).

79. S.M. Parkes, 'The "Steamboat Ladies"', p.91.

80. D. Stopford to Sir M. Nathan, 30 September (University of Oxford, Bodleian, Nathan papers, MS 204, folio 235).

81. D. Stopford to Sir M. Nathan, undated (University of Oxford, Bodleian, Nathan papers, MS 204, folio 260).

82. L. Kelly, *Irish Women in Medicine, c.1880s-1902s: Origins, Education and Careers* (Manchester: Manchester University Press, 2013).

83. L. Kelly, *Irish Women in Medicine*, p.90.

84. D. Stopford to Sir M. Nathan, 18 October (University of Oxford, Bodleian, Nathan papers, MS 204, folio 237).

85. D. Stopford to Sir M. Nathan, 9 December (University of Oxford, Bodleian, Nathan papers, MS 204, folio 239).

86. D. Stopford to Sir M. Nathan, 4/5 April, 12 p.m. (University of Oxford, Bodleian, Nathan papers, MS 204, folio 248).

# CHAPTER THREE

# CASTING IN HER LOT WITH IRELAND: THE TCD YEARS (1918–1921)

By February 1918, Dorothy noted that 'all sorts of upper-class respectable people' were becoming Sinn Féiners. At her Easter break, she planned to go to her mother's house in London and decided to bring food instead of clothes so as not to inconvenience them. She joked that she would produce a 'packet of sandwiches and cube of oxo' when she met Sir Matthew. Affectionate relations between the Nathans and the Stopfords continued. Mary Wordsworth sent a postcard to Dorothy, her aunt: 'Dear Toad, please tell the Man in the Moon [Sir Matthew] to call his kitten Jericho. Jerry for short. Love from Mary'.[1]

Once again, Dorothy was experiencing nightmares which were probably stress related. Hillary Term, 1918, was not enjoyable as work was exam focused rather than undertaken for the 'love of the thing or for any humanitarian purposes'.[2] Sir Matthew boasted that he was still ahead of her with respect to work hours. 'My record for 1917 being 3552 hours which gives a fair quotient when divided by 365. But I don't suppose it is as concentrated work as yours while you are at it. You seem to have some time for fun in between. I am sure I hope so for I like to think you very happy.' He urged her to cross to England at Easter as it was some time since she was there and he wanted to spend a 'long day' with her.[3]

Dorothy asked Sir Matthew to intervene with the British Government with respect to the proposed extension of conscription to Ireland. However, he reminded her that during his year and a half in Ireland, he had advised against conscription and for conciliation and the outcome was a rebellion. Therefore, any intervention by him would be 'not only be ineffectual but might not unreasonably be held to be impertinent ... thanks, dear, for telling me so much of what was happening. Your letter was full of sad interest'. He advised her to stick to her studies as she had wrongly diagnosed him as ill rather than in understandably poor spirits. Instead, he prescribed for himself: 'two sheets of letter from you once a week to be taken after breakfast' and signed off 'with love'.[4]

By the summer of 1918, Dorothy confessed to Sir Matthew that she had 'cast in her lot with Ireland'. She would try and keep a 'sane view' of it but, in the light of her new feelings, she could not take the summer job he had offered as it would not be 'straight' to go and work for the British government. She looked on medicine, however, as absolutely international and she was adamant that she would try to stick to it and keep out of politics as much as possible. The brutal executions of the leaders following the Rising and the 'fairly ruthless repression of searches, raids and curfews' drove many 'hitherto uncommitted persons' into 'the arms of Sinn Féin'.[5] These new converts included Dorothy. Despite her protestations about staying out of politics, her passion for medicine was soon equalled by her new passion for Irish nationalism.

Her sister Alice, too, converted to the Irish cause. In 1918, Alice was contacted by Aunt Alice's secretary Máire Comerford who asked her if she knew of anyone who could take in two men who were 'on the run'. Liam Mellowes and Sean Etchingham came to stay with Alice, Dorothy, Mary and their lodger. Alice was always willing to take in men on the run but she drew the line at housing arms or ammunition. Liam and Sean became frequent visitors and once Dorothy and Alice had to take them by separate train routes to the 'Brown Bread Shop' which was a well-known meeting place. De Valera's secretary 'was in the habit of leaving an extra suitcase' belonging to him in their house. They housed the man himself for a week at one stage:

He had to stay mainly upstairs as I had to negotiate the child's daily governess, a charwoman etc., as well as chance visitors, but he said he was quite happy with his suitcase of books and papers which was already in the house … Miss O'Connell [his secretary] used to come in every day and work with him. I came in one day to find a small Fianna boy in the hall raising the seat of his bicycle to accommodate the president, on which he rode away.[6]

In June, Dorothy sat an examination in political economy and got seven in the viva. 'We melted the examiner's heart by telling him how busy we were. He answered most of the viva questions himself.' Furthermore, in the written exam, the examiner 'tactfully withdrew', allowing the students to help each other. Dorothy was pleased with this acknowledgement that for medical students the arts courses were really a farce. As soon as the war was over, the college could manage without the extra fees and it would be abolished, she believed.[7]

After a whirl of exams, Dorothy went back to Mount Trenchard where once again she revelled in the 'blissful lazy life of a country house … picking blackcurrents [sic], chickens eating gooseberries and pigs rumoured to be eating grapes'. She left this domestic idyll to spend some time in the wilds of mountainous County Wicklow where she fished and swam and camped. She asked Sir Matthew to 'slip over incog for a week?' He could have the run of a picturesque two-room cottage and they wouldn't discuss Ireland. Instead, they'd concentrate on black hackle (a fly for fishing), orange grouse, haymaking and wild raspberries. Sir Matthew didn't join her. He excused himself: 'My dear Dorothy, if it were a little nearer and not quite so windy I would really go to you at Lough Dan for at the moment I feel absolutely of no good here. For three days I have had my new work and have felt perfectly useless.'[8]

While Sir Matthew struggled with his new role as secretary of a commission looking into the possibility of higher wages for women, Dorothy 'performed the triumphal feat' of swimming Lough Dan, accompanied by her Uncle Ned in a boat in 'agonies' in case she developed cramp and required assistance. The distance was 'anything from a quarter of a mile to a mile', she gaily told Sir Matthew. Dorothy followed up this feat by cycling about thirty miles before she went to bed.[9] She enjoyed being a free soul with a tent and a bicycle but, in the end, admitted she preferred company.

In October 1918, Dorothy was distressed by the sinking of the RMS

*Leinster* which had been torpedoed by a German U-boat in the Irish Sea. There were more than 500 deaths.[10] The ship had sailed from Kingstown Harbour bound for Holyhead in Wales. It was about sixteen miles out when it was attacked. Dorothy had done this journey often. She was also very familiar with Kingstown Harbour as she sailed there with the Hannarys. Furthermore, Dorothy's doctor and friend Ella Webb helped those rescued and her accounts were 'pretty terrific'. At home, there were domestic difficulties with servants and coal in short supply.

In November 1918, peace was declared; the First World War had come to an end. Dorothy's cousin, the young doctor Ted Brunton, had died at Loos in 1915, at the age of 25. Other cousins, George Stopford and Geoffrey Young, were safe, while Bob Venables, yet another cousin, had spent 1914 to 1917 in a prisoner-of-war camp in Germany.[11] Dorothy's brother Robert had survived although he was not to be demobilised until June 1919. But, Dorothy was 'too busy with flu' – of which more later – to celebrate.

There was another more welcome distraction for Dorothy that month when Aunt Alice, at the age of 70, left London and relocated to Dublin. She took a 'fine house, 90 St Stephen's Green' for seven years from November 1918. Dorothy was very glad her aunt was coming to Dublin.[12] Her home became a meeting place for scholars, politicians and civil servants. 'She herself [Alice], white-haired and upright, wearing a sixteenth-century Venetian cape negligently flung over her shoulders and with an eighteenth-century pearl necklace and an Arab medieval ornament dangling from her neck, dominated, encouraged and at times intimidated her guests.'[13]

Dorothy found it a 'wakener-up having her in Dublin, she keeps us all up to the mark and is awfully nice'. Robert Barton was chosen as the Sinn Féin candidate for West Wicklow at an impending general election in 1918.[14] Dorothy canvassed for him and wrote a stirring account of a meeting held in the Hibernian Hall of a mountain village:

> a cheer was raised as the candidate entered and groups gathered around him for a university degree, broad acres and different faith create no barriers between him and his fellow countrymen. Belated orator, three hours late … when he arrived, for an hour we sat in breathless silence, swayed now by the deep rich pleading tones, now lashed by his masterly sarcasm, now shaking with mirth at his stories.[15]

She was indignant that candidates could not simply ask the police for a permit to hold a 'free meeting in a free country'. Word was passed from mouth to mouth and assemblies had to be held before the local police had time to draft in reinforcements and stop the meetings. Dorothy sent her diatribe on the electioneering process in Ireland to *The Herald*, the National Labour Weekly, in London. It was rejected for publication.[16] In the end, Robert Barton won the contest and Dorothy enjoyed herself hugely on polling day 'buzzing around a lively constituency … we did 160 miles between 8 a.m. and 11 p.m. and won hands down'.[17]

For her twenty-eighth birthday, Dorothy was presented with a cake on which twenty-eight night lights had been placed in green, white and gold or red, white and blue, 'according to the political opinions of the company'. The birthday party was held in the Grand Hotel in Greystones, County Wicklow, just outside Dublin. She told Sir Matthew that it was a 'horribly swell place where they give you four courses for breakfast, five for lunch and seven for dinner, and, as it is pouring with rain, you have to sit in the lounge and smoke'. Dorothy amused herself by trying to scandalise the Unionist Attorney General, Sir James Campbell who was also staying at the hotel. She would come down to dinner dressed in a 'bright green frock, white collar and gold scarf'. But, to her chagrin, she was not asked to remove herself from this respectable establishment.[18]

Dorothy's stubbornness was a family legend. During her years as a medical student, Edie took Dorothy to Sir John Simon's[19] country house in England for a weekend. The Stopfords had a family connection with Sir John, as his first wife was Ethel Mary Venables, a niece of J.R. Green, Aunt Alice's husband. Simon was anxious to show Dorothy that there were at least some people in England who were 'right-minded on the Irish question'. He took Dorothy and Edie to a dinner, with a couple of hundred guests, organised by the Birmingham Liberal Club. Dorothy was placed between the chairman of the local liberal party and Sir John. Before the speeches, the 'loyal toast' was proposed. Everyone, including Edie, rose to their feet. Dorothy remained seated. According to Edie, Dorothy, who was always 'exceptionally courageous and especially so after her experiences in Ireland', remained calm and 'rooted to her chair'. Sir John seemed amused rather than horrified although Lady Simon, who had remained at home, was 'rather shocked'. The next day, the Birmingham Liberal Club chairman and his wife came to Sunday lunch with the Simons. The chairman was 'obviously entranced' with Dorothy's courage and 'would talk to no-one but her'. Dorothy's 'conquest of Sir John was complete' when she proceeded to beat him at billiards. He afterwards told Edie that Dorothy 'strode' round the billiard table, a cigarette hanging out of one corner of her mouth and curses streaming out of the other.[20]

— ·········· ············ —

Following the constitution of the Irish parliament, Dáil Éireann, Robert Barton procured a ticket for Dorothy to attend the first meeting on 21 January 1919. The handwritten name on her admission ticket was in Irish and seems to read 'Deora Nic Ghiolla an Phairt'.[21] The historian J.J. Lee has described this first Dáil 'consisting of the 27 available Sinn Féin members' as a 'rump parliament' which adopted a 'cryptic five article constitution as well as a "Democratic Programme"'.[22] Robert Barton read the 'Message to the Free Nations of the World'[23] in English and was appointed as the first Minister for Agriculture. He established the National Land Bank which facilitated land redistribution through the co-operative farming societies. Most of the business was done in Irish so it is doubtful how much Dorothy understood of the proceedings. Afterwards, Barton jokingly addressed Dorothy as 'Deora' for a time signing himself 'Riobaird'.

The first Dáil might be said to mark the beginning of the War of Independence which was to continue (mostly as a guerrilla war of ambushes and reprisals) until mid-1922. From January 1919, local Volunteer groups began, sporadically, to assassinate policeman. According to J.J. Lee: 'The British … in collusion with the extremists, drove the elected representatives more into the hands of the gunmen by suppressing the Dáil and Sinn Féin'.[24] The IRA, as the Volunteers began to be known, both retaliated and attacked.

In February 1919, Robert Barton was arrested and held in Mountjoy Gaol, Dublin, for making seditious speeches at Carnew, County Wicklow. From his cell in His Majesty's Prison, Robert wrote to Dorothy. Addressing her as Deora, he was ironic: 'I'm sorry you could not see the arrest take place tho' it was a tame affair. I was so hopelessly outnumbered but to be really expert at this sort of thing one has to have more experience than I have had.' He invited her to spend Easter at his home even if he wasn't there and to do some fishing. His cousin Erskine would be there and he hoped that she would not have to do so many household duties as the last time she was their guest. He continued: 'The principal complaint I have to make of this gaol is that sometimes there is such a racket kicked off by some of these Sinn Féin prisoners in the gaol that I do not get all the rest I had expected!!' Asking her to pass on his love to Mrs Green [Aunt Alice], he said that he would write again in a day or two.[25]

Dorothy evidently sent him in some books and sweets as he thanked her for them and wrote that he had read all of the Wordsworth. However, he could not find one complete sonnet which satisfied him. 'Sometimes the first half, sometimes the last lines stir one but there is always a blemish in the whole, something which impresses limitations and the lack of imagination. There is some touch of Queen Victoria about him,' he complained.[26] While awaiting trial, he escaped on 16 March, using a file smuggled in by Richard Mulcahy,[27] who also arranged for a party of Volunteers to throw a rope ladder over the prison wall. Barton left a dummy in his bed and a note for the governor saying that he felt compelled to leave, due to the discomfort of his surroundings. While on the run, he convinced his cousin Erskine to join Sinn Féin.[28]

At times, it seemed as if Dorothy was leading two lives – one which was caught up with national politics and another to do with college life. Occasionally, the two strands overlapped. For instance, during her Junior Sophister year (third year) Dorothy wrote and carefully preserved an essay simply entitled 'War'. She was optimistic that as an 'articulate democracy' developed, the wars of the future would not be entered upon without the consent of the whole people rather than the politicians and capitalists. She suggested that the 'love of striving' in man, which has been wrongly called the 'love of war', might be 'directed towards fighting disease and solving problems of civilisation'.[29]

There were also battles to be fought in college. At this time, TCD societies remained dilatory in their attitudes towards the admission of women. In 1918, the Dublin University Experimental Science Association (DUESA) was opened to women but 'tactful' arrangements were required as meetings were held in the evenings after the 6 p.m. curfew for women. The female students would gather at the Lincoln Gate to the college and were shepherded in by the lady Registrar who had to remain present throughout the meeting.[30] Newer societies held their meetings in the afternoons so women could attend without chaperones and the women's athletic societies became part of the Dublin University Central Athletic Association.

Dorothy was particularly angered by her exclusion, on grounds of gender, from the Dublin University Biological Society (the Bi).[31] By the time she had entered third year in 1919, she was ready to do battle on behalf of the third-, fourth- and fifth-year women medical students. As secretary to the newly-formed Dublin Women Medical Students Committee, she began to formulate a plan of campaign. The committee also looked for the support of Dr Euphran Maxwell, the female ophthalmology lecturer, who was a role model to many of the women students. Dorothy decided, in the first instance, not to ask for admission to the Bi for first- and second-years as they would not have completed anatomy or done enough hospital work to benefit, but she was confident that they would later gain admission. The attack was to be done quietly, not to be 'talked about by individuals'. She drafted a careful petition to the secretary of the Bi. This read:

> ...we understand there is no provision in the Statute book against the admission of women students to the Bi Assoc the only objection we can see is that it is contrary to the traditions of Trinity, but in the last few years the political and professional position of women in the world has changed. In addition, the increasing numbers of women in the medical school and the concessions of equal advantages granted to them in that school and the Dublin hospitals, and the honours they have gained, they feel justified in forwarding this request.[32]

Dorothy went on to explain in the letter that she had considered the possibility of forming a corresponding society amongst the women but owing to the small number of qualified medical women in Dublin she felt that they could not hope for any great success. Nor did she think that two such societies could co-exist in college. She was adamant that this was not about the social side of the Bi but about women benefiting from, and taking part in, the scientific discussions. She pointed out that the men and women's work as students was identical and when they are qualified would not be dissimilar: 'We therefore seek for every advantage which may be gained during our college course. This fact is recognized by the Academy of Medicine which admits women as student associates.'

And there were some members of the Bi who were clearly in sympathy with Dorothy and her fellow female students. Harold Stofmeyer wrote to Dorothy to 'acquaint her' with the happenings at the meeting. He was sorry to have to tell her that the meeting was definitely opposed to the admission of ladies. Indeed, he had feared this even before going to the meeting and when he got there his fears were confirmed 'immediately I had gazed upon the faces of the assembled throng. In the face of this conservative and prejudiced environment, Dr Solomons got up and proposed a middle course which the Bi, after much discussion, thought it would "consider"'. This proposal was that women should form a Biological Association of their own and hold meetings in the usual way and that the men, in that case, would 'not be adverse to discussion at our occasional mixed gathering subjects of mutual interest'. Hofmeyer suggested that taking this gradual course might allow Dorothy to reach her ultimate goal. He concluded his letter by stating: 'Thou art a "rare plucked 'un"'. Best of luck, yours very sincerely, Harold Stofmeyer'.[33]

The formal reply from the corresponding secretary of the Bi was far less compromising:

> At an ordinary meeting of the association held on the 12th inst your communication was read 'in extremo' to the members by the Record Secretary. In order to obtain an authoritative expression of the attitude of the Association the following resolution was moved: "That the election of women students to the membership and privileges of the DUBA is desirable." After exhaustive discussion this motion was defeated by 120 votes to 2. The views expressed were in no way hostile towards the women students, but the consensus of opinion was that this election would inevitably lead to the disruption or atrophy of the Association.[34]

The response pointed out that the rule of the Association did not discriminate between men and women students but that a candidate could be elected only if a large measure of support was forthcoming. This was clearly not going to be the case for any women applicants and the proposed solution was for them to set up their own society but the suggestion of occasional shared meetings was not mentioned in this letter. It was also pointed out that the Bi was originally founded with infinitely smaller resources than are now available among the women students for the institution of a similar society.

The hard line taken by the Bi towards women was to continue. In November 1929, eight years after Price graduated from TCD, the Bi first allowed female medical students to attend meetings. A further six years later, in 1935, some of Dorothy's work was presented at the Bi but she was not allowed to present it herself. Dr T. Garratt Hardiman wrote to her, thanking her for her notes and her kindness in showing the case. In his remarks to the Bi, he had said that it 'was unfortunate that your sex debarred you from showing the case yourself but I did not notice that anyone said "hear, hear"!! This was no reflection on you of course!! In another 50 years or so we may admit women members?'[35] It didn't take quite that long; in May 1941 women were first admitted to full membership.[36]

While Price's failure to have women admitted to the Bi during her student years must have rankled, she did not have much time to brood. The World War was followed by a pandemic of Spanish influenza with the virus responsible for more deaths than the whole of the First World War. The Spanish flu hit Dublin in 1918. It was terrifying in its virulent symptoms with projectile nose bleeding, the coughing up of blood and the skin turning a blue-black colour. The patients gave off a strange and puzzling stench. As well as producing symptoms that were reminiscent of the plague, the Spanish flu displayed a preference for young adults. In Ireland, more than 20,000 people died and as many as 600,000 people were infected. Doctors and nurses were overworked and exhausted. The cause of the disease was not known, adding to a sense of helplessness and despair among the professionals.[37]

The dreaded flu, with its penchant for young lives, brushed against Dorothy in July 1918, following a whirl of exams, when she, herself, had a 'touch of Spanish flu, cured at night and ignored during the day'.[38] In October 1918, Dorothy, now a third-year medical student, 'exercised her powers cautiously' on the wards of Meath Street Hospital as she knew she was 'horribly ignorant and junior'. She could do little other than what the ward sister suggested. 'I am in her hands and learning a lot. We are packed with influenza cases, mostly DMP [Dublin Metropolitan Police].' Mortality was high as it was a very violent form of the flu, generally ending in pneumonia. However, Dorothy told Sir Matthew that the 'bug' had been found and inoculation was being used for curative purposes although it was too late to say with what success.[39]

At the end of the month, she suffered from 'a private tragedy' when her great friend Cesca Trench died from the flu on 30 October. Cesca, also known as Sadhbh Trinseach, was an artist and illustrator. Like Dorothy, her family were Anglo-Irish and her brothers had joined the British army. Cesca immersed herself in Irish language and culture. She and her sister Margot were members of Cumann na mBan.[40] In 1914, Cesca was staying with the Coffey family in Howth and witnessed the gun-running. After a long courtship, Irish Volunteer, librarian and biographer, Diarmid Coffey[41] proposed to Cesca on 17 March 1918 (St Patrick's day). On 21 March 1918, Cesca's brother Reggie was killed on the Western Front. Nonetheless, Cesca went ahead with her wedding to Diarmid the following month, on 17 April 1918. Both Diarmid and Cesca were described by Dorothy as 'very intimate friends' and she was 'the most splendid and beautiful creature I had ever known'. Cesca was only ill for three days and 'went out like a flash, the last person, full of life and vitality that you could think of dying'.[42] Cesca's death was typical in that this flu was more likely to lead to death among young adults than among the usual flu victims – the elderly and the very young.

In November, the 'general scrimmage of the influenza epidemic' which was 'pretty hot here' continued. Dorothy worked with two nurses on a landing in the hospital where there were about thirty ill patients and the sister had been laid low. The ward was full up with policemen and there were a lot of deaths. 'It was very horrible', she declared, but things seemed to be getting better and most people recovered. Sadly, the sister, who had been 'particularly nice', died.

Dorothy was also impressed by her 'chief', Professor William Boxwell, who was not only 'very clever but also very grand and fine, he is up and about night and day and has pulled a lot of people through'. As for her own contribution, she said it was difficult knowing so little and death seemed very terrible. But she got used to it quickly in the general busyness of ward work and found her feet. The amount of 'odds and ends' of doctoring and nursing that she absorbed in two weeks under pressure was 'rather astonishing and one gains confidence'.[43]

There was some speculation that the disease was something other than flu. Boxwell said that 'from the beginning he had regarded the more severe types as cases of profound septic intoxication'. Dorothy, who was his clinical clerk at this time, witnessed some of the worst symptoms of the flu – the bloody lungs of corpses at post mortem. She found that Boxwell was 'mad on post-mortems'. He tried to get a portion of each lung from the:

> black influenzal pneumonia and at 10 p.m. every night I biked
> down to the mortuary and with or without the aid of a night
> porter carried in about three corpses to the post mortem room,
> and stripped them ready and put them tidy afterwards. They
> were all surreptitious post mortems and once or twice we got
> a fright when someone came to the door which was locked.[44]

Dorothy needed to be strong physically and mentally to manoeuvre a dead adult body and to work alone. 'I well remember nights when the rain came down on the glass roof, and I alone inside trying to get the corpse into its habit and back on to its bench.'[45] Boxwell tried to help but he was too busy and often had to leave at midnight. The results of the post mortems were disappointing as the blood engorging the lungs of the victims of the flu obscured the microscopic picture. Dorothy's experience of frustrating post mortems where lungs were congested, haemorrhaging and leaking purulent fluids was mirrored in other post mortems in Ireland.[46] She recalled these details later and did not mention them in her contemporaneous letters – probably in a bid to spare Sir Matthew the horrific details. Although horrifying, a first-hand experience of a disease of this type of virulence was also valuable to a medical student such as Dorothy. The overstretched resources of the qualified doctors provided opportunities for medical students to test their wings.

By 15 February 1919, Dorothy was finding life very exciting, having attained some self-confidence in her powers of healing. 'I don't believe at all in women doctors not liking to take responsibility, at least I don't see why they shouldn't but it's always charged against them.' It was largely a matter of knowing your work and being careful, she declared, 'the rest is experience, more than brains, with plenty of self-assurance'. She was becoming a 'demon' for work and was in the 'dangerous stage' of taking on anything that offered – she blithely gave ether to a man getting out eleven teeth. Her clerkship went so well that she stayed on a further three months in the Meath Hospital. In March, Dorothy told Sir Matthew that they were having another epidemic, just as bad as the autumn one. 'Five with pneumonia, the latter proving frequently fatal, and the hospital is once more not unlike an evil dream; still lots recover too.' She had a public exam looming in a week's time but was undecided about sitting it as 'this flu business puts one off book work'.[47]

There were also dangers in practicing medicine, and pathology in particular, in this pre-antibiotic era. For instance, the college's first Professor of Anatomy, Alexander Charles O'Sullivan died of blood poisoning in 1924 having infected himself accidentally during a post mortem.[48] Although antibiotics were not available, the new science of bacteriology had taken hold in the college. TCD's School of Physic had good laboratories and clinical facilities, while Adrian Stokes, the first professor of bacteriology and preventive medicine (1919–22), was appointed during Dorothy's student years.[49] However, during Dorothy's early years in TCD, prior to the end of the First World War, many of the medical teaching staff, including Stokes, were absent taking part in the war effort.

Despite all the distractions and lacunae, Dorothy distinguished herself in her clinical practice. Her testimonials from the Meath were glowing. Boxwell wrote that he knew 'Dr Stopford intimately while she was studying medicine at the Meath Hospital. Always keen, and hardworking, she took life seriously, and soon rose above the general class of students; taking the Intermediate Clinical Hospital prize in her second year.' He added that she was 'one of the most helpful clinical clerks' he ever had. She managed the Extern Department with ability during his absence. While at the Meath, she 'made herself familiar with the practical side of the work of a general hospital, carrying out the various necessary operations herself with thoroughness and detail'. She was a 'capable pathologist and has personally conducted a large number of post-mortem examinations'. Boxwell noted that Dorothy had a 'shy personality; with courage and determination, and is a cultivated lady in the highest sense'.

Dorothy enjoyed working in the Meath Hospital and she also began to 'dip into' the conditions of sick children in the city. She was influenced by a number of female doctors including Ella Webb, who ran Baby Clubs which had been founded under the auspices of Lady Aberdeen's Women's National Health Association. Webb allowed Dorothy to help out in her slum dispensary on Tuesday evenings. Later, Dorothy was to work with Webb in

St. Ultan's Hospital which had been founded by Dr Kathleen Lynn and Madeleine ffrench Mullen.

— ........... ...........  —

Dorothy's intimacy with Sir Matthew had waned. In January 1920, she wrote to him musing that she has not heard from him for so long that she wondered whether he had already left for Australia where he had been promised the governorship of Queensland. The tone of the letter was, as always lightly ironic, but now it was also that of someone filling in an old friend on recent happenings in which he did not play a part or about which he had not been consulted.

She had seen little of his old friends, the Webbs, but had new 'inhabitants' now – the Childers, who were to 'throw in their lot with this country. Mrs Childers is going to be a great help over social work, babies clubs and hospitals etc and they are a good addition'. On politics, Dorothy was brief – Lord French was established as the Lord Lieutenant in the Viceregal Lodge but she had never seen him. Her interests had expanded beyond Castle politics and she expected Alderman Tom Kelly MP to be the new Lord Mayor: 'He is residing now in Wormwood Scrubs awaiting trial or rather awaiting a charge to be preferred against him. So, things are looking lively but no immediate rising is likely, the people are very patient and forbearing.'[50]

Dorothy had not travelled to London that Christmas as she was in residence at the Meath Hospital and did not get a holiday. Constance had come over to Dublin instead. The residency at the Meath had left Dorothy 'much the wiser'. She wrote that she had: 'chiefly learnt not to be afraid of tipsy people who streamed in at all hours of the day and night to be patched up. I have also added a commanding note to my otherwise charming voice, which is part of the trade and acquired in dealing with the aforementioned "drunks".' Dorothy earned an odd guinea or two 'assisting swells to operate on private patients'.[51]

She moved from the Meath Hospital, on the south side of Dublin city, to undertake her obstetrical placement in the Rotunda Hospital on the north side. She could 'be seen at any moment of the day or night emerging into the district carrying a small bag' ready to assist at a home delivery.[52] At the Rotunda, as elsewhere, there were teaching fees to be paid and, here, they supplemented the salary of the Master. The hospital had a personal resonance for Dorothy as her grandfather had been a Master there. It was also a prestigious place to study as it enjoyed a reputation as being one of best lying-hospitals in the United Kingdom.[53]

Dorothy also began to socialise: 'making excursions into the life proper of a medical student – a world in itself'. So, Dorothy was able to reassure Sir Matthew that there was 'little time left for politics and bomb throwing and you will not see me lodged in jail quite immediately' although she joked that if she had a little spare time she would 'hop in for a bit'. She had passed her BA degree which entitled her to a university vote but she didn't expect to have much opportunity to exercise it. At 30 years of age, she was also entitled to vote in the general elections.[54]

Dorothy 'shaved' through part one of the final medical exam, coming last on the list. She was, once again, going into residence in 'her hospital', the Meath. Nevertheless, she told Sir Matthew that she would not allow hard work to get in the way of what he would call mischief. He was appointed as Governor of Queensland in Australia in June 1920 and Dorothy's last letter to him prior to his departure noted that she would not see him before he left as she was not planning a trip to London. 'Don't forget me. I shan't you', she added.

Dorothy wrote this letter soon after having her appendix removed. She had been working in surgery and 'apparently caught appendicitis from her patients'. Her 'chief', Billy Taylor carried out the operation and she was 'only eleven days in hospital'. She was amused by having all her friends in the Meath around but it meant that she could 'barely hope for a pass in surgery' even if she was ready to take the exam. Dorothy went to the Pen-y-pas Hotel, Llanbene in North Wales to recuperate. Her mother, Constance, and a Cambridge friend accompanied her. The letter drew to a close with the wish that Sir Matthew would not be lonely in Australia and that, when he returned, he would come and visit 'our Republic' and, perhaps, by then, she would be able to entertain him in Merrion Square (the apogee of medical addresses). She signed off 'yours affectionately'.[55]

The friendship of the past six years had dwindled to a gentle end. Perhaps, it had foundered on Dorothy's burgeoning nationalism, maybe it was the difference in their ages, the divergent paths that they had chosen or Dorothy might have found out about Sir Matthew's other liaisons. His Jewishness may have played a part although it is not mentioned in the correspondence. She may have transferred her affections to Robert Barton

– the Stopfords thought that she might marry him – while Sir Matthew, who never married, was enjoying a most indiscreet liaison with a fellow civil servant, the Fabian Amber Pember Reeves.[56]

Christmas 1920 was enlivened for Dorothy's sister Alice by the presence of Liam Mellows and Sean Etchingham. Alice remembered: 'how much they frightened me by not getting in until after curfew on Christmas Eve because they had been buying presents for my daughter's Christmas stocking'.[57]

The year ended with a significant political development. In December, the Government of Ireland Act, which J.J. Lee described as 'Lloyd George's response to the Irish crisis', proposed the establishment of parliaments in Dublin and Belfast with powers of local self-government. In Lee's view, it 'formally established a six-county Northern Ireland. Partition had long existed in the mind. Now it existed on the map'.[58]

––– •••••••••••• •••••••••••• –––

Even as her clinical exam loomed, distractions to Dorothy's medical studies continued. By 1921, there were some '40,000 soldiers in the country but much of the fighting was borne by 7,000 Black and Tans and 6,000 Auxiliaries, ex-soldiers and ex-officers recruited for a "police" operation, who began arriving in March and August 1920 respectively.'[59] Dorothy, who was now a member of the university branch of Cumann na mBan[60], which had been outlawed in 1919, told her mother that, as Diarmid and Mrs Coffey were away, she was staying with Margot Trench, the sister of Cesca, Diarmid's late wife and a fellow member of the Cumann. Mrs Coffey was 'not well, has the wind up in a gale and so I came to oblige her … M's mother also got wind up and wired for her to go over (to London)…'. Constance had evidently not urged Dorothy to take similar action: 'Imagine my pride to get such a fine letter from my Ma – much the bravest of the lot – I was proud of you and am so grateful – our "old lady" is the best of the lot to be so good and calm and not fuss us. There is no danger for us at present. But the poor men.' The house was raided by the British military on the first night of Dorothy's stay. She said Margot was as 'brave as a lion' but a 'bit jumpy' so it was much nicer to have two people to laugh at the event. There was also a Dr Watson and his mother occupying a floor in the house.

At 2.30 a.m., Dorothy heard continued knocking – all the paint came off the door where they rapped their rifles and kicked. She and Margot put on their dressing gowns: 'I had borrowed a gaudy Japanese silk one, orange and green!' Dorothy also had a pigtail. The soldiers 'rushed in with bayonets pointed at Margot and revolvers cocked'. They were very angry because of the long delay in answering the door. About six men and officers came in 'fierce and rude and blustery'. They shouted at Margot to turn on the lights. In the end, all they could find to take away were three pairs of gloves and a book of poems by a Mr Nevinson, (presumably Henry Wood Nevinson).[61] Dorothy told her mother that Mr Nevinson was delighted when she informed him the next day as he said it was a 'great advert'.

Dorothy wrote: 'My impressions were not fear (except a little thrill going down) but it is a horrid insult to have these Tommies running in and out of your room smoking fags and doing what they please to you in very sketchy attire'. Mrs Coffey was not due back for a while and Dorothy stayed on with Margot as she had 'no nerves, in fact I find it rather bracing. Of course, if there were anyone really in danger in the house it would be quite another matter … Alice I may say is green with envy!'[62]

There was further excitement in March 1921. Just as Dorothy's student years were drawing to close, the Headquarters of Cumann na mBan asked her to go to West Cork to lecture on first aid to their Kilbrittain branch. She was eager but somewhat apprehensive as she had passed all her final examinations and was 'anxious not to get into trouble' until TCD had actually conferred her medical degree. She wondered if the university authorities would confer a degree *in absentia* to someone 'who was in Mountjoy [gaol] for political reasons'.[63] Dorothy decided to go ahead with the assignment but to try and be as inconspicuous as possible. She travelled to Cork by train and, at Bandon station, she was met by two women, Maud O'Neill and 'Baby' Lordan, a qualified nurse. They 'guessed her' as there were few travellers. All three women waited until the platform was empty before they approached each other. Then Maud and Baby conveyed Dorothy in a trap to O'Neills in Maryboro, about eight miles distant. O'Neill's home was known to the British as a Sinn Féin hotbed and Dorothy knew that if she was found there she would be 'damned off-hand'.

Dorothy was highly unusual in this company. She spoke with an English accent. She was one of Ireland's few female doctors as well as a member of the Anglo-Irish ascendancy. Despite her upbringing with its emphasis on the avoidance of the taint of an Irish accent, Dorothy, like her sister Edie, found herself increasingly at ease among those with an Irish brogue and, as an adult, she did not allow class distinctions to temper her friendships and loyalties. She slept at O'Neill's, sharing a bed with Baby. She gave separate sets of lectures to sixteen girls in the open air in the grounds of Ardacrow House while she spoke to the 'lads' at one or other farmhouses. 'To this day, I still remember the delicious hot brown bread [at Calnan's] and the pain after devouring it.' The 'lads' included Captain Jackie Neill and Adjutant Jim Mahony of the local Kilbrittain Company along with volunteers and scouts and occasional visits from Battalion officers and even Dr Lucey, whom Dorothy thought (correctly) might be the medical officer to the Flying Column.

She concentrated on the essentials of battle medicine including the demonstration of a rough and ready method of stopping haemorrhages. One of the lads, John Murphy or 'Scaife' whose 'brains had all gone to brawn' ripped off his coat, displaying 'gigantic' biceps and challenged Dorothy to stop the blood flow. She was watched in breathless silence as she applied a tourniquet to the brachial artery and twisted and twisted a pencil to tighten it. Dorothy recalled: 'Yes, the pulse stopped and I was accepted as worthy to doctor the West Cork IRA.' Despite this heroic demonstration, Dorothy realised that the real needs of the men centred on personal hygiene rather than medical measures. (However, later, during the Civil War, Jackie O'Neill did apply a tourniquet to the wrist of a man which probably saved his life as he was two hours' drive from medical help).

On her last day in Cork, Dorothy was relaxing with some of the girls, and was out in the fields riding a hunter called Peacock when they were warned that the Essex regiment were raiding O'Neill's farmhouse and wanted to talk to her. They stuffed the first aid notes in a wall and Dorothy went in. She told the Captain that she was applying for the post of Kilbrittain dispensary which was vacant and had been mentioned to her by one of the O'Neill sons who were in Dublin. 'This story half went down' but they wanted to know why she had a pipe in her luggage which they had evidently searched. She replied, 'with perfect truth, "I smoke one, do you want a demonstration?"'. Some of the soldiers laughed and the Captain told her to clear out, whatever her business was. The next day, she went to Bandon Railway Station to catch a train to Dublin. She had dispatches for Dublin in her case and, in the station lavatory, transferred them to her person. The Essex regiment were parading up and down the station but did not bother her.

On her return to Dublin, Dorothy duly informed the Headquarters of Cumann na mBan, where Mrs Wyse Power[64] was presiding, that the West Cork Column did not want dressings or first aid supplied. Instead, they needed sulphur powder, instructions on bathing and the treatment of scabies which plagued them as they darted around the countryside without the luxury of proper baths.[65] Cumann na mBan were astonished.

At the end of March, Dorothy went, once again, to Mount Trenchard to stay with the Monteagles. On 5 April, the Ballyhahill lads called for Mary [Spring Rice] as they had a wounded volunteer. Dorothy and Mary went there at 9 p.m. and Dorothy drove on to the bogs, over the border into Kerry, she reckoned. 'There in a remote farmhouse was a fine fellow with a bad bullet wound in his jaw, luckily in and out, but it needed attention badly after five days of amateur nursing'. She fixed him up and the 'boy' slept on the kitchen table while Dorothy nodded on a hard chair near a 'grand circular turf fire'. Just before dawn, she redressed the wound and showed the lads how to make a chair with their hands to carry the wounded volunteer to the nearby road. At daybreak, she was given a bike to cycle back to Mount Trenchard. Two days later, she dressed the wound again, having been instructed to tell her hosts, if questioned, that she was off in search of goose's eggs.[66]

Dorothy's clandestine activities did not come to the attention of the college authorities and she graduated in April 1921. She was one of sixteen graduates, including one other woman, conferred with *Baccalaurei in Medicina et in Chirugia et in ante Obstetricia*.[67] But she was still worried about her clandestine activities and when a press photographer took a snapshot of herself and the South African Donald Lathan, she asked Donald not to give her name. He 'spun a yarn' that Dorothy was Miss E.C. Smith and he was the first Jamaican student to qualify in TCD. Dorothy was clearly gleeful as she noted that the picture appeared the next day in *The Irish Times* and the *Freeman's Journal*. In the latter, the caption of the photograph was 'Dr congratulates Dr' and a short paragraph elaborated: 'Mr. D.V. Lathan, the first Jamaican to obtain the M.B. degree at Dublin University congratulates Miss E.C. Smith, who has also just obtained her degree'.[68]

In her official graduation photograph, which is among her medical papers in TCD, 31-year-old Dorothy looks younger than her years. She is pretty with dark hair drawn sleekly away from her face and confined under her mortar board. Her glasses, with their light frames, are barely visible. She seems slightly surprised, with a pleasantly determined light in her eyes.

With her graduation over, Dorothy needed employment but she could not get a job in Dublin. She was not alone in her employment difficulties. Irish medical schools were producing more graduates than Ireland required. Dorothy decided to return to Kilbrittain dispensary to work there 'in earnest'. There was no competition for a job which had lain vacant for the preceding six months after the incumbent reportedly ran away in his slippers during a raid by the Auxiliaries, who took 'pot shots at him with revolvers as they ran'. 'Anyone was welcome, even a "gurral [girl]"'.[69]

## NOTES

1. D. Stopford to Sir M. Nathan, 3 April 1918 (University of Oxford, Bodleian, Nathan papers, MS 204, folio 247).

2. D. Stopford to Sir M. Nathan, 4/5 April, 12 p.m. (University of Oxford, Bodleian, Nathan papers, MS 204, folio 248).

3. M. Nathan to D. Stopford, 18 February 1918, Sir Matthew Nathan letters (NLI, MS 15341(1)).

4. M. Nathan to D. Stopford, 29 April 1918, Sir Matthew Nathan letters (NLI, MS 15341(1)).

5. E. Price Unpublished Memoirs (NLI, MS 11426(1)).

6. A.K. Wordsworth, Witness Statement (BMH, WS 1242).

7. D. Stopford to Sir M. Nathan, 1918 (University of Oxford, Bodleian, Nathan papers, MS 204, folio 255).

8. M. Nathan to D. Stopford, 4 September 1918, Sir Matthew Nathan letters (NLI, MS 15341/1).

9. D. Stopford to Sir M. Nathan, 1918 (University of Oxford, Bodleian, Nathan papers, MS 204, folio 258-60).

10. *The Irish Times*, 11 October 1918.

11. C. Cullen (ed.), *The World Upturning: Elsie Henry's Irish Wartime Diaries, 1913–1919* (Dublin: Irish Academic Press, 2013), p.4.

12. D. Stopford to Sir M. Nathan, 17 October 1918 (University of Oxford, Bodleian, Nathan papers, MS 204, folio 273).

13. R.B. McDowell, *Alice Stopford Green: A Passionate Historian* (Dublin: Allen Figgis, 1967), pp.109–12.

14. P.J. Dempsey and S. Boylan, 'Robert Barton', in *Dictionary of Irish Biography* online, (accessed 29 September 2012).

15. D. Stopford, 'Electioneering in Ireland', 11 December 1918 (NLI, MS 15346).

16. D. Stopford, 'Electioneering in Ireland', 11 December 1918; Rejection slip from the *Herald*, London (NLI, MS 15346).

17. D. Stopford to Sir M. Nathan, 1918 (University of Oxford, Bodleian, Nathan papers, MS 204, folio 271).

18. D. Stopford to Sir M. Nathan, 1918 (University of Oxford, Bodleian, Nathan papers, MS 204, folio 269).

19. Sir John Simon was a British barrister and politician who held senior cabinet posts. He campaigned against the Black and Tans in Ireland. His first wife, who had died, was Dorothy's cousin.

20. E. Price Diary (NLI, MS 11426/1).

21. Blue Admission Card (NLI, MS14341(2)). Written in Irish, granting Deora Nic Giolla Phairt permission to be present at Dáil Éireann, An Chéad Tionól, 21 Eanáir, 1919. Signed by R. Mulcahy. The name Deora Nic Giolla Phairt is handwritten and difficult to decipher.

22. J.J. Lee, *Ireland, 1912–1985: Politics and Society* (Cambridge: Cambridge University Press, 1990), pp.41–3.

23. D. Macardle, *The Irish Republic* (Dublin: Irish Press, 1951), pp.924–6. Full text of the 'Constitution of Dáil Éireann' and 'Message to the Free Nations of the World', issued in Irish, English and French, 21 January 1919.

24. Macardle, *The Irish Republic*, pp.924–6.

25. R. Barton to D. Stopford, 26 February 1919, Prison Correspondence 1919–24 (NLI, 15341 (3)).

26. R. Barton to D. Stopford, undated, Prison Correspondence 1919–24 (NLI, 15341 (3)).

27. R. Fanning, 'Richard Mulcahy', in *Dictionary of Irish Biography* online, (accessed 13 October 2013). Richard Mulcahy (1886–1971) was a revolutionary and politician. He was Chief of Staff of the IRA. In 1921, he was a supporter of the Treaty and became Minister of Defence in the Free State government.

28. Dempsey and Boylan, 'Robert Barton'.

29. D. Stopford, 'War' (NLI, MS 15346).

30. S.M. Parkes, 'The "Steamboat Ladies", the First World War and After', in S.M. Parkes (ed.), *A Danger to the Men? A History of Women in Trinity College Dublin, 1904–2004* (Dublin: The Lilliput Press, 2004), pp.101–2.

31. Parkes, 'The "Steamboat Ladies"', p.97.

32. D. Price, Testimonials (NLI, MS15343 (1)).

33. H. Stofmeyer to Miss Stopford, 13 December 1918 (NLI, MS 15343(1)).

34. Allen, corresponding secretary DUBA to the Secretary of the Women Medical Students' Committee, 14 December 1918 (NLI, MS 15343(1)).

35. T. Garratt Hardiman to Dr Price, 4 April 1935 (TCD, Price papers, MS 7534(74)).

36. J.F. Fleetwood, *The History of Medicine in Ireland* (Dublin: Skellig Press, 1983), p.290.

37. To read more about the flu, see C. Foley's book *The Last Irish Plague: The Great Flu Epidemic in Ireland, 1918–1919* (Dublin: Irish Academic Press, 2011); G. Beiner, P. Marsh and I. Milne, 'Greatest Killer of the Twentieth Century: the Great Flu in 1918-19', *History Ireland* (March-April 2009), pp.40–3. For poignant first-hand accounts from flu victims read I. Milne, 'Through the Eyes of a Child: Spanish Influenza remembered by Survivors', in A. Mac Lellan and A. Mauger (eds), *Growing Pains: Childhood Illness in Ireland, 1750–1950* (Dublin: Irish Academic Press, 2013).

38. D. Stopford to Sir M. Nathan, 6 July 1918 (University of Oxford, Bodleian, Nathan papers, MS 204, folio 256).

39. D. Stopford to Sir M. Nathan, 17 October and 2 November 1918 (University of Oxford, Bodleian, Nathan papers, MS 204, folio 272-4).

40. For a full account of Cumann na mBan, which held its inaugural public meeting on 2 April 1914 and was outlawed in 1919, see C. McCarthy, *Cumann na mBan and the Irish Revolution* (Cork: The Collins Press, 2007).

41. Diarmid Coffey did a BA in 1910 and was called to the Bar in 1912. He joined the Irish Volunteers in 1914. He participated in drills and was on board *The Kelpie* which landed guns at Kilcoole, County Wicklow in August 1914. Later, he was a clerk of the Senate, later working in the Public Records Office (now the National Archives). He was an author and editor.

42. D. Stopford to Sir M. Nathan, 2 November, year not given (University of Oxford, Bodleian, Nathan papers, MS 204, folio 275).

43. D. Stopford to Sir M. Nathan, 2 November, year not given (University of Oxford, Bodleian, Nathan papers, MS 204, folio 274).

44. L. Price, *Dorothy Price. An Account of Twenty Years' Fight against Tuberculosis in Ireland* (Oxford: Oxford University Press, 1957), p.4. For private circulation only.

45. Ibid., p.4.

46. Ibid., p.93.

47. D. Stopford to Sir M. Nathan papers, 19 March, year not given (University of Oxford, Bodleian, Nathan, MS 204, folio 265).

48. P. Gatenby, *The School of Physic, Trinity College Dublin: A Retrospective View* (Dublin: Trinity College, 1994), p.21.

49. Ibid.

50. D. Stopford to Sir M. Nathan papers, undated (University of Oxford, Bodleian, Nathan papers, MS 204, folio 285).

51. D. Stopford to Sir M. Nathan, 25 January 1920 (University of Oxford, Bodleian, Nathan papers, MS 204, folio 282).

52. Ibid.

53. L. Kelly, *Irish Women in Medicine, c.1880s–1902s: Origins, Education and Careers* (Manchester: Manchester University Press, 2013), pp.92–3.

54. In November 1918, the Parliament (Qualification of Women) Act, 1918 (8&9 Geo. V, c.47) entitled women to vote and become members of parliament. In December 1918, Sinn Féin were successful and Constance Markievicz became the first woman to be elected to the Westminster parliament. She did not take up her seat.

55. D. Stopford to Sir M. Nathan, undated (University of Oxford, Bodleian, Nathan papers, MS 204, folio 290).

56. Ó Broin, *Protestant Nationalists*, pp.159–60. Amber Pember Reeves letters to Sir Matthew are preserved in the Bodliean library, Oxford. Ó Broin suggests the Stopfords would have been 'surprised' by Sir Matthew's liaisons, while Dorothy would have been 'mortified'.

57. A. Wordsworth, Witness Statement.

58. Lee, *Ireland, 1912-1985*, p.43.

59. Ibid., pp.43–5.

60. E. McCarvill, Captain of University Branch Cumann na mBan, witness statement (BMH, WS 1752).

61. Henry Wood Nevison (1856–1941), born in Leicester, England, was educated at Shrewsbury School and the University of Oxford. He was a social activist, journalist, author and poet. Nevison campaigned against the Black and Tans in Ireland.

62. D. Stopford to C. Stopford, undated (NLI, MS MS15341 (8)). This letter was written in late 1920 or early 1921 and sent from 21 Pembroke Road, Dublin.

63. D. Stopford, Kilbrittain, unpublished memoirs D. Price (NLI, MS MS15341).

64. Jennie Wyse Power (1858–1941) was a nationalist and suffragette.

65. D. Stopford, Kilbrittain, unpublished memoirs (NLI, MS 15341), p.2.

66. Foynes, D. Stopford (NLI, MS 15341).

67. 'University of Dublin: Conferring of Degrees', *The Irish Times*, 20 April 1921.

68. 'Degree Day at Trinity: Dr. congratulates Dr.', *Freeman's Journal*, 20 April 1921.

69. D. Stopford, Kilbrittain, unpublished memoirs (NLI, MS 15341), p.2.

CHAPTER FOUR

# OF SEA PINKS, BLACK AND TANS, AND MEDICAL MATTERS: THE KILBRITTAIN YEARS (1921–1925)

*'Dearest mother, everything is perfect and*
*I am extraordinarily happy...'*[1]

In May 1921, Dorothy seemed delighted to have closed the textbooks and left Dublin city to live in rural Kilbrittain, County Cork, in the south-west of Ireland. She anticipated summer swims and long walks. The nearby cliffs were:

> ...low and covered in sea pinks and you can climb down to little strips of sand and rocks every now and then. It is so peaceful and the sea so blue. I could sit here forever. I hope very few people will be sick so that I have loads of time to loaf here and dream. I think I shall make a success of it and be all right in every way...[2]

Dorothy basked in the sun as she addressed this lyrical description of west Cork to her mother. She had walked along the cliffs and was sitting, staring towards the Atlantic between old Kinsale Head and Courtmacsherry. 'It is perfect, you see all the liners go past.' She found inland 'lovely too'. If only there was peace, Constance might visit her. Indeed, if Dorothy got a house, she hoped her mother would come anyway.

Somewhat optimistically, or perhaps with deliberate mendacity, she told Constance that Kilbrittain was 'a quiet quarter, no raidings and everything very peaceful'.[3] The reality was far different. Military law was in force. Letters could be confiscated and read so Dorothy was very careful about the content of any letters she posted in Kilbrittain Post Office. By 1920-21, more than 500 members of the British forces had been killed in Ireland and almost 1,000 wounded. More than 700 civilians died between January and July 1921.[4] The War of Independence primarily involved Dublin and Munster. Peter Hart has described the 'guerilla war' in Cork as a 'kind of total war in miniature, with fewer and fewer barriers to violence and the burden of suffering falling on civilians'.[5] He suggests these barriers were breaking down for both the IRA and the British forces. Dorothy's new job placed her right in the heart of this volatile situation.

The IRA in Cork was divided into seven battalions organised around the main towns, while each battalion comprised several companies. Flying columns were engaged in guerrilla type warfare. The memoirs of Tom Barry, the commander of the West Cork flying column, describe shootings, killings, retaliations, ambushes, arson and torture.[6] (There were acts of terror and counter-terror committed on both sides.) Barry described Liam Deasy, the Brigade Adjutant of the Bandon Brigade, to which Barry belonged, as the 'best brigade adjutant in Ireland'.[7] In Barry's opinion, Kilbrittain Company was the best company in Ireland. Dorothy's new home was in the midst of this IRA hotbed: Kilbrittain had hosted an IRA training camp in late 1920 that led to the establishment of the West Cork flying column. According to historian Michael Hopkinson, a successful column was a matter of local pride.[8] Meanwhile, the barracks where the Black and Tans were established at Kilbrittain was strongly fortified and surrounded by barbed wire. It was the subject of many IRA attacks.

Following what Barry described as the 'twelve dark days' of February 1920 when eleven officers and men of the Bandon Brigade[9] were killed, and the IRA retaliated in kind, he wrote about his perception of the necessity for the killing of four of the 'enemy' and the wounding of four others: 'This reality of death to the enemy was all that mattered, for as surely as a subject people never got an iota of freedom from British Imperialists without killing British troops, so too was it a fact that the only way to make British troops behave with even a modicum of decency, was to pump those principles of humanity into their bodies with bullets attached.'[10]

Among Dorothy's papers in the National Library of Ireland there is a detailed account of the history of the Sinn Féin movement in West Cork, demonstrating that she was well aware of the history of the area, including the active part taken by men she called friends in iconic ambushes such as Crossbarry.[11] Dorothy was still a member of Cumann na mBan which supported the activities of the IRA. She was associated with some of the senior figures in Sinn Féin and the IRA. Indeed, she had difficulties in the beginning convincing the IRA that she had returned to take up a real job in Kilbrittain. The British were equally sceptical.

Nonetheless, Dorothy's new position involved three days a week in Kilbrittain dispensary and one day at Ballinadee which was about three miles away. In addition, she had been offered the post of registrar of births, deaths and marriages.[12] Her first concern was to find transport – she hoped to use a motorbike but would start with a bicycle. To her surprise, she was refused a permit for an 'ordinary bike' but thought it was a mistake. Meanwhile, she borrowed a pony and trap. Cork was under military law so Dorothy drove into Kinsale to enquire again about a permit. She sent in her card to the Colonel and he sent word out to the gate that he would not grant her a pass on any conditions. 'Good, says I, we know where we are, no need of further camouflage, I'm in the open now and it's much easier.' Dorothy did not allow matters to rest at that. She knew that the British House of Commons had heard denials that motor permits had been refused to doctors in Ireland. She wrote out a statement of what happened to her and had it witnessed by our 'good and friendly C of I clergyman' and sent it to her sister Edie, who was secretary of the Peace with Ireland Council. As she worried that the ordinary post was unsafe, Dorothy sent this missive via 'Republican post underground' but it never reached its destination.[13]

Denied a bicycle, and without transport, the IRA supplied Dorothy with a horse and a saddle. The letter which accompanied a small grey cob was signed by the 'Adjt Ist Batt. 3rd Cork Brigade'. It informed 'Miss Dr Stopford' that the Brigade and Battalion staff wished her to have the animal and its belongings for a present 'not including the saddle'. When she got a car, they wished her to return the saddle.[14] Dorothy named the little cob Maria, after her niece Mary. The pony was very well suited for 'jogging the roads' and could jump too although Dorothy had no time for such 'frivolities'.[15] There were wild strawberries in the ditches but from her vantage point on Maria's back she couldn't reach down to pluck them. However, Dorothy told her mother that she really preferred a horse and had brought down riding gear. A Dr Thomas Watson gave her some leather saddlebags which she put on under the saddle and these 'flapped around the horse's middles as he jogged along, filled with bottles and instruments'. There was a mild sensation the first day she arrived in Bandon in this fashion. Her attire was also of use in drumming up business: the first day she held a dispensary in Kilbrittain no patients showed up. The next day 'a flock of persons' came along with 'trumped up complaints' wanting to have a look at the 'doctoress' and her riding breeches, 'both novelties in those parts'. Dorothy fell off Maria quite a lot. She relied on local farmers to 'appear over a hedge' and put her up again. It was thirsty weather and she was given a glass of milk at every halt. This bucolic practice should have been idyllic but the War of Independence was in full dangerous flood. 'If only there wasn't death waiting round every corner for the lads,' she mused.[16]

Although she was ten miles from a butcher and the roads were blocked with trenches,[17] Dorothy managed to get a newspaper every second day delivered by a bread cart from Bandon. She asked her mother to send on an illustrated paper occasionally as it would be passed from hand to hand. She had no time to read books other than medical tomes. Indeed, she had no wish for reading. On the long summer evenings, she was out until 10 p.m., usually sitting in a hayfield with 'the two daughters of the house,' possibly Cissie and Birdie Crowley, chatting and sewing. She would go to bed, then, after a cup of cocoa. Some of the days were lazy with walking on the cliffs, a dip in the sea and the occasional patient. Other days were more strenuous as she was on call all the time both for her patients – attending childbirth if necessary, setting bones, calling to the bedridden – and for IRA casualties.[18]

During the summer, roses and honeysuckle were growing in the ditches and it was pleasant riding out but she quickly realised she needed to get a car as Maria was dropping with fatigue.[19] Dorothy's finances were looking up – she had private patients in addition to the dispensary salary. She told Constance she had £76 in the bank and had another £60 due by the end of September. She reckoned she could make £500 a year, thereby doubling her salary. Meanwhile, Dorothy was looking around for a trap and said she would enjoy taking Constance around in it, if she got one. She described herself as 'fat and rosy and very fit, the life suits me down to the ground as you may guess'.[20]

She lodged with Mrs John Whelton of Flaxford, whose son Billy was out with the IRA flying column. Very soon after she moved in, the house was raided by the British military twice. The first time, a 'cyclist corps dropped on us out of the skies' at 9 p.m. They searched the entire house except for her room and didn't speak to her. The very next night, Dorothy was out late on a case and had just come home and was sitting in the kitchen about 11 p.m. She was smoking a cigarette after her cup of cocoa and was reading her letters. She had been warned that the military were coming and had time to burn a selection of letters before a 'sub'(subaltern or junior officer) walked in.

'He said "good evening" and leaning across the table he picked up a pile of letters and started reading them very carefully. I ignored him (smiling inwardly) and went on sitting and smoking. Then he and the Tommies searched my room, very minutely.' They found nothing and Dorothy averred that they never would. The men, all except one sergeant, were very polite. They enquired as to whether she liked the place and had she been on a sick call. Her English accent may have been an asset here.[21] However, she knew how these 'devils' had behaved on a raid ten minutes previously. She expected that they wouldn't trouble her much – they would probably do another raid on her new house and then drop it. Later, the soldiers asked Mrs Whelton for tea for six. Major A.E. Percival, of the Essex Regiment, which had devised its own mobile columns in response to the IRA's flying columns, appeared for a cup of tea. She had wanted to meet him and ask why her permit was refused but he kept in the background. Dorothy described Percival as their Mephistopheles and told her mother that she would refer to him in future letters as 'Elizabeth's husband'.[22]

In Dublin, Aunt Alice, too, was raided. Her historical work and manuscripts were carried off by the Black and Tans to Dublin Castle but some of the documents were returned, along with 'heaps of stuff' belonging to other people. She hadn't sorted them out before she was raided again. Once again, documents were removed and returned, with some missing, and new ones added.[23] According to Edie, the raids occurred after the two maids and Aunt Alice, who was then over 70 years of age, had gone to bed. The Black and Tans would beat on the door with their knuckle busters until it was opened. Aunt Alice insisted on preserving the marks they made on the door. Dorothy's sister Alice also came under scrutiny as her house provided shelter to people on the run, including de Valera, Liam Mellowes,

Sean Etchingham and Erskine Childers. The army council of the IRA also met there and Alice's daughter Mary recalled seeing Michael Collins, Dick Mulcahy and 'Ginger' O'Connell. Mary remembers one raid where the Black and Tans left a gun upstairs but Alice was wise to that trick and told them they had left something behind. One of the officers asked about Dorothy who had 'gone south'. He wanted her address but Alice replied that she did not give out addresses.[24] Alice, Mary and Frances, their 'gallant old cook' went into the drawing room to collect themselves when Alice suddenly remembered that papers had been left in for 'Mr Doyle' (Liam Mellows). The papers were sitting safely on top of the desk which had been rifled by an army officer.[25]

In West Cork, Dorothy believed that the British were on the run when she went to work there in 1921. Their numerical superiority did not match the guerrilla tactics of a much smaller force which had the *entrée* to most homes and cottages. Major Percival's Essex column was not so very mobile, according to Dorothy, as they always knew at least half an hour in advance when they were between Bandon and Kinsale. A boy or girl on a bike or horse would let the IRA know. Dorothy met with the 3rd Cork Brigade staff and officers of the flying column, 'names to conjure with' although ranks were not divulged to her at that time. Local scouts and volunteers, who were not in the flying column, were often around Flaxfort where she was staying. Minor engagements such as an attack on Kilbrittain barracks made life 'exciting'.

Dorothy's job as a dispensary doctor began with some 'fairly easy cases'. People were curious and interested in the 'Lady Doctor' and came 'for the fun of it' at first. However, practising medicine alone, immediately after college, was challenging. She had to send one small boy with pleurisy and bronchitis to hospital and worried whether her diagnosis was correct as she had to write it down. She found herself enthralled by her work and forgetting about the outside world. It was 'very responsible if you get a puzzling or serious case and no one to fall back on, then your lack of experience comes in'. But she told her brother Robert she hadn't had a 'hideous crash' yet and she was getting plenty of work. She worried about an old man who died after she had given him a 'powder'. Although she knew it couldn't have killed him, she went around the next day with her heart in her mouth and found, to her relief, that he hadn't taken the powder. On another occasion, she had to sign a death certificate for an infant but was unsure as to the exact cause of death. This was the first case she had seen of tuberculosis in an infant and in her student days she had not been taught that infants might die of generalised tuberculosis.[26] In 'puzzled ignorance', she decided it was due to 'tuberculous diathesis [diathesis means hereditary predisposition]', as the infant's mother had tuberculosis. Later, she wrote that this was incorrect. Indeed, she added, there was 'no such thing'.[27]

She had another worry when the plaster cast she had put on the leg of a 4-year-old slipped. She had heard that there was a doctor on the beach and decided to seek him out. There, she found Dr Welpy of Bandon and asked him to help. She gave the anaesthetic and they 'fixed the whole thing again'.[28] Dr Welpy was 'Edinburgh, very nice, about thirty-five and very smart, the Oxford type, says I must send him all my cases and I am to help operate and give anaesthetics'.[29] As well as providing Dorothy with another stream of income, this gave her the opportunity to link into the wider medical community.

The desire for a visit from her family was never far from Dorothy's mind. Her brother Robert graduated from Cambridge which he had attended after discharge from the army. He only achieved a 'third' but Dorothy consoled him that was good enough especially as he had secured a job already. She wished he would come over for a week as she had purchased a trap and was getting it painted. They could have great fun going around together. Neither Robert nor Constance visited despite Dorothy's obvious desire for visitors and her many invitations.

As well as her regular work, Dorothy was often engaged in the time-consuming work of tending to wounded IRA men. She was advised not to come out if she heard shots, but to wait until the 'lads' sent for her. When her services were needed – for instance, when the facial burns on a volunteer turned septic – hiding her movement from the British forces made the task more arduous. Looking after the burns victim entailed daily trips to Murphy's farm in the townland of Scaife – this was the headquarters for the 1st battalion (Bandon) of the Cork 3rd Brigade. To get there, Dorothy had to travel on horseback from Flaxford to James O'Mahoney's farm at Cloundereen. Mary O'Mahoney, 'one of the best of C[umann] na mBan' or Ellen, who helped there and about 'whose courage a volume could be written', would escort Dorothy across several fields, crossing the road from Timoleague to Bandon. This was the 'only point of real danger as lorries might be passing'. They went down a deep cutting of furze and up to

Scaife on the other side of a stream – a matter of two miles or so. Dressing the wound and trekking back took the whole afternoon. It was not safe to approach by road on horseback.[30]

Her grey cob lived on a farm near the Whelton's cottage and was 'foddered' from another farm and 'fetched out' to Dorothy each morning and evening. This distributed the expense of its keep. 'The lads [the IRA] arranged all this. All I had to do was get on the horse and off it again.' She describes her first meeting, in mid-May 1921, with Mick Crowley and Denis Lordan, members of the local IRA flying column. They were to become firm friends. Denis was only 18 or 19 years old but Dorothy was so impressed by his sober bearing and good sense that she asked him for his opinion as to her costume – riding breeches and a rich red jumper. She wondered how her attire might affect the local community's opinion of her as a reliable doctor.[31]

A month in the saddle left Dorothy with 'leg muscles like whips and in great condition'. She rode into Bandon in a pink jumper Constance had made, 'a skirt (very ineffectual), breeches, gaiters and all. I will have to discard the skirt, it's a perfect nuisance but don't want to create much [more] sensation at first'. By 1 July, Dorothy had secured her own house and found 'a very nice girl [Kitty] to "do" for me … she lives in a nice cottage close by here and she was a patient of mine and I know her and she is the very thing'. Harbour View house was large and 'perfect' with three windows on the top floor and one either side of the hall door.[32] There were two more houses attached – empty when she moved in but she anticipated that they might become occupied by summer visitors. 'You look across the road down the cliffs straight on to sea, lovely and sunny and such a view. It is beautiful. There is a grass garden and fields and cliffs all around with a few summer residents scattered about.'[33]

She had a range but no coal, so she proposed to manage for the summer with a small oil stove reinforced by a primus and oven. 'My nearest neighbours are famers (also patients) … I am simply delighted … five bedrooms, stabling for two horses and a coach house … the furniture is quite good and the crockery etc splendid.'[34] Patients often gave her gifts. On 4 July, she came home with a pot of jam, a whiskey bottle filled with cream, and a dozen eggs. She also 'raked in' £5 for bills paid.[35] She joked about an old lady of 84 who was trying to marry her to her 'good-for-nothing about 50-year-old son, handsome waster addicted to [drawing of a bottle]'. She was rather enjoying the fun as he was the owner of a very fine telescope which she would regard as 'fair spoil'. 'I loathe him but we want the telescope. It would be grand for seeing Atlantic liners.'[36]

This rural idyll was punctuated by occasional ugly events such as the time when Percival and his column burned down O'Mahoney's farm at Cloundereen and took James Mahoney, who was more than 70 years old, hostage. They sat him in a pony trap and put a goat in the seat opposite him. He was paraded around the local area for several hours while his house burned and he was unsure whether his son had been shot. Luckily, his son, and wife, the 'jolliest' old lady that Dorothy knew were safe. Mrs Mahoney's greatest regret seemed to be the loss of an empty Players cigarette packet. It carried the coveted 'four stars' and, if sent back to the manufacturer, would be rewarded with a '100-tin' free. Dorothy, a dedicated fellow smoker, sympathised with Mrs Mahoney, who also 'dearly loved her "fag"'.[37]

Dorothy seems to have far less sympathy for Lord Bandon, a Justice of the Peace whose much grander home was burned and who was kidnapped by the IRA. 'The more the British raided, the more the poor old fellow had to be moved,' she wrote. Once, when a British column almost came upon him, the wife of a farmer was 'popped' into bed beside him with a nightgown over her clothes. According to Dorothy, he 'probably discovered more about his neighbours in Co Cork than he had learnt in seventy odd years living amongst them in his castle'.[38] Tom Barry named Sean Hales and Jim O'Mahoney (both well known to Dorothy) as being in charge of the party which kidnapped the Earl of Bandon. There were other IRA kidnappings too – three coastguards, three Royal Marines and three more Justices of the Peace. The Justices of the Peace were to be executed should the British 'shoot or hang any IRA captive'.[39] Dorothy had to dress a bad petrol burn in the middle of the night when the Coast Guard station at Howes Strand was burned out and the coastguards kidnapped.[40] An IRA lieutenant William Foley had received facial and hand burns and had to be tended by Dorothy for a few weeks.[41] Afterwards, she received an 'embarrassing souvenir' – a Union Jack that had once flown over the Coast Guard station. The last engagement of the flying column was on 26 June 1921 when one volunteer and a number of Auxiliaries were wounded in Rosscarbery. The next day, Tom Barry met Liam Deasy and some others and they read in the daily newspaper of the invitation sent by Lloyd George to de Valera to explore peace settlement possibilities.[42]

On 8 July, Dorothy caught the train to Dublin – nominally she was going to see a sick friend in County Limerick but in reality, she was going to Dublin 'on urgent business, very urgent!' She lamented that Alice and Mary were out of town so she would not see them. Away from Kilbrittain, she told her mother that it had been horrid not being able to write freely to her and recited to her the story of the two raids at Flaxfort but reassured her that she had been doing splendidly. She was on excellent terms with all the gentry and Protestants whom she found 'very nice and broadminded'. She was going to Church more frequently than usual and had been invited to tea by many of the Protestants. However, she was making more real friends among her Catholic neighbours. She had discovered there was 'no such thing as class or religion amongst sensible people'.[43] She was 'studying the world and enlarging my views and my heart. I am accepted as one of themselves' by the Catholics.[44] Her only complaint about remote Kilbrittain was that there was insufficient intellectual stimulation to make living there a long-term prospect.

In Dublin, on the unspecified urgent business which probably involved delivering papers or verbal intelligence, she stayed with Mollie Childers and saw B ['Bob', Robert Barton] every evening. In January 1920, he had been re-arrested in Dublin, tried under the Defence of the Realm Act (DORA) and sentenced to penal servitude in Portland Convict prison. He was released in July 1921 to help negotiate a truce with the British. Dorothy told her mother that Bob was 'well, but God, one can realise by his face what they did to him but he is all right now and in great spirits'. They had 'such fun in odd moments and he behaves like a school boy. There is great coming and going. It will be awful going back but I have a lot of work so must go.'

On 11 July 1921, the coming and going between Dublin and London resulted in a truce between the British and the Irish forces. Dorothy Macardle, historian and friend of Dorothy Stopford, later wrote that this brought 'a sudden return to normality, release from a prolonged and almost intolerable strain ... to thousands of homes in the towns, villages, and lonely countryside men were returning who had been long away with the "columns" and in hourly danger of death'.[45] In West Cork, there was relief, too, for the British and their supporters. Three of the four Justices of the Peace who had been kidnapped were released when the peace talks began. Lord Bandon was held prisoner until after the Truce became operative.[46]

The Peace with Ireland Council in London, where Edie worked, also called a truce and Edie came to Ireland on holiday, meeting up with Dorothy in Alice's house. They drove to Kilbrittain through counties Carlow, Tipperary and Cork. Edie recalls an 'amazing journey' that took a whole day. Long detours were necessary as bridges had been blown up. She noted houses burnt down by the Black and Tans and police stations burnt by the IRA. Edie spent a few weeks in Kilbrittain attending céilís and meeting with farmers and their families as well as IRA members. Patriotic Irish songs were sung and dancing was strictly traditional Irish dancing.[47]

Alice and Mary also came to stay with Dorothy. The weather was hot but Alice was very fit and enjoying life. Dorothy was busy. There were thirty or forty babies waiting to be vaccinated as no vaccinations had been done for ten months. The registration of births and marriages had got into 'an awful muddle' and she had to straighten it out. Dorothy spent two mornings packing empty bottles into cases and despatching them off and restocking the dispensary. She was feeling very settled.[48] With the truce, life was immeasurably easier. In July, it was glorious, with the moon light flooding across the water as she lay in bed. Alice and Mary amused themselves fishing in Dorothy's small boat. It seemed everyone was ill and Dorothy couldn't write a long letter but the busyness would save her missing Alice and Mary, when they left. Meanwhile, 11-year-old Mary was 'dancing her legs out every night'.

On 14 July, Dorothy had the money to buy a car but she decided to wait a little while. If peace came, she would buy the car. If it was war, she would buy a second horse. She asked Constance not to send her any more money as she would soon be a millionaire.[49] Although the truce had made a 'wonderful difference' with everyone 'so free and happy', Dorothy felt lonely sitting luxuriously in her new house. She had no visitors, no work and the girl was out. She told her mother of another friend, Cissie Crowley. She was very fond of Cissie but hadn't mentioned her prior to the truce for fear of drawing trouble on her. For Dorothy, the Crowley's home, Ivy Lodge, was where the best of all warm hearts in Kilbrittain resided. She enjoyed sitting around the table in a rather narrow room. Mr Crowley taught her how to throw up a gun and shoot a bird on the wing, while Mrs Crowley was the 'youngest and gayest of them all. It was a wonderful household – not forgetting Mick and Con running in and out armed to the teeth.'[50] This contrasts with Tom Barry's poignant description of a visit by himself and three others in the flying column to Cissie's parents, early in 1921. Mrs

Crowley was sitting on a stool in the yard gazing on the remains of her 'blown up and burned out' house. Mr Crowley was attempting to fix up a henhouse. They were alone. Their son Paddy, Cissie's brother, had been killed a week previously. Another son Denis, known to Dorothy as "Sonnie", lay 'badly hurt in a British jail after a merciless beating by his captors'. A fourth son, Con, whom Barry describes as one of their best fighters, was also a prisoner under the false name of Patrick Murphy. Mick, who had been seriously wounded early in the War of Independence, was a 'leading Flying Column Officer, and his chance of survival did not appear to be high…'. Barry writes that the two daughters, 'Ciss and Birdie, among the most excellent of our Cumann na mBan', were absent on IRA work.[51]

During the truce, Dorothy and Cissie enjoyed meals in the kitchen of Dorothy's house, Harbour View while the dining room functioned as a surgery and the drawing room was a general sitting room with books and papers. She said it was 'really very jolly. You would laugh seeing Cissie and me tackling the horse up in the mornings and feeding her, I have a rick of hay in the field which I bought'. The trap was a tub painted black and green and Dorothy found it a 'great ease'. Although Cissie was a 'dear and great company', Dorothy feared for the peace and told her mother she longed for a visit from her own family. Perhaps Edie could come or Aunt Alice if it was not too rough for her in the cooking line. Dorothy consoled herself with the companionship of a pure white kitten called Mrs A Griffiths sired by a tomcat called Bobbie Childers.[52]

In another twist, Dorothy was asked by the local sergeant to apply for the appointment of Medical Officer to the Royal Irish Constabulary barracks in Kilbrittain. She did so as it would mean £20 a year and they were all 'on very good terms' now. However, the sight of Black and Tans outside the barracks could still strike fear into the local population. A third-person account of a visit by the Black and Tans, written by Dorothy, provides an insight into a summer evening. 'At her gate, stood four Black and Tans. Now no-one who had lived in Ireland for four or five years previously could ever see a Tan without their heart leaping into their mouth.' It turned out one of them, 20-year-old Constable Baker, was 'bleeding like a pig' from his ear – he had impaled himself on the barbed wire outside of the barracks. Meanwhile, Billy [Whelton], 'debonair, late of the column' sauntered up the road to see what was up. Luckily he had no gun, only a rabbit. In the back kitchen, Jim [presumably O'Mahoney], the Adjutant, whose 'temper and hair corresponded with the terse description foxy' waited impatiently. When the wound was dressed and the Tans departed, Kitty, the girl who helped in the house, boiled mussels, Billy shelled them, Dorothy, her sister (probably Edie) and Jim examined the fishing lines. Then, Dorothy, her sister, Jim and Billy set off fishing with 'the girls' pulling the boat as darkness crept down over the bay. This and other scraps of writing would seem to indicate that Dorothy had the intention to write a memoir about her time in Cork, perhaps in the form of a fictionalised account. She never followed through and, indeed, she did not even file a statement with the Bureau of Military History which was set up in 1947 to gather accounts of people's experiences of the movement for independence between 1913 and 1921.

On 16 July 1921, Dorothy sent her mother photos of Volunteers and Cumann na mBan girls. Dorothy had 'motor loads of them the last few days coming in for chats and incidentally minor ailments to be treated'. She told Constance that if there was any more fighting she need not be afraid for her. They were looking after her well and she was on the right side. The brigade staff sent the local battalion special orders that they were to look after her and see that she got no abuse from anyone so she was safe as they [the IRA] had the 'whip hand' there. Although the peace was a relief, Dorothy mused that she would 'hate anything in the nature of a come down settlement yet do long for peace as otherwise all these fine men will be killed. However, extermination war is better than slavery and to continue under the present brutal rule. We know now what to expect from England...'[53] She loved all the boys and girls like brothers and sisters. The adjutant was a great friend. She had some Volunteers in to tea most days since the truce. 'It is just fine after all the guarded way we had to meet before.'[54]

On 24 July, it was back to work. Dorothy went to Bandon and gave three anaesthetics for Dr Welpy, earning £3-3-0/- in almost an hour. He was 'awfully nice, rather smart but the right sort', and she lunched with the Welpys whenever she was in town.[55] She noted that living was cheap in Kilbrittain, with neighbours helping to clean out the stables, chop her sticks and do all sorts of odds and ends for her that otherwise she'd have to pay for. They got a jug of cream nearly every day. She asked Constance to send on a couple of sheets and pillow cases, a table cloth and also a bath towel. These would be useful for visitors.

On 4 August, Aunt Alice arrived with Edie. It was 'lovely having the house full but is very busy workwise ... I am very flourishing if dropping'.[56]

Edie was 'vastly amused if nothing else' by Dorothy's lifestyle and there was plenty to eat. Edie helped with tackling and feeding the horse and with the work around the house. She got up at 5 a.m. and made Dorothy a cup of tea when she was called to a forceps birth. 'Edie is a perfect angel and I love having her,' enthused Dorothy, writing to her mother and signing herself as Dodo.

Meanwhile, at national level, negotiations were continuing with letters going back and forth between de Valera, and the British Prime Minister, Lloyd George. On 3 September, there was a letter from Riobaird (Robert Barton) who was in Gairloch, in Scotland. He had gone there with a letter for L.G. (Lloyd George) and was waiting for a reply. He adjured Dorothy to 'be kind to the Black and Tans and give them sweetened medicine'.[57]

On 9 September, Dorothy was 31 years old. Her mother sent her £3, a 'noble birthday present', and she hoped Constance hadn't been 'running yourself short'. Edie was still in Kilbrittain and Dorothy now had the loan of a little two-seater car. She told Constance she would be sending her a present of money soon but would have to wait until she had bought a car and sorted her finances.[58] She had six old ladies on her books now, one had broken her arm and the rest had coughs and colds but all were getting well. There were also lots of babies to be seen to. On 16 October, Dorothy noted that Edie was still there and would stay until the following Friday although she wished she would stay on. They went to a Féis in Ballinadee in the pony trap. Meanwhile, Dorothy was learning to drive a motor car. She believed she could easily manage a Ford but had not yet fixed on a car. She told Constance not to be 'a bit alarmed' about her driving, as she was very good and especially slow around corners. She had a mechanic for nearly a fortnight so she had learnt very well.[59]

In Dublin, events were proceeding apace as the Sinn Féin cabinet accepted an invitation from Lloyd George to come to London for a convention. Historian J.J. Lee notes that 'ominous splits' occurred immediately.[60] Of the cabinet's seven members, Cathal Brugha and Austin Stack refused to go to London. De Valera also baulked. On 8 October, an Irish delegation including Michael Collins and Robert Barton departed for London. Erskine Childers was the secretary for the Irish side. Alice wrote to her 'Dear Dodo' that she, Mary (her daughter), and Aunt Alice went to Westland Row (now Pearse Street train station) to see the departure of the delegates. Alice talked to Bob (Robert Barton) for a while and Bob said he would go and see Constance if he had the time. 'They all looked well and cheerful but they have been working at terrific pressure lately and were working until 4 o'clock this morning.' Alice also noted that Desmond Fitzgerald was asking for Edie: 'He evidently has his eye on her.' At the last minute, someone suggested that the Stopfords should go to Kingstown (now Dun Laoghaire) with the delegation. There was only time to 'bundle Aunt Alice into the train as it was moving' and Mary and Alice were left behind with Máire Comerford, who was Aunt Alice's secretary from 1919 to 1922. There was a fair crowd at the station and they gave a cheer as the train moved out.[61]

At the end of October, before Edie left, Dorothy took the plunge and bought a car from some ladies in Bandon. It was an almost-new Ford, a black five-seater, registration number IF2499, for which they had paid £310 and she, in turn, got for £200, almost her entire annual salary. She only bumped one cow on the way home! The somewhat worn car was 'the joy of my life. It starts itself and has very good lights and good hood and screens at the side so I can keep very dry. Edie and I are delighted with it. I am really a very good driver and very cautious'. They drove into Cork city, 'twenty-five miles in great style'. Dorothy stressed that she wouldn't do anything rash as she didn't want to smash up £200.[62]

When Edie left, she missed her terribly although she acknowledged that it was rather dull for visitors at that time of year. Dorothy consoled herself with 'grand fishing in the bay' at the end of October. She went out every night for five nights, usually from 4 or 5 p.m. to 10 p.m. Her small boat held three people and she had two 'lads' who came out with her. They also stayed with her while they recuperated: one had 'a heart and the other a lung' problem. Dorothy had to do most of the pulling. After eight to ten miles a night for five nights her biceps were 'considerably improved'. It was worth the effort – they caught eleven large fish one night. She was enjoying every minute of outdoor activity. The two boys were great company in that line. 'Men have their uses certainly,' she noted dryly. Reverting to a more feminine type, she added that she had bought a new coat in town, 'soft grey cloth, with a squirrel collar – very smart, the latest thing. I didn't really want it only Kitty made me get it, she thought I looked too shabby for the car. It was only £5-5-0/-'. In November, the fishing ended and Dorothy asked Constance for yet more bedclothes as she had constant visitors. She also wanted magazines for the waiting room. When lovely new blankets arrived, she scolded her mother for not sending on old ones, and said she would regard them as Christmas presents. She sent Constance a photo of Billy Whelton who was staying with her. He was not very strong and was acting as her chauffeur. She also sent a photo of 'Jim' (presumably O'Mahoney) who was 'nicest of all'.[63] Sadly, none of the photographs seem to have survived.

In November, rural life was turning somewhat sour. Kilbrittain now seemed to be a 'dreary place in the wet and storm ... Waves sky high and driving rain'. The car, with its hood and side screens, was warm and dry compared with the pony trap. Again, she asked her mother to come over although she noted she had someone staying with her for most of the time – usually to convalesce.[64] Then Billy had to go to Dublin for hospital treatment but Jim O'Mahoney, with his 'desperate heart', might return. Jim was her best success: he had *angina pectoris* and 'nearly popped off a couple of times – luckily he was in the house here and I was on the spot for the attacks and we hope for a complete cure'.

With all her patients recovering, she asked the lady doctor from Ballineen to come and stay. She was young, just qualified and going to England after Christmas. Dorothy had only met her once but she seemed very nice. 'We are trying to fill up gaps until the family come at Christmas, as it would be lonely to be here alone, Kitty and I'. There were problems with the post and strikes on the railway line. Dorothy shifted from her sunny room with its low window looking out over the sea to a 'small snug inner room for the winter which is much warmer and the windows don't rattle or the wind howl all night now'. She told Constance that she hated 'having this lonely life' and not sharing it with her: '...It's not all lovely sometimes it is very hard and I have to drag myself out when I don't want to but on the whole it is very jolly and I have such good friends,' was her somewhat contradictory summation.[65] They enjoyed 'great gambling for halfpence – not bridge or such like but other democratic games which you would have never heard of'. She went to a work party at the Rectory and sewed an apron and they had prayers and sang hymns. She was much amused and rode over on Maria and met all the ladies of the parish. The 'next minute', she was fishing and ferreting with the IRA. 'You can guess which I prefer,' she added. However, she was sternly refusing all efforts, including Kitty's, to convert her to Catholicism and said that she would prefer to go to hell.[66]

> They then all exclaim that they know it's wrong but they can't
> believe I will go to hell. We have great sport ... everyone is

very natural here and says what they think. It is so much easier. They think you very hard if you don't cry when moved. I'm not sure it isn't the best way, to shew your emotions if you feel them … good night now, my dearest little mother; I do so long to have you here.'[67]

On 16 November, Robert Barton wrote to Dorothy from London. He thanked her for a photograph she had sent of herself in uniform, complete with rifle, astride a horse. He commented that she seemed more at home with the horse than the rifle and asked if she had ever expected to see herself 'in such a turnout?' Again, the photograph does not seem to have survived. Robert talked of poor Ulster being 'in the soup' and said that if ever there was a 'ruthless hun on earth', it was Lloyd George. He warned Dorothy not to publish the letter as it might be considered provocative or even a breach of the truce. 'These canaille are getting more and more exacting in their claims.'[68]

At the end of November, Dorothy gave a series of first aid classes to the IRA.[69] These included the treatment of gunshot wounds, haemorrhage, pressure points, burns and scalds, shock, fractures, putting an arm in a sling, looking after a sprained ankle, strains, head injuries, and lifting. She told the men how to distinguish entry from exit wounds and about the risk of haemorrhage, sepsis and shock. They learned how to wash and care for the wounds without excessive probing. She was against the use of spirits for shock.[70]

On 6 December 1921, after two months' of negotiation and an ultimatum from the British side of all-out war within three days, the Irish delegates signed a treaty conferring dominion status on the Irish Free State. Robert Barton wavered and then signed reluctantly. The Treaty was met with controversy and recriminations. Three members of the Cabinet were in London and four in Dublin. De Valera's decision to remain in Dublin was questioned as was the lack of communication between the London delegates and the Dublin cabinet ministers.[71]

Meanwhile, Christmas was looming. Constance sent on a parcel of chocolate biscuits and Dorothy was surprised and delighted as they were so unexpected and so rare. She saved them up until Saturday when Jim was returning. Meanwhile, she and Kitty had three each! She was looking forward to Christmas, when her sister Alice would bring plum pudding and two turkeys. Dorothy reckoned she would get more turkeys as presents and told Constance she would send one on to her. Meanwhile, she had been summoned to attend a Republican Court in Bandon where she had to give evidence. A man 'punched another man off his horse and gave him a fearful black eye and nearly broke his skull. It will be great fun. I am driving our sergeant in, he is 6 foot 6 ins.'[72]

Her brother Robert sent her a pair of silk stockings from the United States. Dorothy had never possessed such a thin pair and vowed to wear them with an air, telling people 'oh those are only Cincinnati stockings'. However, for the past week, she had been busy pursuing mucky work that was not conducive to the wearing of such fine stockings. She had been lying on her back under the car and:

… pulling my boat and flopping my feet in fish and water and mess at the bottom of it … It is a grand life here – I hope to have some photos soon to startle you with my goings on … the wild duck and curlew are tumbling over each other under my windows … they want me to join the hunt on Thursday but I don't think I will – my pony is not up to the mark and I can't afford to keep a hunter…[73]

Alice and her daughter Mary spent Christmas 1921 in Kilbrittain with Dorothy. She took them to an IRA céile and they danced through the night. Eleven-year-old Mary's chief dancing partner was a tall young farm labourer. Dancing finished at dawn and the dancers went to 7 a.m. mass on the way home. Mary told Leon Ó Broin that she remembered Dorothy driving the trap out of a yard in the cold light and them all calling out 'Thank God we're Protestants' for they could go straight to bed.[74]

On 27 December, Robert Barton wrote to Dorothy saying the treaty would go through but if de Valera stood 'clear and firm on independence another generation will win through where we have failed'. He sounded defeated, saying it was a 'sad story'; it was not what he went to gaol for, and he was retiring to 'home and oblivion'.[75] Having voted for the Treaty, under stress, he now rejected it and joined the Republican side. Later, he wrote that many a time he wished he had died in Portland prison.[76]

The seeds of civil war were sown. Towns, villages, and families split into pro- and anti-Treaty factions. Dorothy, along with Robert Barton and Erskine Childers, aligned herself with the Republican side, pro-de Valera, while Edie and Aunt Alice became supporters of the new Irish Free State. Historian Peter Hart suggests that, 'with few exceptions, the men who fought the British in the Tan War went on to fight the Free State'.[77] Most of Tom Barry's column became Republican. Cumann na mBan, too, aligned itself virulently with the Republican side. So it's probably not surprising that Dorothy also opted for Republicanism. When Robert Barton wrote to Dorothy to congratulate her on remaining a Republican when so many of her relations had 'gone wrong', he was understanding. 'Aunt Alice is dreadful, so sure she is right! I suppose we are equally dreadful, so sure she is wrong'.[78] Edie noted that family relations were 'rather strained' for some time.[79]

Evacuation of the British troops from the twenty-six counties which comprised the new Irish Free State began in January 1922, although the British felt it was necessary 'in view of the Republican attitude' to retain large numbers in Dublin, the Curragh and Cork. The evacuation of the Auxiliaries and Black and Tans and the disbanding of the Royal Irish Constabulary also began.[80] In February, Cumann na mBan asked pro-Treaty members to resign.[81] The IRA began to split into pro- or anti-Treaty brigades and divisions. An uneasy pact between de Valera and Michael Collins attempted to calm the warring factions and a fragile peace held.

In February 1922, Dorothy found it impossible to discuss all the events taking place. Therefore, she wrote to Aunt Alice as 'niece to aunt, not as dispensary doctor to historian or Irishwoman to Irishwomen', leaving 'the really interesting things aside concerning the changes taking place'. But, she cautioned that every day down there they were getting further from the Free State and more Republican.

All the 'lads' (IRA) were established in barracks in Bandon and the country was transformed and very dull. There was no more 'flying around, sleeping and eating here and there. They are a more disciplined and proper corp if less attractive'. She visited them in their new barracks and after inspecting the whole place they had a game of cards. Dorothy decided to leave Harbour View which was too lonely and go to lodge at Cloundereen. The new house was very splendid and she would have her own suite with separate entrance. Nobody was getting sick so she was very idle. There was some shooting with woodcock until the cartridges ran out. She joked that she thought she would look for a 'nice homely wife' as this was the matchmaking season. 'In a moment of great confidence I have discovered that I should be worth a 200 or 300 acre farm, having a profession and being strong and active!'[82]

The political climate was darkening. Tensions were rising between pro-and anti-Treaty factions. Then, in April 1922, a series of horrific killings must have shocked Dorothy. It seemed to begin with a group of IRA officers from the Bandon battalion, led by Michael O'Neill of Kilbrittain, breaking into a Protestant household at 2 a.m. in the morning. O'Neill was shot dead. A series of attacks on Protestants commenced. In what Peter Hart describes as an 'unprecedented massacre', over the next three nights ten Protestants were shot dead and another wounded. Hart ascribes these deaths to anti-Treaty members of the IRA. Dorothy's friend, Denis Lordan, later admitted it was 'our fellows'.[83] Another of Dorothy's friends, Dorothy Macardle recorded that these murders 'created shame and anger throughout Ireland'. Hundreds of Protestants went into hiding or abandoned their homes. The boats and mail trains leaving Cork for England were packed with Loyalist refugees, many of whom only returned to settle their affairs before departing forever.[84]

The Irish civil war between the IRA and supporters of the Free State began in June 1922 when the national army opened fire on the Republican army which was occupying the Four Courts in Dublin. Dorothy may have remembered writing that essay on War in her Sophister year in TCD when she declared: '…civil war is the most terrible so perhaps it is the most righteous war'. The fighting spread to the city centre. This initial battle in Dublin lasted some eight days. Edie's employer, The Peace with Ireland Council, had been wound up and Edie had gone to live with her sister Alice in Bray, County Wicklow. Hearing the rumours of civil war, Edie and Alice travelled into Dublin, some twelve miles away. They found a 'silent city, except for the tramp of innumerable Dubliners as they patrolled the streets endlessly in order (like us) to get some idea of what was happening'. There was a 'sulphurous and ominous feeling in the air, as before a thunderstorm'. There were no incidents that day although they were intrigued to see a Ford car dashing down O'Connell Street, and 'in it, in professional white coat, our sister Dorothy, who had put her professional skill at the disposal of the rebels'. The next day, Edie once again travelled into the city centre, lunched with Aunt Alice and, together, they went to watch the battle at the Four Courts. They stood on O'Connell Bridge, assuming they were out of range, when a burst of machine gun fire churned up the river twenty yards away. They withdrew to a 'respectful distance' and the next day the Four Courts fell to the Government forces. War had broken out in Cork within a few hours of the opening salvos in Dublin. Apparently, while hurrying back to Cork, Dorothy was arrested with Mrs Tom Barry and held in Kilkenny temporarily.[85]

Back at work in Cork, she had a professional battle on her hands. In September 1922, a complaint was filed against Dorothy by a parish priest, William Murphy who was school manager in northeast Ballinaspittle. He was incandescent that she 'off her own bat' visited the school and then closed it down. Dorothy ably defended herself saying that she had closed the school for disinfection after a child, in the desquamation (skin shedding) phase of scarletina, had attended the school. She couldn't get in touch with the parish priest who was seven miles away and she claimed that the Medical Officer of Health (MOH) 'in cases of urgency' had the right to close any school or public place on his own authority. She was rebuked in a letter from Bandon District Council which pointed out that an MOH had no power to close a school. His duty was 'confined to making a recommendation if he considers it necessary to the manager of the school'.[86] Dorothy had overstepped the mark and was, no doubt, smarting as a result of the rebuke.

Another even greater humiliation was in store. On 6 December 1922, the Irish Free State was established and the Republican side, which Dorothy supported, had officially lost. Between 1917 and 1923, the toll of dead and wounded reached 7,500. In Cork, more than 700 people were killed, 400 of them by the IRA. The IRA killed 200 civilians including some 70 Protestants. Historian Charles Townshend noted that compared with other civil wars, the violence in the Irish civil war was constrained although he qualifies this by stating that the toll went far beyond 'simple bloodshed. It represented the culmination of a process in which, over three years of guerrilla conflict, violence permeated society'. While he agrees that the Protestant community felt the 'threat of harm and dislocation' acutely, a 'sense of apprehension ran much wider as the fighting continued'.[87]

The Protestants who remained in Ireland included Aunt Alice, who was one of the first nominees to the new Irish Senate, a position she held until her death in 1929. Another Protestant, the poet and mystic William Butler Yeats was a fellow senator. He was enthusiastic about the role of the Senate, believing that it was a distinguished body and would get 'much government' into its hands.[88] Aunt Alice and Yeats set up a Senate committee to organise a scheme for editing, indexing and publishing Irish language manuscripts.

Alice also appealed for reconciliation between the warring parties in the civil war.

On the losing side, Dorothy had to continue with the mundane tasks associated with her job. Transport was still heavily regulated. On 19 January 1923, Dorothy was issued with a motor permit by Óglaigh na hÉireann allowing her to drive her Ford car (registration IF 2499). She was described as a lady of 30 years of age – a slight under-estimate – of medium build with dark hair. The permit was issued subject to the following regulations: 'That the holder of the permit does not engage in any activities prejudicial to the elected government of the people; that the vehicle in respect of which this permit is granted will not be used for any purpose prejudicial to the elected government of the people.'[89] She also had to procure permission to purchase and use motor spirit. In July, she was issued with an Irish Republican Army motor permit, signed by F. (presumably Florence) Begley.

Between 17 November 1922 and the end of January 1923, fifty-five Republican prisoners were executed. Large numbers were imprisoned in gaols and internment camps including Robert Barton, Denis Lordan and many more of Dorothy's friends. Liam Deasy signed an appeal for surrender. On 30 April, de Valera was authorised by an army council to offer a suspension of hostilities. Throughout the ensuing negotiations, the Irish Free State continued to hold its untried Republican prisoners. In July 1923, it was estimated that there were more than 11,000 military prisoners.[90] Dorothy's sister Edie noted that good men were lost on both sides of the civil war with the Republicans losing Erskine Childers, who was executed for carrying arms and Michael Collins who was killed in August 1922. Gradually, 'events went back to normal'.[91]

By the end of 1922, Dorothy had decided to leave Cork and widen her professional horizons by seeking employment in Dublin. Her contribution during the War of Independence and the civil war was valued and, later, marked by the IRA in the form of a gold watch presented to her when she left Cork in 1923.[92] In Dublin, Dorothy kept in touch with her Cork friends. Writing to Birdie Crowley, she signed herself off as 'the Doctoreen', telling her amusing anecdotes of a fiddler playing outside Mary Spring Rice's door and a morning spent washing the black Ford car. 'She [the car] is glorious looking, the hose is great sport.'[93]

Throughout 1923, Dorothy had a stream of correspondence from her friends in prisons and internment camps.[94] She was kept busy reading and answering letters and making up parcels. Denis Lordan, who had been arrested at Bandon on 26 December 1922, was now prisoner number 1856 in Hut 19, Newbridge Barracks, County Kildare. He described the camp as 'quite a little town of all male inhabitants'. He had met several friends, also some of Dorothy's friends. He was endeavouring to start a debating class and warned Dorothy to be prepared for trouble when they met again.[95] He told Dorothy that Birdie Crowley and Co. were rather disgracefully running after the new MD, Dorothy's replacement, and joked that it would be a relief to Sonnie if he had Birdie off his hands.[96] In February, he thanked her for sending on some macramé twine and promised her some articles he would make with it. 'Ciggs' and tobacco were a 'godsend' as all the lads were 'short of smokes' when they came in.[97] In his next letter, he reminded her that his twenty-fifth birthday was on 21 May.[98] Her response was evidently satisfactory as he called her 'Dear Fairy Mother' and thanked her for the sweets and ciggs.[99] In September, Denis asked Dorothy to get in touch with Maud (possibly a relation) and ask her to send him a pair of boots, size nine, as it was difficult to stay well while walking around in bare feet. He was studying Irish and said that pencils and notebooks were hard to come by. He was worried about finding a job when he was released and he asked Dorothy to keep a look out for any vacancies 'from a private secretary to a farm labourer with a preference for motors or engineering'.[100]

In October 1923, more than four hundred prisoners went on hunger-strike in Mountjoy. Hunger strikes spread to other prisons and internment camps.[101] Denis Lordan duly joined them. He told Dorothy that he was in 'cheery mood' and was striking for their 'immediate and unconditional releases … ciggs are our only comfort now with an occasional sip of tepid water'.[102] He wrote to Dorothy saying that he would telephone her when he was released although he did not expect to be very strong.[103] She sent in health salts and cigarettes as requested. When he came off strike, Denis asked Dorothy to send in a tonic and 'some nourishment such as brown bread, cornflour or what you know to be most suitable, we can have such things cooked here'. He sounded despondent and asked her to excuse his short note as he did not feel like writing much.[104] Denis Lordan was released on 8 November 1923. He travelled to Cork with Dan Buckley and met Birdie Crowley in Bandon. Then they all motored to Kilbrittain. A plebiscite was taken there to ask for the release of the remaining prisoners and they got 600 names.[105]

Robert Barton, who was interned in Harepark, the Curragh, County Kildare, wrote to Dorothy in early November, thanking her for the medicines which she had sent in. Dorothy had motored to his house in Annamoe, County Wicklow to see his sister. He thanked her for being so good to his sister and told Dorothy to tell her he had enough clothes and not to send any more. He was pleased Dorothy had moved to Dublin and was very glad she was successful. She had a flat in Fitzwilliam Square and 'the address certainly calls for high fees,' he wrote. He asked her to pass on his love to Aunt Alice.[106]

At the end of 1923, Liam Deasy was in Mountjoy jail. He wrote more formally to 'Dr Stopford' thanking her for advice which he had not followed. He had been on hunger strike too and said the hardest part had been abstaining from potatoes for ten days, as he 'always had a great desire for them; also the porridge which is a food one loves to get in prison'.[107] He sent Dorothy a hand drawn Christmas card, a tricolour with an illustration of barred windows. The text read: 'Greeting from Mountjoy, Christmas 1923'.[108]

The internments were not just confined to men. The struggle for independence had also pushed women into prominent roles in the public sphere. Indeed, William T. Cosgrave, head of the Free State government during the civil war, blamed the war on interference by these women, whom he described as 'no ordinary women'. His response was to instigate a so-called 'war on women'.[109] Some 250 women were arrested. Prisoners included Máire Comerford, Aunt Alice's former secretary, who went on hunger strike while detained in Mountjoy. Dorothy Macardle, who was a member of Sinn Féin and Cumann na mBan, was also imprisoned. She was an active Republican and worked on the staff of *An Phoblacht*, a newspaper founded in January 1922 by Erskine Childers. In March 1923, she too went briefly on hunger strike.[110] While no letters from these women prisoners to Dorothy Stopford were found among her correspondence, she may well have been in touch with them, and she, undoubtedly, would have been aware of their plight.

Outside prison, other former Volunteers were also in distress. Sonnie Crowley, who had been badly beaten by soldiers of the Essex regiment, had been hospitalised because of his weak back. It was later confirmed that he was suffering from tuberculosis. In May 1923, he wrote to 'My dear, dear doctoreen' telling her how much he missed her. '...anyway Doctor we all

liked you very very much, loved you in fact…' He told her to wear the watch
the IRA had given her with pleasure. '… you deserved it and got it with a
céad míle fáilte from some of the best and most true of Ireland's soldier
sons who I know were all glad that you were so pleased with such a small
token of gratitude for your services to Cork 3.'[111] In October, Dorothy had
an attack of asthma and Sonnie wrote to commiserate. He remembered her
having an attack in Cork and wished he had visited her every day, however,
at that time he 'hadn't penetrated that stone wall'. He had hung on and
waited for her to come to them as he didn't want to interfere.[112]

Writing from the Bon Secours Hospital, in Cork, he teased Dorothy that
he would not marry her and in fact, always knew that it was his money
she was after. '"I will not marry you" and hope that you will cease your
unwelcome attentions for the future'. He told her he must marry a lady
and his failure to make her one put her out of the running. Turning more
serious, he said he was sure she was worn out from her exertions to help the
hunger strike. He was very pessimistic about the whole business himself.[113]

In 1924, Sonnie went to a sanatorium in Leysin, Switzerland, in search
of a cure for tuberculosis which continued to afflict him. His spirits were
high and he told Dorothy that he hoped to meet a nice lady-patient with a
well-filled purse and would, in due course, invite Dorothy out to take her
chance at meeting a 'millionaire soft-hearted enough to fall victim' to her
'wily self'. He told Dorothy of a regime of fresh air, sunshine and wound
dressing and thanked her for helping his brother, Mick, who was back
in college, studying engineering.[114] The Irish White Cross[115] was paying
towards Mick's education; it was also funding Sonnie's stay – he reckoned
it was costing about £3 a week without extras such as baths which cost five
francs each. Sonnie provided Dorothy with details of Dr Rollier's innovative
light treatment, however, at this time tuberculosis was not a priority in her
professional life.

Although Dorothy remained committed to the Republican cause for
the remainder of her life, she began to put most of her energies into her
medical career once she returned to Dublin. She began a small private
practice but she found her true professional home in St Ultan's Hospital,
Dublin which was founded in 1919. Initially conceived by Madeleine ffrench
Mullen and Kathleen Lynn as a hospital to treat the country's increasing
number of syphilitic infants, this hospital expanded to treat infants with
other conditions. St Ultan's Hospital was predominantly Protestant and the

founders and medical committee comprised some of the most politically active women in Ireland. Lynn had worked as a medical officer during the 1913 Lockout. Three years later, as a captain in the Irish Citizen Army, Lynn participated in the 1916 Rising. Madeleine ffrench Mullen was also active in the Rising. Ella Webb, who had been Dorothy's doctor during her student years in TCD, was on the medical board. In addition, she ran a Women's National Health Association of Ireland (WNHA) dispensary to distribute pasteurised milk to women and children.[116] Alice Barry, the only Catholic on the medical board, had preceded Dorothy to Kilbrittain, County Cork, and had been active on behalf of the Irish revolutionary leader Michael Collins in Dublin in 1920.[117] Dorothy's Aunt Alice had been an early supporter of St Ultan's. In 1920, she wrote the introduction to the *Leabhar Ultain* which was compiled by Katherine MacCormack of the all-female Dun Emer Guild[118] and sold for the benefit of the hospital. This richly illustrated book is a collection of poems, drawings, and pictures by Irish artists and writers, including Jack B. Yeats, Harry Clarke, AE, Douglas Hyde and Maude Gonne MacBride.[119] St Ultan's Hospital practised gender discrimination in favour of the employment of women and Margaret Ó hÓgartaigh has aptly described the hospital as a 'women's medical republic'.[120] In the days prior to legislation with respect to gender discrimination, St Ultan's could express its preference for female employees openly in job advertisements.[121]

Dorothy was appointed as house surgeon at St Ultan's for two months from 31 July 1923; she was paid 15 shillings per week instead of board and lodgings. In December 1923, the hospital offered Dorothy the position of assistant physician, the duties as follows: 'to lecture and examine nurses, to do one dispensary a week, to take the duty for members of the staff when requested and to attend emergency calls if needed'. In March 1924, Dorothy attended her first medical committee meeting. From then on, she was a diligent attender, and vocal participant, at the monthly meetings.[122] Importantly for Dorothy's career, the hospital had credentials reaching beyond the political. It was research oriented and encouraged experimentation. Staff were encouraged to travel, gain experience and attend postgraduate courses on the continent.[123] This was unusual at a time when specialisation was largely an *ad hoc* process and many consultants did not possess postgraduate qualifications.[124] Initially Dorothy's medical interests centred around the common complaints of childhood such as gastroenteritis, a common and often fatal illness of infants in the 1920s.

In her leisure time, Dorothy loved to hill walk in Wicklow, and on one of these excursions in 1923 she met Liam Price. He was a tall, thin man with a slight limp. A photograph of him in the National Library of Ireland collection shows him on a motorcycle, quite dashing in a trench coat with a thick thatch of hair parted at the side. Like Dorothy, he wore glasses. Born on 23 February 1891, he was named 'William George'. He had one sister, Kathleen, born two years after him. Liam's father was George Roberts Price, a graduate of TCD in classics and a lawyer. The children were brought up in the Church of Ireland and, like the Stopfords, their gaze was towards Britain. Liam went to Aldenham Public School in England and, later, graduated in classics from TCD. Again, following his father, Liam became a barrister. During the Easter Rising, Liam was serving with the British Army Pay Corps and, stranded in Dublin for the weekend, he observed events. In 1918, he served in France briefly. As signified by his name change from William to Liam, he, like Dorothy, was converted to Irishness. Diarmid Coffey, the widower of Cesca Trench (Dorothy's friend who had fallen victim to the Spanish flu) was one of a circle of people who influenced this change in Liam. Her friend Robert Barton was also on the outskirts of this circle.[125] So, perhaps it was inevitable that Liam and Dorothy met through their mutual acquaintances and their interest in Irish nationalism. However, unlike Dorothy and Robert Barton, Liam was a supporter of the Free State. Dorothy and Liam wisely agreed to differ when it came to Irish politics.[126]

In the autumn of 1924, while walking at Luggala, a hill which falls away abruptly into the dark depths of romantic Lough Tay in County Wicklow, Dorothy and Liam decided to get married. They hurried to Bray to tell Alice and Mary.[127] Dorothy's Republican friends in Cork were very gracious about the proposed wedding. A letter signed by a veritable who's who of the West Cork IRA – Sean Buckley, Liam Deasy, Mick Crowley, Jim Hurley, Jack O'Neill, John Lordan, Liam O'Buachalla, Tadg O'Sullivan, Sean Lehane, Thomas Kelleher and Dan Holland – told Dorothy that they had heard of her forthcoming marriage with great pleasure and 'we feel that you who have shared with us the burden of the struggle for the independence of our Motherland will appreciate this little token to remind you of our esteem and affection'. They wished her every happiness in the new life that was before her and wrote that they would 'always treasure the memory of the sacrifices you made for us and for the cause we all love and we trust that friendship made in times of danger shall continue to the end. From the men of the

Old Cork 3 Bde'.[128] A list of wedding gifts compiled by Dorothy includes a clock from 'Liam Deasy and the 3rd Corks'.[129] She also received a silver photo frame from Sean Buckley. Mr and Mrs Dan Buckley sent her a silver fruit salver. Another old Cork friend and colleague, Dr (and Mrs) Welpy gave Dorothy a silver soup tureen. A poignant letter from Mollie O'Neill (now Walsh and living in Kilountain, Bandon, County Cork) accompanied a present of a little cushion which was intended for the chair Dorothy used most. It didn't deserve the name of wedding present and was 'only a gentle reminder of a warm-hearted and grateful friend … you don't belong to us down here anymore but we love you just the same'. Mollie assured Dorothy that she would feel a 'deal more comfortable' now that she had someone to lean on and to share her joys and reverses. She told Dorothy that Denis Lordan had stayed with her for a few weeks and now had work driving a lorry but hoped to better himself.[130]

The strained relations with her family, due to Dorothy's Republican allegiance, had evidently been overcome and the wedding list included £10 from Alice, £30 from her mother Constance as well as a set of silver brushes from Edie and Constance. Liam gave Dorothy a fur coat, an appropriate gift for a winter wedding.[131] The day before the wedding, Dorothy's purchases for the marriage and honeymoon were stolen from her car while she visited Aunt Alice, who was ill. Generous Aunt Alice replaced everything. On 8 January 1925, Dorothy and Liam got married in the beautiful St Ann's Church, on Dawson Street in Dublin city centre. Their best man was their friend, Diarmid Coffey. Dorothy's niece, Mary was their bridesmaid. Directly after the ceremony, Dorothy and Liam hurried away to catch the morning mail boat – they were going to honeymoon in Italy. Diarmid took the Stopfords (Mary, Alice, Edie, Robert and Constance) and the Prices (Liam's mother and sister, Kathleen) to breakfast. Aunt Alice's illness prevented her from attending.[132]

The wedding came as a surprise to at least one of Dorothy's friends. An astonished Dorothy Macardle dashed off a letter: 'me Da [the wealthy brewer of McArdles ales] says you are married! I'm out of breath!' She wondered: 'Did you take it into your head and propose all of a sudden or was it premeditated?' As long as Dorothy promised not to give up her medical practice, she was assured of her friend's approval and blessing. 'I do hope you won't leave Dublin as I should miss you dreadfully'. She didn't even know the name of Dorothy's bridegroom. 'Me Da says he is a judge,' she wrote.[133]

A year prior to their wedding, Liam had been appointed as a District Justice in the Wicklow circuit, a post he remained in until retirement.[134] Dorothy and Liam remained in Dublin and Dorothy continued to practise medicine. Indeed, in later years, when medicine occupied her time to the detriment of her wardrobe, Dorothy may have been used by her friend as the model for the pragmatic, unfashionable and drily humorous Dr Stack in Dorothy Macardle's 1945 novel *The Unforeseen*.[135]

The Stopford years were over. Dorothy Stopford became Dorothy Price. This is the name associated with her professional work on tuberculosis which began about five years after her marriage and blossomed into international renown.

## NOTES

1. D. Stopford to C. Stopford, undated [May 1921], (NLI, MS 15341 (8)).

2. Ibid.

3. Ibid.

4. J.J. Lee, *Ireland 1912–1985: Politics and Society* (Cambridge: Cambridge University Press, 1990), p.47. For an account of the War of Independence, see M. Hopkinson, *The Irish War of Independence* (Dublin: Gill & Macmillan, 2004).

5. P. Hart, *The IRA & its Enemies: Violence and Community in Cork 1916-1923* (Oxford: Oxford University Press: 1999), pp.102–3.

6. T. Barry, *Guerilla Days in Ireland* (Dublin: Irish Press, 1949).

7. Barry, *Guerilla Days*, p.17.

8. M. Hopkinson, *The Irish War of Independence*, p.73. Hopkinson suggests that Tom Barry was a 'maverick' who was suspicious of outside control, relating principally to the men of his column.

9. These officers included Lieutenant Patrick Crowley of Kilbrittain, one of a family of four brothers and two sisters who were to become close friends of Dorothy's.

10. Barry, *Guerilla Days*, p.104.

11. D. Stopford, History of the Sinn Féin Movement in West Cork (21pp), 1915–1918 (NLI, MS 15344).

12. J. O'Mahoney, Clerk of Union and Rural District Council, Bandon, to D. Stopford, 10 May 1921 (NLI, MS 15341 (1)). He asked her to take up duty on 26 May 1921.

13. D. Stopford, Kilbrittain, unpublished memoirs (NLI, MS 15341 (2)), p.2.

14. Ibid.

15. D. Stopford to C. Stopford, 29 October undated year (NLI, MS 15341 (8)).

16. D. Stopford, Kilbrittain, unpublished memoirs (NLI, MS 15341 (2)), p.3.

17. Hart, *The IRA & its Enemies*, pp.102–3. The IRA tried to disrupt roads, bridges, railways, telegraph and telephone communication. From the winter of 1920, communication and travel were 'paralysed'.

18. D. Stopford to C. Stopford, undated letters (NLI, MS 15341 (8)).

19. Ibid.

20. D. Stopford to C. Stopford, 2 June undated year (NLI, MS 15341 (8)).

21. R. Jacob diaries (NLI, MS 32,582 (39)). Rosamond Jacob describes meeting Dorothy in 1912. Despite her English accent, she seemed 'all right'.

22. D. Stopford to C. Stopford, 8 July 1921, written on Cork train to Dublin (NLI, MS 15341 (8)).

23. Bea to D. Stopford, undated (NLI, MS 15341 (8)).

24. A.K. Wordsworth, Witness Statement (BMH, WS 1242).

25. E. Stopford, unpublished memoirs (NLI, MS 11,426 (1)); L. Ó Broin, *Protestant Nationalists in Revolutionary Ireland: the Stopford Collection* (Dublin: Gill & Macmillan), pp.179–80.

26. L. Price, *Dorothy Price. An Account of Twenty Years' Fight against Tuberculosis in Ireland* (Oxford: Oxford University Press, 1957), p.86.

27. Price, *Dorothy Price*, p.13. For private circulation only; also cited in M. Ó hÓgartaigh, 'Dorothy Stopford-Price and the Elimination of Childhood Tuberculosis', in M. Ó hÓgartaigh (ed.), *Quiet Revolutionaries. Irish Women in Education, Medicine and Sport, 1861–1964* (Dublin: The History Press Ireland, 2011), p.109.

28. D. Stopford to R. Stopford, 27 June undated year (NLI, MS 15341 (8)).

29. D. Stopford to C. Stopford, 8 July 1921 (NLI, MS 15341 (8)).

30. Scaife, handwritten account, D. Stopford (NLI, MS 15341).

31. Ibid.

32. D. Stopford to C. Stopford, 1 July undated year (NLI, MS 15341 (8)).

33. Ibid.

34. Ibid.

35. D. Stopford to C. Stopford, 5 July undated year (NLI, MS 15341 (8)).

36. D. Stopford to C. Stopford, 8 July 1921 (NLI, MS 15341 (8)).

37. D. Stopford, Kilbrittain, unpublished memoirs (NLI, MS 15341 (2)), p.3.

38. Ibid.

39. Barry, *Guerilla Days*, pp.216–7.

40. D. Stopford, Kilbrittain, unpublished memoirs (NLI, MS 15341 (2)), p.3.

41. W. Foley, Witness Statement (BMH, WS 1560).

42. Barry, *Guerilla Days*, pp.219–21.

43. D. Stopford to C. Stopford, undated (NLI, MS 15341 (8)).

44. D. Stopford to C. Stopford, 8 July 1921 (NLI, MS 15341 (8)).

45. D. Macardle, *Irish Republic* (Dublin: Irish Press, 1937), p.477.

46. Barry, *Guerilla Days*, pp.216–7.

47. E. Stopford, Memoirs (NLI, MS 11,426 (1)).

48. D. Stopford to C. Stopford, Monday evening, undated (NLI, MS 15341 (8)).

49. D. Stopford to C. Stopford, Friday, undated (NLI, MS 15341 (8)).

50. D. Stopford to B. and C. Crowley, 27 December, undated year [early 1950s as address is Herbert Park] (NLI, Crowley papers, Acc 4767).

51. Barry, *Guerilla Days*, pp.212–3.

52. D. Stopford to C. Stopford, 15 January 1922 (NLI, MS 15341 (8)).

53. D. Stopford to C. Stopford, 17 July undated year (NLI, MS 15341 (8)).

54. Ibid.

55. D. Stopford to C. Stopford, 24 July undated year (NLI, MS 15341 (8)).

56. D. Stopford to C. Stopford, 4 August undated year (NLI, MS 15341 (8)).

57. R. Barton to D. Stopford, 3 September 1921 (NLI, MS 15341 (1)).

58. D. Stopford to C. Stopford, 21 October undated year (NLI, MS 15341 (8)).

59. D. Stopford to C. Stopford, 16 October 1921 (NLI, MS 15341 (8)).

60. J.J. Lee, *Ireland, 1912–1985: Politics and Society* (Cambridge: Cambridge University Press, 1990), p.48.

61. A. Stopford to D. Stopford, 8 October 1921 (NLI, MS 15341 (1)).

62. D. Stopford to C. Stopford, 22 October 1921 (NLI, MS 15341 (8)).

63. D. Stopford to C. Stopford, 6 November undated year (NLI, MS 15341 (8)).

64. D. Stopford to C. Stopford, 9 November 1921 (NLI, MS 15341 (8)).

65. D. Stopford to C. Stopford, 19 November (NLI, MS 15341 (8)).

66. D. Stopford to C. Stopford, undated (NLI, MS 15341 (8)).

67. D. Stopford to C. Stopford, undated (NLI, MS 15341 (8)).

68. R. Barton to D. Stopford, 16 November 1921 (NLI, MS 15341 (4)).

69. Staff Lieut, Medical Services, 1st Batt. to D. Stopford, 13 November 1921 (NLI, MS 15341(4)).

70. D. Stopford, First Aid Notes (NLI, MS15346).

71. Lee, *Ireland, 1912–1985*, pp.50–5.

72. D. Stopford to C. Stopford, 24 November undated year (NLI, MS 15341 (8)).

73. D. Stopford to R. Stopford, Saturday, undated (NLI, MS 15341 (8)).

74. Ó Broin, *Protestant Nationalists*, p.187.

75. R. Barton to D. Stopford, 27 December 1921 (NLI, MS 15341 (4)).

76. R. Barton to D. Stopford, 20 March 1922 (NLI, MS 15341 (5)).

77. Hart, *The IRA & its Enemies*, pp.265-7.

78. Ibid.

79. E. Stopford unpublished memoirs, pp.28–30 (NLI, MS 11,426 (1)).

80. D. Macardle, *Irish Republic*, p.653.

81. Ibid., p.658.

82. D. Stopford to A. Stopford Green, 11 February 1922 (NLI, MS 15131(1)).

83. Hart, *The IRA & its Enemies*, pp.273-92.

84. Ibid.

85. *Irish Press*, 2 February 1954.

86. D. Stopford notes, 29 December 1922; letters from Kinsale District Council and Bandon District Council (6 January 1923).

87. C. Townshend, *The Republic: The Fight for Irish Independence* (London: Allen Lane, 2013), p.452.

88. Ó Broin, *Protestant Nationalists*, p.202.

89. Owner's Permit (NLI, MS 15346).

90. Macardle, *Irish Republic*, p.862.

91. Ibid.

92. Ó Broin, *Protestant Nationalists*, pp.194-5. According to Ó Broin, Denis Lordan emigrated to South America and thirty years later, when he was back in Cork, Dorothy gave him back the

watch for him to give it to his daughter.

93. D. Stopford to B. Crowley, undated (NLI, Crowley papers, Acc. 4767).

94. William Kearney was a regular correspondent and Dorothy sent him in sugar, tea, copybooks and envelopes. He was prisoner No. 1866, Hut 39, Newbridge Camp. Jack O'Neill also wrote: there were letters from a woman addressing Dorothy as 'Doctor Darlint' and signed 'H' which told Dorothy of Jackie being on hunger strike and her worries about his health.

95. D. Lordan to D. Stopford, 10 January 1923 (NLI, 15341 (3)).

96. D. Lordan to D. Stopford, 8 February 1923 (NLI, 15341 (3)).

97. D. Lordan to D. Stopford, 21 February 1923 (NLI, 15341 (3)).

98. D. Lordan to D. Stopford, 5 May 1923 (NLI, 15341 (6)).

99. D. Lordan to D. Stopford, 21 May 1923 (NLI, 15341 (6)).

100. D. Lordan to D. Stopford, 5 September 1923 (NLI, 15341 (3)).

101. Macardle, *Irish Republic*, p.867.

102. D. Lordan to D. Stopford, 22 October 1923 (NLI, 15341 (6)).

103. D. Lordan to D. Stopford, 21 February 1923 (NLI, 15341 (3)).

104. D. Lordan to D. Stopford, 29 October 1923 (NLI, 15341 (3)).

105. D. Lordan to D. Stopford, 12 November 1923 (NLI, 15341 (6)).

106. R. Barton to D. Stopford, 2 November 1923 (NLI, 15341 (3)).

107. L. Deasy to D. Stopford, 20 December 1923 (NLI, 15341 (3)).

108. L. Deasy to D. Stopford, December 1923 (NLI, 15341 (3)).

109. J. Molidor, 'Dying for Ireland: Violence, Silence and Sacrifice in Dorothy Macardle's Earth-Bound: Nine Stories of Ireland, 1924', *New Hibernia Review*, 12, 4 (Winter 2008), pp.1–2.

110. See N.C. Smith, *Dorothy Macardle: A Life* (Dublin: The Woodfield Press, 2007) for an account of Dorothy Macardle's life.

111. S. Crowley to D. Stopford, 23 May 1923 (NLI, 15341 (6)).

112. S. Crowley to D. Stopford, 27 October 1923 (NLI, 15341 (6)).

113. S. Crowley to D. Stopford, 27 November 1923 (NLI, 15341 (6)).

114. S. Crowley to D. Stopford, 14 November 1924 (NLI, 15341 (6)).

115. A. Ceannt, *The Story of the Irish White Cross, 1920–1947* (Dublin: At the Sign of the Three Candles, 1948). The White Cross, an apolitical organisation, was formed towards the end of 1920 to provide aid to volunteers and their dependents. Its executive committee included R. Erskine Childers, Thomas Foran and Mrs Sheehy-Skeffington. The general council

included Alice Stopford-Green (Aunt Alice), Dorothy Macardle, Miss Barton and Lord Monteagle. The White Cross received substantial funding from America.

116. For an account of Kathleen Lynn's life and work in St Ultan's, and for insights into ffrench Mullen, see M. Ó hÓgartaigh, *Kathleen Lynn: Irishwoman, Patriot, Doctor* (Dublin: Irish Academic Press, 2006).

117. Alice Barry, witness statement (WS), Bureau of Military History (BMH) (National Archives of Ireland (NAI), BMH/WS 723); F. Clark, 'Barry, Alice Mary', in *Dictionary of Irish Biography* online, (accessed 28 July 2010).

118. The Dun Emer Guild was an Irish arts and crafts venture founded by Evelyn Gleeson and the two Yeats sisters.

119. St Ultan's Hospital Board Minutes and Agenda Books 1918-84 (RCPI, SU/1).

120. Ó hÓgartaigh, *Kathleen Lynn,* p.154.

121. Minute Books of St Ultan's Hospital Medical Committee, 30 June 1919-11 December 1935 (RCPI, SU/3/2/1). Text of advertisement placed in the *British Medical Journal* (1929) inviting applicants for the post of bacteriologist and pathologist, woman preferred.

122. Minute Books of St Ultan's Hospital Medical Committee, 30 June 1919–11 December 1935 (RCPI, SU/3/2/1).

123. *St Ultan's Annual General Reports 1919-30* (RCPI, SU/1/1); *St Ultan's Annual General Reports 1931–39* (RCPI, SU/1/2); *St Ultan's Annual General Reports 1940–49* (RCPI, SU/1/3); *St Ultan's Annual General Reports 1950-59* (RCPI, SU/1/4).

124. W.R.F. Collis, *The State of Medicine in Ireland* (Dublin, 1943), p.28; J.F. Fleetwood, *The History of Medicine in Ireland* (Dublin: Skellig Press, 1983), p.271.

125. Ó Broin, *Protestant Nationalists*, p.198.

126. L. Corlett and M. Weaver (eds), *The Price Notebooks* (Dublin: Dúchas, 2002), pp.ix-xxvi.

127. Ó Broin, *Protestant Nationalists*, p.199.

128. M. Crowley to D. Stopford, 2 January 1924 (NLI, MS 15341 (9)).

129. D. Stopford, List of presents, undated, notepaper headed 33, Fitzwilliam Square, Dublin (NLI, MS 15341).

130. M. Walsh to D. Stopford, 1 January 1925 (NLI, MS 15341 (9)).

131. D. Stopford, List of presents, undated, notepaper headed 33, Fitzwilliam Square, Dublin (NLI, MS 15341).

132. Ó Broin, *Protestant Nationalists*, pp.199–200.

133. D. Macardle to D. Stopford, 9 January (NLI, MS 15341 (2)).

134. A. O'Brien and L. Lunney, 'Price, Liam', in *Dictionary of Irish Biography* online, (accessed 28 July 2010).

135. D. Macardle, *The Unforeseen* (London: Peter Davies, 1945).

# PART II

# THE
# STOPFORD PRICE YEARS

# CHAPTER FIVE

# PATIENTS WHO 'COULD NOT TALK BACK': PRACTISING PAEDIATRICS (1925–1935)

*I sit here during the rest hour, 2-3 p.m., at my bedroom window looking at an impossibly lovely view, across a valley in the foreground, to Austria ... well this is very amusing here. I got so frightened yesterday I very nearly didn't come; I had to screw up all my courage...*[1]

The first decade after Dorothy and Liam married brought joy, in that their marriage thrived, and sorrow, in the form of the death of Aunt Alice in 1929. To Dorothy's lasting regret, she and Liam had no children as she was unable to conceive.[2] Liam, too, would have liked a family. However, Dorothy and Liam developed new and absorbing interests. As Dorothy left behind the rural delights and alarms of a single-handed dispensary practice and the doctoring of wounded IRA lads and began to specialise in paediatrics, she became excited about medical research. After working on some of the commoner problems in infants, she settled on tuberculosis as the topic on which she would, increasingly, expend her energies. Liam, meanwhile, became more and more engaged with antiquarianism, place names and folklore, with a particular focus on County Wicklow where he worked as a district justice. Both of them were to forge national reputations in their fields, with Dorothy becoming an internationally renowned medical expert.

Life was not all about work though. Liam and Dorothy had fun: parody and invention were very much part of their lives according to Dorothy's great niece Sandra Lefroy, the daughter of Mary who had been born in India. The Stopfords and Liam enjoyed writing and talking to each other, using a language that employed a light-hearted play on words. Liam and Dorothy also amused themselves constructing crosswords. Dorothy had a great sense of humour and was a 'tremendous giggler'.[3] Sandra says that many people remember Liam as austere – Dorothy, too, has been cast as formidable, and, indeed, in a professional capacity, she was not to be trifled with – but, in private, they were easily amused and amusing, 'very straightforward people'. Male visitors were more welcome to Dorothy than female and as Dorothy aged, Sandra suggests that she 'thought like a man' and dressed in an unfeminine manner. A photograph taken at Sandra's mother's wedding bears this out. Liam is svelte in a crisp top hat and tails, with a white shirt and elegantly striped tie; Dorothy, who had put on a little weight, is wearing a sensible dark cardigan and skirt with a white blouse and white gloves. Her ensemble is topped off by a small hat with a ribbon. The hat and the ensemble are mismatched – in fact, it looks as if she grabbed the hat, at random, off a rack on the way to the church. Overall, the effect is as if she is dressed for comfort rather than elegance. Her earlier interest in clothes seems to have been lost somewhere down the years. However, she is smiling and looks like the sort of dependable aunt you could confide in and call upon in any emergency.

Dorothy and Liam were financially secure and could afford to keep a staff, to own motor cars, and to holiday abroad. They had a large circle of friends and they entertained and were entertained. Their outings were often recorded in *The Irish Times* and they were part of a group of well-to-do professionals who attended various charity functions, the theatre and other public events.

—— ·········· ···· ········ ——

The newly-married couple moved into a flat in 41 Fitzwilliam Place and, a few years later, they bought an entire house, number 10, on the same road.[4] Now mostly business premises – the Price's former home is presently the headquarters of the Irish Medical Organisation – the beautifully proportioned Georgian houses in inner south Dublin were, at this time, an enclave of doctors, judges and other higher professionals. The Prices' house was large and they employed a cook, two maids and a parlour maid to housekeep. Dorothy and Liam drove their own cars, a luxury beyond the means of most at this time. Neither of them believed the other could drive so this was a source of ongoing argument. It was also somewhat ironic as Liam, who was a 'very fast and rather alarming driver himself' was known as a District Justice for being 'hard' in the matter of driving offences.[5] It wasn't just driving: Dorothy and Liam bickered endlessly about 'trifling domestic things' but wisely agreed to disagree over the more major controversial topics such as their different political allegiances.[6]

Dublin is close to the Dublin and Wicklow mountains, especially with the use of a car, and both Dorothy and Liam continued to enjoy hill walking, while Dorothy loved to fish. Liam had a limp from an accident during his school days at Aldenham Public School and Dorothy persuaded him to go for a hip operation. This was partially successful as the limp diminished but Liam still used a walking stick which doubled as a scale in the photographs and sketches that appeared in the field notebooks that he used to document place names and antiquities.[7] Liam's interest in antiquarianism grew and in 1926 he was elected as a member of the Royal Society of Antiquaries in Ireland. Indeed, it was said that Liam's interest in ancient Ireland, its archaeology and place names 'took precedence over his formal work, so that, in the minds of his contemporaries, he appeared to be a scholar of note whose hobby was the law'.[8]

Close relations with both families – the Prices and the Stopfords – continued. Aunt Alice lived nearby in St Stephen's Green where, despite her declining health, she continued to hold dinner parties and her house was a meeting place for civil servants, ministers, scholars and visitors from England. As Aunt Alice's health failed, Dorothy's sister Alice acted as co-hostess. This was probably a challenging role as Aunt Alice, who terrified most people,[9] was, like Dorothy, particularly partial to the company of men and would always try to make sure women did not take centre stage. Aunt Alice's political career as a senator placed her in the midst of contemporary debates about Ireland's future. In June 1925, some months after Liam and Dorothy married, W.B. Yeats declaimed an iconic speech in the Senate, defending divorce. He wanted the state to legislate for individual freedom and allow the minority Protestants to retain this right. Stirring though it must have been to listen to him, there was cold comfort for Protestants in the decades to come as contraception, birth control and divorce were outlawed by a conservative State in thrall to Catholic mores.

Aunt Alice died in 1929 and her death prompted a variety of responses in the media, ranging from the effusive to the critical. The *Irish Statesman* carried the line that she was 'one of the most noble, generous and disinterested Irish women of her time', while *The Times* was less generous. True to type, Aunt Alice left most of her money to the male member of the family – Dorothy's brother Robert – although she also willed a share to the others. Dorothy's sister Alice used some of the money to send her daughter Mary, now aged 19, to Cambridge University, where she read modern languages. There was enough left for Alice and Mary to go on a world tour prior to Mary's departure to university. Robert was working abroad with his cousin Sir John Simon on a series of political and economic problems.

For Dorothy, Aunt Alice's death brought a slew of letters from old friends in its wake. Sonnie Crowley wrote from Ivy Lodge, in Kilbrittain – he sounded depressed, he had been ill, the weather was bad and he had to help in the shop – the shop with attached post office and café, in the centre of Kilbrittain village, is still owned by Crowleys – as Birdie and his mother were not very strong although he was glad to have Birdie and her husband Denny at home. He condoled with Dorothy on the death of Aunt Alice, who would be honoured as a 'genuine patriot' but remarked that it was a pity she favoured the 'stepping-stone policy' that is, moving gradually towards a thirty-two-county Ireland. The 'jolly crowd of boys and girls' whom Dorothy had met in Kilbrittain were now scattered all over the globe in order to earn a living, he noted.[10] Sonnie had evidently not been in touch with Dorothy for some time as he also mentioned the death of Dorothy's friend Mary Spring Rice whom he heard had died unexpectedly. Mary, who had been involved in the Howth gun-running, died of tuberculosis in a sanatorium in North Wales in 1924, five years prior to Aunt Alice's demise.[11]

Dorothy wrote to Sir Matthew to tell him of Alice's death and received a warm reply: 'It is good when something comes back to your life that one had treasured and that had seemed to go out of it. That is what I felt when I had my mail this morning and feel more on rereading the letter it brought from you.' He was sorry to hear of the death of Aunt Alice with whom he had been friends 'since we foregathered at the beginning of the century'. In a more light-hearted vein, he told her that it interested him greatly to hear of Dorothy's three interests: 'First of all the husband of whom you told me something of his work'. Sir Matthew sympathised 'greatly in the archaeological pursuits'. He teased Dorothy that as she became more familiar with the subject, she would be content 'with these 730 circles or crosses in the year to which you tell me you are at present limiting yourself'. Secondly, he congratulated her on her medical practice, state and private, for which 'you gave yourself such long and careful preparation and lastly there are the politics of which I always suspect you to care more for the way the machine works than for the stuff it turns out'. Admitting he might be doing her an injustice in this last analysis, he added that 'at any rate it is a joy for me to hear that you are really extremely happy'.[12]

At this time, Sir Matthew had returned to England from Australia and was sitting on a Commission to report on the Governmental system of Ceylon. He also continued to guide the Infant Welfare Association with which he was connected when Dorothy lived at Chelsea. He invited Dorothy and Liam to come and stay with him in the old and pretty house which he had bought twenty-two years ago and slyly added that they might do so when Dorothy could bring herself to visit 'oppressive, wicked, effete and in every way abominable England'.

Dorothy and Liam did visit England occasionally but their lives were firmly grounded in Dublin: they entertained and attended public social events. The comings and goings of Dorothy and other prominent doctors – in particular the annual summer absences and autumnal returns – can be charted through *The Irish Times* Court and Personal column. The Prices' names also occasionally featured in the social columns in the *The Irish Times*. They went to concerts and 'at-homes' in the Rotunda Hospital. Dorothy and Liam were among the guests listed at the German Consul-General's garden party in Northumberland Road, Dublin, in August 1928. The German connection continued when they attended a celebration of German national day in August 1932. Three years later, *The Irish Times* recorded that Dorothy wore 'a dark grey suit and blue hat' to a reception held by the German Minister. Her outfit clearly did not impress the paper's correspondent who commented favourably on other ensembles, using adjectives such as 'pretty', 'tailored', 'smart', 'becoming' and 'graceful'.[13] Dorothy's outfit did not elicit any such praise.

Dorothy played bridge and took part in charity tournaments organised by Professor and Mrs Rowlette.[14] She and Liam attended events such as

the opening of the Royal Hibernian Academy's annual exhibition in the
Metropolitan School of Art, Kildare Street, Dublin.[15] They were invited
to State events also: in 1932, Dorothy received an invitation from the
Government of the Free State to attend a reception in honour of His
Eminence, the Papal Legate, at the Thirty-First International Eucharistic
Congress, Dublin. This Eucharistic Congress was a major international
event in the Catholic calendar each year. The Dublin Congress exceeded
expectations and was one of the largest Eucharistic congresses of the
twentieth century. While the invitation was preserved in Dorothy's papers,
there is no record of whether she attended or not. However, she could not
have missed the event with its thronged public parades wending their way
through the streets of the city centre. The following year, Dorothy and Liam
were listed among the guests at a state reception at Dublin Castle.

In addition to attending public events, the Prices were socially active
in a private capacity. The guest list for their dinner parties included, as
might be expected, doctors, antiquarians, members of the literati as well
as Republicans such as Dorothy Macardle, S.T. O'Kelly,[16] Frank Aiken[17]
and Rosamond Jacob.[18] Many of their neighbours were well-regarded
Dublin physicians and surgeons. When Dr and Mrs Leonard Abrahamson
celebrated the return of Mrs Abrahamson's brother and sister-in-law from
Palestine, Dorothy and Liam had only to walk up the road to Number 40
to attend the crowded entertainment in the 'large and beautifully decorated
rooms'.[19] Glimpses of the Price's private social life in the early 1930s can be
gained from the entertaining, gossip-laden, occasionally malicious diaries
of Signe Toksvig, a Danish writer married to Kilkenny-born author Francis
Hackett.[20] On 17 April 1932, she places them in Ballyvolan Fort, in County
Wicklow, scrambling over 'indeterminate earthworks and rubble heaps'
wondering if they were 'round or angular and was the masonry Norman or
pre'. While Signe and Liam photographed the remains, Dorothy and Francis
picked primroses and talked politics behind a gorse bush. Signe described
Liam as obstinate though gentle in manner while describing Dorothy
as 'rather intelligent'. All in all, she summed them up as 'fairly soothing
people'.[21] Next month, the Prices went to tea with Signe and she said they
were '*petillant* (he was), pleasant, really simple and friendly'. They brought
along that 'solar myth', folklorist James Delargy.[22] At the end of May, Signe
was invited to the Prices for dinner. She was not impressed by their decor:
'finely proportioned rooms, chillily decorated and sparsely furnished'.

Then, she went with them to a meeting of the Royal Antiquarians of which Liam was an enthusiastic member. Deliciously malicious, she described the talk: 'A Neolithic relic named Buckley opened meeting. McAlister away on bog. A fossilised mind, a school inspector, subjected us to seemingly endless torture'.[23]

In October, Signe dined once again in the Price's chilly house – this time, the Millington Synges[24] were there for dinner. Her ready pen recorded: 'Didn't like him. Perverse, gritty, silent. She dull-seeming'. They were joined by a crowd after dinner; one attendee, Dr M, turned out to be an anti-semite. Liam, Signe and two other guests 'went for him'. Signe praised Liam as 'so straight-forward and shyly sweet and she [Dorothy] had herself well in hand, was a good hostess.' All in all, Signe judged it a good evening.[25] On 16 December 1933, she once again dressed to dine at the Price's. This time, Dorothy came under fire: 'Dorothy jabs at L.P. the whole time, but rather childlikely.' She followed up this observation with the rather cryptic remark: 'No brains, but good enough.' The party went on to a music hall show where the tobacco smoke choked them.[26] As a smoker, Dorothy may not have noticed – indeed, she probably contributed her share to the smoke cloud. Signe undoubtedly preferred Liam to Dorothy and records other pleasant social events involving Liam or Liam and Delargy. In 1935, she was openly exasperated by Dorothy: 'And oh the lucubrations of Dorothy Price! "My friends [Fianna Fáil] are in power now. Irish have temperament. Danes have none.' Perhaps, the 'warm oysters' and 'stodgy dinner', provided by the Prices, added to Signe's exasperation.[27]

Although many people suggest Dorothy got on better with men than women, her papers includes gossipy letters to and from other women with whom she maintained long and close friendships. There are other glimpses of Dorothy's female friendships: for instance, Rosamond Jacob's diaries record an intimate conversation she and Dorothy had when she called to tea in July 1932. They talked of the 'vogue of homosexuality among women in Paris – men too troublesome, so women use one another'.[28] Rosamond's friend Ruby was 'clingingly, selfishly in love' with her but Rosamond wrote that she, herself, was not homosexual. Later, Dorothy helped Rosamond to get Ruby into a nursing home for a period.

As well as women friends and colleagues, Dorothy also got on well with her own sisters although Sandra Lefroy suggests that Edie, who was lamed in a horse riding accident on Callary, in County Wicklow, became reserved and a little difficult in later years. Alice remained in Dublin and was close to Dorothy.

With all of the social whirl and outdoor activities, it seems that there must have been little time left for work. In actual fact, during this decade, Dorothy was extremely busy. She held a number of appointments in hospitals as well as running a private practice and engaging in philanthropic work. Her job in St Ultan's prospered and she was appointed as a full physician. She took on appointments in the Royal City of Dublin Hospital, in Baggot Street, the Sunshine Home, Stillorgan, and as a medical officer at the preparatory school Coláiste Moibhí. Dorothy's medical practice brought her into close contact with many of the social problems that faced young women in Ireland. Unwanted pregnancy, with its associations of shame, was a huge difficulty, often solved by families placing their daughters into the care of religious orders. Strict moral codes made it easier to hide problems than to deal with them. The laws inherited by the new Irish Free State in respect of the perceived problem of juvenile prostitution and immorality were outdated and in June 1930, the Cumann na nGaedheal government appointed a Committee on the Criminal Law Amendment Acts (1880–5) and Juvenile Prostitution under the chairmanship of King's Counsel William Carrigan. This committee, which became known as the Carrigan committee, had a reasonably balanced membership, including representative of the Roman Catholic and Church of Ireland clergy as well as four lay members – two women and two men. Twenty-nine witnesses were called, of which nineteen were female. These women gave evidence on behalf of a variety of professional and philanthropic organisations, including the Irish Women Workers' Union, Saor an Leanbh, the Irish Women Citizens and Local Government Association, the Leeson Street Magdalen Laundries, Dublin's Lock Hospital and the National Society for the Prevention of Cruelty to Children. Dorothy and Dr Delia Moclair Horne, representing the Irish Women Doctors' Committee, presented a memorandum signed by fifty-four female doctors. Along with her colleague, Dorothy highlighted young Irishwomen's 'remarkable' ignorance of the facts of life. They called for enhanced instruction and both Dorothy and Delia cited personal knowledge of 13-year-olds who had become pregnant.

Dorothy and Delia related the secrecy with which many unmarried women responded to pregnancy to the under-reporting of sexual crimes against women and children. Both women argued that in their professional experience young girls only disclosed rape or assault if they became pregnant. Incarceration was portrayed by many witnesses, including female witnesses, as a protective response for women in trouble. The final Carrigan Commission report, by and large, ignored the views of the female doctors. According to historian James M. Smith, the Carrigan report's 'evasion' of their testimony 'suppressed these professional women's call for education', particularly for impoverished girls or those who were institutionalised.[29]

In the end, the report was alarmist in many of its conclusions and embarrassing to the Government. For instance, it stated: 'The testimony of all the witnesses, clerical, lay and official is striking in its unanimity that degeneration in the standard of social conduct has taken place in recent years. It is attributed primarily to the loss of parental control and responsibility during a period of general upheaval, which have not been reversed since the revival of settled conditions.'[30] Dance halls were a 'crying evil', while public immorality was 'rampant in defiance of priests and police'. The twenty-one recommendations were a mixture of progressive and regressive measures: it was suggested that the age of consent be raised from 16 to 18 years and contraception was to be outlawed. However, the Department of Justice was unimpressed and issued a memo advising against publishing the report.[31] The report was duly suppressed. Dorothy publicly suggested that it was more important for the recommendations of the report to be implemented than for it to be published. When a new Fianna Fáil-led government came to power in 1932, the eventual Criminal Law Amendment Act of 1935 differed significantly from the Carrigan report.

Dorothy and Liam were not particularly interested in formal religion but Dorothy became associated with a number of primarily Protestant philanthropic endeavours. Many of her female professional colleagues were already leading the way in child welfare and philanthropy. Ella Webb, who was now a colleague of Dorothy's at St Ultan's Hospital, was instrumental in setting up the Sunshine Home in Stillorgan, Dublin, in 1925 to provide care for children with rickets. At that time, there were no official figures for children with rickets but the condition was prevalent among the children of Dublin's slums. These children were often bow-legged, with knees knocking against each other; as the condition worsened and the soft young bones set into hard deformed shapes, the children could be crippled. Rickets is a childhood illness caused by a lack of Vitamin D which is necessary for bone building. Poor diets, consisting mainly of bread and tea with few vegetables or fruit as well as a lack of exercise and over-crowding, with concomitant lack of exposure to sunshine, were thought to contribute to the disease.[32] Dorothy, too, worked with the Sunshine Home which was a small-scale operation, providing a glimpse of what might be achieved if more funding was available. Dorothy's bluff kindness could sometimes be construed as patronising as, in 1928, when she expressed a typically forthright opinion that the children of Dublin 'used too many clothes, and to get their clothes off them when they came there [the Sunshine Home] was a relief to them'.[33] However, the home, with its primarily Protestant doctors, did not proselytise. It plugged a gap in State provision and part of its aim was to produce what Price described as 'healthy useful citizens'.

Dorothy was genuinely concerned about the plight of the poor, a topic that had claimed her attentions since she left St Paul's School and worked as a lady almoner. She began to join another St Ultan's colleague, Kathleen Maguire, in her work in slum dispensaries. Dorothy was also associated with the Protestant Orphan Society and the National Society for the Prevention of Cruelty to Children. In 1933, at the annual meeting of the Cottage Home for Little Children, in Kingstown, which, for many years, catered solely for Protestant children, Dorothy praised the work of the home which seemed to her to be a 'real home of happy, natural children' and she emphasised the importance of children getting pure milk.[34] Dorothy was a member of the Clean Milk Society which attempted to ensure that infection was not spread through imbibing contaminated milk. Some of the bigger farmers in County Dublin had begun to tuberculin-test their dairy cattle and, according to Dorothy, the idea of tubercle-free milk with a very low bacterial count was beginning to spread. The children's hospitals encouraged the use of this 'pure milk'. In 1933, the committee of the Clean Milk Society decided to approach the Minister for Local Government and Public Health, Seán T. O'Kelly, to attempt to persuade him of the necessity for a clean milk bill. To the chagrin of the committee, chaired by J.W. Bigger, professor of bacteriology and preventive medicine at TCD, they were fobbed off with a meeting with the parliamentary secretary Conn Ward. As the only Republican on the committee, Dorothy had direct access to Seán T. O'Kelly: she visited him privately, explaining to him that he 'must himself see the deputation'. This intervention was successful and he duly met them with his 'accustomed courtesy and good after-results'.[35] The Clean Milk Society was wound up in 1934, as they were satisfied with the legislation that was passed. However, the problems of impure milk were not solved for some time to come: legislation with respect to pasteurisation of milk was finally enacted in Ireland in 1957.

— ............ ............ —

Meanwhile, working in a hospital for infants was often disturbing and difficult as gastroenteritis, pneumonia and tuberculosis killed many young patients. The death rate for children under one year of age was 70 per 1000 in Dublin in the late 1920s. There were few cures for infectious diseases prior to the late 1940s when antibiotics began to become available although rest, diet and some therapies did offer relief. In June 1928, Dorothy noted that of 179 admissions to the hospital, 61 died but cases were taken in that appeared to be 'moribound' (dying). Such cases were never refused, according to her, as it was never certain that they were going to die.[36] In 1929, Dorothy was promoted from assistant physician to full physician in St Ultan's Hospital. Dr Kathleen Maguire, whom Dorothy had joined in her slum dispensary, was also a major stimulus to intellectual endeavour, inculcating an interest in medical research and encouraging 'any never-so-feeble evidences of an inquiring mind'.

> ...for nine years I had imbibed wisdom from her in St Ultan's Hospital, making a point of doing her round with her, when she would pause at the last cot, with the baby clutching her fingers whilst she drifted off into a very interesting discourse, drawing on her great experience and her wealth of reading. She was a very clever woman and Sister Mulligan and I enjoyed these bedside talks, when she would range far and wide, as when, over a case of epispadius [a rare congenital defect of the urethra], she spoke of John Ruskin (known to her people, the Alexanders, and to my grandfather, Dr Kennedy; Ruskin had stayed with him at Belgard).[37]

Dr Maguire had urged Dorothy to take the trouble to 'find things out and to read and publish'. Dorothy took these injunctions to heart, and in 1930, her first research publication appeared in the *Irish Journal of Medical Science* – it detailed the results of a series of vaccinations to treat diarrhoea. This work was spurred on by her observation that breast-fed babies seemed to fare better in the recurrent epidemics of summer diarrhoea in Dublin. They evidently had some immunity as a result of the breast feeding and Dorothy decided to induce artificial immunity to some strains of bacteria that she perceived as causing the illness. She developed autogenuous vaccines – these were personalised vaccines made from cultures of bacteria grown in the laboratory from specimens taken from each baby. All of the babies recovered and she took full credit, claiming, in one case, to have saved the infant's life.[38] Dorothy was lucky – the diarrhoea was probably self-limiting and dried up with time and the vaccines did not produce any adverse side-effects. This type of research would, today, be subject to rigorous scientific and ethical review and consent processes. Dorothy's early research work was not subject to a formal peer review process in St Ultan's Hospital. This is not surprising, as hospital ethics committees were not put in place in Ireland until the 1980s.[39] Dorothy did, however, seek parental consent. She published and presented her work, and, in this manner, it was open to peer review and scrutiny. At the time, Dorothy's research approach was typical of the work being done in other Irish and European hospitals and institutions: medical ethics and rules on experimentation were not clearly defined or codified in the laws of most countries prior to the Second World War.[40]

Dorothy's work on autogenous vaccines was part of a wider endeavour by St Ultan's to cure or prevent illness using vaccines made in the hospital. The hospital appeared to embrace an optimistic view of the value of these products. In 1933, and again in 1936, Dorothy wrote, on behalf of the hospital staff, to the army headquarters asking for half a pint of blood from each of two soldiers who had definitely had measles and who had tested negative for syphilis. The type of blood did not matter, she added, as they were giving adult serum (the liquid component of blood without red blood cells) in an outbreak of measles 'which is deadly amongst our young babies'.[41] Other measures were taken in St Ultan's against infectious diseases: that same year, nurses with colds were asked to wear masks on duty and to stay off duty if they were at the 'streaming stage'.[42] Dorothy had previously proposed that any infants admitted with a temperature of over 100°F should be isolated in a separate ward.[43] The issue of colds among staff was not resolved and some form of vaccination was introduced. In 1936, the eighteenth annual report of the hospital noted that the hospital had, again, achieved 'very satisfactory results' from their scheme of immunisation against the common cold. 'In order to banish as far as possible this evil from our midst, we immunised not only the nursing staff but the maids and laundry staff, and we have practically reduced the morbidity from this ailment to zero!'[44] If this was true, then St Ultan's would have made world medical history – an effective vaccine against the common cold still, in 2014, does not exist. Again, the hospital was lucky that the patent vaccines they made and administered to staff and patients did not result in illness or death.

In May 1930, Dorothy was offered the position of medical officer at Coláiste Moibhí, a preparatory college for Protestant boys and girls, which educated its pupils to become primary teachers who were fluent in the Irish language. Her duties were to include weekly attendance at the college to see to the health needs of pupils and to meet with the head teacher to discuss any important cases. The matron kept a sickbook and Dorothy had to examine each pupil whose name was in the book. She had to write a weekly report on the health of the pupils in general and a separate report about each student whom she examined. If necessary, she committed sick pupils to hospital, making sure that he or she got there safely and the Department of Education had to be notified about pupils in hospital. For this, she was offered the sum of £60 annually with no pension and no bonus. The college was Irish speaking and the letter of appointment to Dorothy was written in Irish, a language that she did not speak fluently. Nonetheless, Dorothy took on the post, procuring a translation of the correspondence (possibly from Liam who was competent, if not completely fluent, in Irish) and experimenting with various versions of her married surname in Irish including 'Praidheas, Praoidheas and Prioidheas'. She settled on 'Doirinn Praoideas'.[45] Dorothy's lack of linguistic competence was noticed and a query was sent to the Minister for Education asking if it was a fact that the doctor at Coláiste Moibhí was not an Irish speaker and, if so, whether it was proposed to continue with this arrangement. The reply simply stated that the discretion in choosing a doctor lay with the principal and that the doctor whose service had been obtained for the past six months knew Irish and, it was understood, conversed in Irish with the students under treatment. Dorothy remained in the post for years to come: it was a busy appointment with outbreaks of infectious diseases such as influenza and measles. In addition to providing Dorothy with additional income, and some interesting clinical work, this school served as a valuable source of 'control' subjects for her research work with tuberculin testing. In Dorothy's words: 'these pupils, comprising boys and girls between the ages of 14 and 18 years, are required to be perfectly healthy as they are training to be primary teachers'.[46]

— ·········· ···········—

On 1 August 1931, a notice appeared in *The Irish Times* Court and Personal column informing readers that Dr Dorothy Price had left 10 Fitzwilliam Place for a month.[47] Dorothy and Liam took the train to Cobh, County Cork, and boarded an oil-fired German liner, the *Milwaukee*, in order to go on a walking tour in Carinthia in southern Austria. Dorothy wrote a full account of this trip, which was to mark the beginnings of her first serious interest in the diagnosis and treatment of tuberculosis in children.[48] From Cuxhaven, the Prices travelled to Munich and on to Heiligenblut, a 'delightful little village under the Grossglockner glacier and mountain in Austria'. From there, they got a bus to Klagenfurt where they joined up with Dr Adolf Mahr and his family who were holidaying there. Adolf,[49] an archaeologist and later Nazi activist, was curator of Irish Antiquities in the National Museum in Dublin. Liam and Adolf, who shared a common interest in archaeology, took a trip down the Dalmatian coast to Split while Adolf's wife, Maria, and Dorothy journeyed to Vienna where Maria acted as Dorothy's guide. Dorothy stayed in the Hotel Holler and Maria stayed with friends. Dorothy noted down various useful German phrases including *Möchten sie gern rauchen?* – a useful phrase for a heavy smoker such as Dorothy. Every morning, Dorothy got up at 7.30 a.m., refreshed herself with a glass of hot coffee *mit schlag* (with cream) and a roll, and then she visited various hospitals. She signed up for a series of post-graduate courses – skin, surgery in infants, diabetes in children, feeding in children – under the auspices of the American Medical Association. The lectures were in English and excellent. Dorothy took copious notes. However, she 'had no note on

Hamburger [Professor Franz], with whom I went around one morning with an American doctor who took me. What I saw went too deep to need notes'.[50]

What she saw was a method of diagnosing tuberculosis which can be difficult to diagnose, particularly in children where common symptoms include fever, abdominal pain, anorexia and weight loss. These symptoms could belong to a number of conditions, not just tuberculosis. Tuberculin testing helped to provide a differential diagnosis. In its first incarnation, tuberculin was a fairly crude substance: an extract of tubercular protein, extracted by autoclaving, filtering and concentrating a laboratory culture of the bacterium *Mycobacterium tuberculosis*.[51] Tuberculin testing is based on the fact that the introduction of tuberculin into an animal or human that has been previously exposed to tuberculosis leads to a response, great or small, depending on the route of exposure and the dosage. In young children, a positive tuberculin test invariably meant a primary infection. The tuberculin test was therefore particularly useful for this cohort in the first half of the twentieth century before widespread use of the BCG vaccine which could prevent tuberculosis (people vaccinated with BCG became tuberculin positive).[52]

Tuberculin testing had been around since the late 1800s but it was only in 1907 that a tuberculin skin test was developed by Clemens von Pirquet, in Vienna. This skin test produced a local reaction rather than one which would affect the whole body, so it was convenient and safe to use. Following this watershed, the continental medical profession began to incorporate tuberculin testing into its diagnostic algorithms.[53] Professor Hamburger, who was von Pirquet's successor, used an ointment containing tuberculin to check if children had been previously exposed to tuberculosis. If the skin reddened, the test was positive. If the test was negative, he followed it up using a more sensitive technique – the Mantoux test – where tuberculin was injected.

Dorothy was fascinated by the roof of Univeristätskinderklinik, where, right in the heart of the city, there nestled an open-air school, with 'glass sleeping wards, and semi-clad little kids, sun-burned through gradual, not violent exposure to the sun, either in bed resting or doing a few lessons in the fresh air at little desks'. Hamburger, whom Dorothy described as a 'small fair stern silent man' progressed through the ward, rewarding children with sweets if their schoolwork was good. He slapped the face of a child with a bad report. Dorothy made no comment on this disciplinary measure.

During the visit, she bought a tube of Perkutan (or Hamburger's ointment) and a glass slide, with a millimetre rule on it, to measure skin reactions.[54] In addition, she purchased various textbooks in German, and had to procure help in translation although, very quickly, she learned to read and speak the language, as she considered the German medical literature on tuberculosis essential. She mused:

> It is extraordinary that tuberculosis in children should have been a closed book to Ireland for 20 years after methods of diagnosis were well established on the continent, and at least ten years after methods of treatment had been evolved. One can only ascribe it to the fact that doctors in Ireland did not read or visit German-speaking centres, and took everything via England.[55]

Despite the epiphany that Dorothy experienced in the Kinderklinik, she did not immediately put Hamburger's methods into use. She was busy with other work such as measuring the haemoglobin content of infants from birth to one year. She also developed a device to measure the blood-pressure of infants. Then, in 1932, Dr Nora O'Leary joined St Ultan's and she and Dorothy together began to diagnose and treat patients with tuberculosis. In Dorothy's opinion, Nora had a 'very good analytical brain and an inquiring turn of mind'.[56] In 1933, twin brothers Peter and Louis came under the care of Dorothy and Nora. Their illness was perplexing. Peter had a high temperature 'without physical signs and without being excessively ill'. At the suggestion of 'a young doctor' from the laboratory in TCD, Price did a tuberculin test. It was only then that the knowledge and materials Price had brought back from Vienna were first put to use in a clinical environment. She used the Perkutan ointment that she had procured in Vienna and got a strongly positive reaction. Subsequently, when tested, Louis was negative but he soon developed a fever and his tuberculin test became positive. These two cases of primary tuberculosis were the 'first and also the most outstanding examples of initial fever' that Price was to meet.[57] Thus, it was the concatenation of two chance events – following Hamburger on a ward round and, two years later, seeing twin boys develop primary tuberculosis – that interested Price in tuberculin testing.

The boys were sent by their parents to recuperate in a sanatorium in Scheiddeg in Germany. Nora O'Leary accompanied them. Her enthusiastic report on the treatment regime there prompted Price to enrol on a ten-day postgraduate course. Initially, she was apprehensive about taking up a course in a language of which she had only a rudimentary knowledge. She had to 'screw up all her courage'. However, she was glad she did so as everyone was very welcoming: 'This place is great for Hitler. Being Irish I find it is an open Sesame'. In a letter to Liam, she confided that listening six hours a day to German lectures was a strain and, of course, she missed some of the information. However, she had acquired a reading list and would make up for it when she returned to Ireland. In wifely fashion, she reminded Liam that the servants would want their wages of two pounds nineteen shillings each, or four pounds thirteen shillings (presumably there were different rates of pay for the maids and the cook) before she came home. She ended the letter with 'lots of love my Ducksie to you…Goodbye, auf wiedersehen, Do'.[58]

Turning her attention back to the immediate, and studying alongside thirty Danish, Swiss and German postgraduate colleagues (several women were also on the course), she became even more convinced of the correctness of the continental views on tuberculosis, particularly with respect to diagnosis using tuberculin.[59] This contrasted with what she had been taught as a medical student in TCD. Professor V.M. Synge summed up the helplessness felt by the Irish medical profession in the face of tuberculosis in children at that time:

> Cases of tuberculous glands in the neck, tuberculosis of bones and joints, and tuberculous peritonitis, many of which recovered after a long illness. He also saw numerous cases of tuberculous meningitis and miliary tuberculosis. Nothing could be done for such cases – the victim always died in a few weeks. How a child acquired tuberculous meningitis or miliary tuberculosis was obscure. Tuberculin reactions were brushed aside as unreliable if not misleading.[60]

Tuberculosis is often presumed to be a chronic pulmonary disease affecting the lungs of adults but the disease also affected children. In children, non-pulmonary forms of the disease are more common than lung disease. Any part of a child's body can be affected including bones and joints, the abdomen and the membranes surrounding the brain as well as being disseminated throughout the body in millet-seed-sized nodules in a form of the disease known as 'miliary' tuberculosis. In 1922, the year in which the Free State was founded, there were 4,613 deaths from tuberculosis in the country, with 611 of these among children under 15 years of age. By 1930, this had fallen to 537 (total deaths 3,825). But, for most of the first half of the twentieth century, tuberculosis was the third leading cause of death among Irish children, eclipsed only by gastroenteritis and pneumonia.[61] It is no wonder that Dorothy began to channel her time and energies into finding out more about the disease.

Dorothy improved her German language skills and continued to read German medical textbooks. Her handwritten translation of most of the second edition of *Praktisches Lehrbuch der Kindertuberkulose*[62] can still be found among her medical papers in TCD's archives. She became increasingly convinced that tuberculin testing, followed by x-ray, provided valuable evidence of infection with tuberculosis. She and Nora began to use Hamburger's ointment on 'all and sundry', testing 100 inpatients in St Ultan's and later extending the work to 246 outpatients at St Ultan's and the Royal City of Dublin Hospital in Baggot Street where, in 1932, Dorothy joined the staff as physician to the children's dispensary. Paediatricians did not have beds in the hospital and when children required admission, they were admitted under the care of the physician or surgeon on duty. Dorothy was appointed as the 'children's specialist' with the right to hold a dispensary every Friday morning.[63] One of Dorothy's successors to the post, Barbara Stokes, later commented that 'All the consultants felt that paediatrics was a non-speciality. We were rather like vets – our patients could not talk back...'[64] Dorothy's work was to render paediatrics visible at national level and contributed, to some extent, to its acceptance as a separate speciality.

At the time she was working in St Ultan's and the Royal City of Dublin Hospital, Baggot Street, she was seeing tuberculosis wreak havoc among her young patients. She believed that early diagnosis of tuberculosis in children, facilitated by tuberculin testing, was essential for their treatment. Many children who were infected with tuberculosis recovered completely

and were symptomless throughout their primary infection; however, in others the disease progressed and rest was considered essential for recovery. Children could be cured if they were diagnosed at the early or primary stage of the disease, according to Dorothy. For her, the two crucial elements of treatment were the removal of infants from 'all possible tuberculous contact' and bed rest, both of which could be achieved by admission to a hospital or sanatorium, although there was a shortage of such beds.

In 1933, Dorothy decided to investigate how healthy subjects would react to tuberculin and to tie in these reactions to x-ray findings. She tuberculin tested all fifty-five pupils in Coláiste Moibhí using the Moro skin test, whereby diagnostic ointment is rubbed onto the skin. Her colleague Dr T. Garratt Hardman in Baggot Street x-rayed the girls and boys – five pupils were sent down every Monday to have a chest and abdominal x-ray taken. As MO to the college, Dorothy knew the 'family and personal history of each pupil'. They discovered two cases passing through 'mild primary tuberculous infection' and Dorothy instituted a partial rest treatment. There were difficulties interpreting a calcerous gland and Dorothy went to London to consult Peter Kerley who, under the auspices of the British Medical Research Council, was working on a radiological study of the chests of 1,000 healthy young people.[65] In 1934, Dorothy decided to expand the scope of her tuberculin testing investigations. She wanted to get a total of 500 cases for publication so she tested twenty children in the Sunshine Home. Then, she and a colleague tuberculin tested the patients in the children's pavilion in Peamount Sanatorium, Dublin.[66] A surprise was in store: it was expected that all of the children, who had been sent to the sanatorium because they had tuberculosis, would be tuberculin positive. Fourteen out of fifty-three children reacted negatively. Dr Alice Barry, the Peamount superintendent, gradually sent these children home with a note to their County Medical Officer of Health (CMOH) explaining that they were not tubercular. Neither tuberculosis officers (TOs) nor CMOHs, who would have referred the children to the sanatorium, routinely used tuberculin tests at this time (1933–4). All subsequent entries to Peamount children's pavilion were tuberculin tested on entry and the negatives were not admitted.[67] However, there was no onus on other sanatoria to follow suit. Admission policies were developed at an institutional level rather than on a national basis, so children who may not have had tuberculosis continued to be admitted to institutions where they were immediately placed in contact with infectious cases of the disease.

A year later, on 23 March 1934, Dorothy presented her findings on the 500 tuberculin tests at the Medical Section of the Royal Academy of Medicine in the Royal College of Physicians. T. Garratt Hardman presented a parallel paper on the x-ray findings. Their colleagues were, by and large, unimpressed. Dorothy recorded:

> Some slight interest in the subject was evinced, but in general I do not think anyone regarded it as having any relation to reality and certainly the Department of Health and the local authorities showed no enthusiasm for skin-testing as a public health measure by their Tuberculosis Officers.[68]

The other big surprise with Dorothy's work concerned the tuberculin test results of Coláiste Moibhí students. At this time, it was thought that all adolescents had been exposed to tuberculosis and would be either infected or immune, and therefore test positive with tuberculin. However, there was a low rate of positivity among the adolescents, aged between 14 and 18 years, indicating that they had not previously been exposed to tuberculosis, and therefore, had no immunity.[69] This study was important in that it disproved the belief among the medical profession that all healthy young Irish adults had been exposed to tuberculosis.[70]

The emerging interest in the diagnosis and treatment of tuberculosis in Irish children paralleled and contributed to the development of paediatric medicine in Ireland as a specialism. The Irish Paediatric Club, which later became the Irish Paediatric Association, was set up in 1933 by some of the staff of the three children's hospitals in Dublin – Temple Street, Harcourt Street and St Ultan's and was reinforced by specialists in various branches connected with children. There were no subscriptions and no *bunreacht* (constitution).[71] Dr Robert Collis,[72] a colleague and friend of Dorothy's, was one of the founding members, and the first meeting was held in the Price's home. The Paediatric Club was to prove a significant development in the study of childhood illness in Ireland. Writing in 1967, John Mowbray, a paediatrician at the Children's Hospital, Temple Street, Dublin, asserted that this club, with its 'pitifully small but indomitable membership', was responsible for the paediatrician 'being recognised as the equal of the consultant physician, surgeon and obstetrician'.[73] Dorothy and Robert Collis shared a strong interest in the diagnosis and treatment of childhood tuberculosis.

In Sweden, in the early 1920s, Swedish paediatrician Professor Arvid Wallgren had commenced his influential work with tuberculin testing and the preventive BCG vaccine in Gothenburg.[74] By the 1930s tuberculin skin tests were in universal use in Scandinavian schools, hospitals and other institutions. Robert Collis had visited Sweden in 1932 and brought Arvid's work to Dorothy's attention.[75] Dorothy became even more convinced of the value of approaches to tuberculosis that differed from the Irish and British perspective. She synthesised her knowledge into a thesis, and in January 1935 she was awarded the postgraduate qualification of Doctor of Medicine (MD) by TCD for a thesis entitled 'The Diagnosis of Primary Tuberculosis of the Lungs in Childhood'. Her thesis included a summary of how childhood tuberculosis was dealt with in France, Germany, Austria, Switzerland and Ireland. It stated baldly that 'in comparison with other countries we have to admit that in the 26 counties much remains to be done' with respect to children and tuberculosis. There was no provision for children with lung infections other than a fifty-bed wing in an adult sanatorium.

> There is no place for these children to go except amongst cases of open phthisis, and there is no greater danger for a primary case while passing through a state of lowered resistance to be placed in proximity to patients with open phthisis. No tuberculin tests are done in schools nor in the tuberculosis dispensaries, and there is no attempt at protection for children from infection at school, should there be a classmate with open phthisis sitting near them. The Tuberculosis Officers in cities and counties are not equipped with tuberculin tests, and seldom with xrays...[76]

In May 1935, Dorothy had a further opportunity to study the manner in which continental countries tackled tuberculosis when she attended an international hospitals conference in Italy. She attended lectures, visited hospitals in Turin and Milan and took detailed diligent notes. However,

Liam later noted that it was largely a waste of time as she did not observe any new approaches to tuberculosis.

— ··········· ············ —

Dorothy's first decade in Dublin, with her work in St Ultan's, the Royal City of Dublin Hospital and Coláiste Moibhí, was instrumental in directing her towards serious medical research. Dr Kathleen Maguire would have been delighted that Dorothy had taken her admonition to observe and to publish to heart. By the end of 1935, after a dozen years in Dublin, Dorothy had begun to work with tuberculin testing to diagnose tuberculosis, she had completed her MD thesis, published five papers in medical journals, including articles on autogenous vaccines, the feeding of infants with gastroenteritis, tuberculin testing and a paper on primary tuberculosis of the lungs in children. However, Irish medical practitioners were not convinced of the value of tuberculin testing and Dorothy would have to work hard to persuade them.

NOTES

1. D. Price to L. Price, 3 September 1934 (TCD, Price papers, MS 7534(61)).

2. L. Ó Broin, *Protestant Nationalists in Revolutionary Ireland: The Stopford Connection* (Dublin: Gill & Macmillan, 1985), p.204.

3. Interview, Sanda Lefroy, December 2011.

4. *The Irish Times*, 6 May 1925.

5. Ó Broin, *Protestant Nationalists*, p.200.

6. Ó Broin, *Protestant Nationalists*, p.198; Interview, Sandra Lefroy, December 2011.

7. C. Corlett and M. Weaver (eds), *The Price Notebooks* (Dublin: Duchas, 2002), pp.xi–xii.

8. Obituary, *Annual Report of the Royal Irish Academy 1966-7*, cited in Corlett and Weaver, *The Price Notebooks*, p.xiv.

9. Interview, Sandra Lefroy, December 2011.

10. S. Crowley to D. Price, 23 January 1929 (NLI, MS 15341 (9)).

11. B. Hourican, 'Spring Rice, Mary', in *Dictionary of Irish Biography* online, (accessed 14 October 2013). Mary Spring Rice (1880–1924) was a fluent Irish speaker, a member of the Gaelic League and a nationalist.

12. M. Nathan to D. Price, 28 September 1929 (NLI, MS 15341 (1)).

13. *The Irish Times*, 2 May 1935.

14. *The Irish Times*, 8 November 1930.

15. *The Irish Times*, 14 April 1931.

16. P. Maume, 'O'Kelly, Seán Thomas', in *Dictionary of Irish Biography* online, (accessed 14 October 2013). S.T. O'Kelly (1882–1966) was a devout Catholic, founder member of the Irish Volunteers, cabinet minister and later Tánaiste in the post-1932 Fianna Fáil government, elected President of Ireland in 1945.

17. R. Fanning, 'Aiken, Francis, Thomas', in *Dictionary of Irish Biography* online, (accessed 14 October 2013). Frank Aiken (1898–1983) was a farmer, a member of the IRA and, later, a politician. He was elected Minister for Defence in the Fianna Fáil government of 1932.

18. Rosamond Jacob Diaries, 21 October 1927 (NLI, MS 322,582 (58)). With thanks to Dr Clara Cullen for alerting me to the references to Dorothy in the Jacob diaries.

19. *The Irish Times*, 7 December 1936.

20. L. Pihl (ed.), *Signe Toksvig's Irish Diaries 1926–1937* (Dublin: The Lilliput Press, 1994).

21. Pihl, *Signe Toksvig's Irish Diaries*, p.172.

22. Ibid., p.176.

23. Ibid., p.187.

24. Victor Millington Synge (1873–1976) was a professor of medicine and a nephew of the playwright John Millington Synge.

25. Pihl, *Signe Toksvig's Irish Diaries*, p.213.

26. Ibid., p.277.

27. Ibid., p.311.

28. R. Jacob Diaries (NLI, MS 32,582 (70-1)).

29. J.M. Smith, 'The Politics of Sexual Knowledge: The Origins of Ireland's Containment Culture and the Carrigan Report (1931)', *Journal of the History of Sexuality*, 13, 2 (April 2004), pp.208–33.

30. The full text of the Carrigan Report may be read at http://the-knitter.blogspot.ie/2005/06/full-carrigan-report_24.html, (accessed 14 October 2013).

31. F. Kennedy, 'The Suppression of the Carrigan Report: a Historical Perspective on Child Abuse', *Studies*, 89 356 (Winter 2000), pp.354–63.

32. For an account of the Children's Sunshine Home, read L. Kelly, 'Rickets and Irish Children: Dr Ella Webb and the Early Work of the Children's Sunshine Home, 1925–1946', in A. Mac Lellan and A. Mauger (eds), *Growing Pains: ChildhoodIllness in Ireland, 1750–1950* (Dublin: Irish Academic Press, 2013).

33. *The Irish Times*, 4 June 1928.

34. *The Irish Times*, 26 May 1933.

35. L. Price, *Dorothy Price. An Account of Twenty Years' Fight against Tuberculosis in Ireland* (Oxford: Oxford University Press, 1957), p.7. For private circulation only; *The Irish Times*, 1 June 1928.

36. Ibid.

37. Price, *Dorothy Price*, pp.4–5; also cited in M. Ó hÓgartaigh, 'Dorothy Stopford-Price and the Elimination of Childhood Tuberculosis', in M. Ó hÓgartaigh (ed.), *Quiet Revolutionaries. Irish Women in Education, Medicine and Sport, 1861–1964* (Dublin: The History Press Ireland, 2011), p.113.

38. D. Price, 'Autogenous Vaccines in Intestinal Infections of Infants', *Irish Journal of Medical Science (IJMS)*, 6, 2 (1930), pp.59–64.

39. *The Irish Council for Bio-Ethics 2002–2005 Term of Office Report* (Dublin, 2006), p.8; D. Dooley, 'Medical Ethics in Ireland: A Decade of Change', *The Hastings Centre Report* 21, 1 (1991), p.20, pp.18–21; www.bioethics.ie., accessed 29 August 2009; EU directive 2001/20/EC, *www.eortc. be/services/doc/clinical-EU-directive-04-april-01.pdf*, (accessed 29 August 2009).

40. R. Porter, *The Greatest Benefit to Mankind: A Medical History of Humanity from Antiquity to the Present* (London, 1999), pp.650–3; E. Shuster, 'Fifty Years Later: the Significance of the Nuremburg Code', *New England Journal of Medicine*, 337, 220 (1997), p.1439; A. Hedgecoe, 'A Form of Practical Machinery: the Origins of Research Ethics Committees in the U.K., 1967–1972', *Medical History*, 53, 3 (2009), pp.331–50; 'The Vaccine Trials', in *Third Interim Report of the Commission to Enquire into Child Abuse* (Dublin: Commission to Enquire into Child Abuse, 2003), pp.209-28.

41. Minutes of Medical Committee, St Ultan's, 8 July 1933, 8 Nov 1936 (RCPI, SU/9/1).

42. Minutes of Medical Committee, St Ultan's, 13 December 1933 (RCPI, SU/9/1).

43. Minutes of Medical Committee, St Ultan's, 18 September 1929 (RCPI, SU/9/1).

44. St Ultan's Hospital, 18th Annual General Report, 1936 (RCPI, SU/2/1).

45. Correspondence between Coláiste Moibhí and D. Price, May-November 1930 (TCD, Price papers, MS 7534/13-20). For an account of the innovative Coláiste Moibhí, see V. Jones, *A Gaelic Experiment: the Preparatory System 1926–1961 and Coláiste Moibhí* (Dublin: the Woodfield Press, 2006).

46. D. Price, Investigation into Tuberculin Skin Tests of 33 Normal Adolescents (TCD, Price papers, MS 7534/39).

47. *The Irish Times*, 1 August 1931.

48. Price, *Dorothy Price*, pp.1–3.

49. P. Maume and D. McGuinness, 'Mahr, Adolf', in *Dictionary of Irish Biography* online, (accessed 14 October 2013). Adolf Mahr's (1887–1951) appointment as senior keeper of antiquities in the Irish museum in 1927 was partly due to a desire in independent Ireland to avoid an over-reliance on British professionals. He was an active and talented archaeologist. Mahr had a son and three daughters with his wife, Maria van Bemmelen. He joined the Nazi party on 1 April 1933, later spending the war years in the German foreign office.

50. Price, *Dorothy Price*, p.2.

51. S. R. Rosenthal, 'Tuberculin Sensitivity and BCG Vaccination', in S.R. Rosenthal (ed.), *BCG Vaccine: Tuberculosis, Cancer* (Boston and New York: Little, Brown, 1980), pp.183-4.

52. D. Price, *Tuberculosis in Childhood* (Bristol: Wrights, 1942), pp.31–2.

53. R.Wagner, *Clemens von Pirquet: his Life and Work* (Baltimore: the John Hopkins Press, 1968), pp.66–9.

54. Price, *Dorothy Price*, pp.2–3.

55. Ibid., p.3.

56. Ibid., p.5.

57. Ibid.

58. D. Price to L. Price, 3 Sept 1934 (TCD, Price papers, MS 7534(61)).

59. Ibid.

60. V.M. Synge, 'Introduction', in Price, *Dorothy Price*, p.v.

61. A. Mac Lellan, 'The Penny Test: Tuberculin Testing and Paediatric Practice in Ireland, 1900–1960', in A. Mac Lellan and A. Mauger (eds), *Growing Pains: Childhood Illness in Ireland 1750–1950* (Dublin: Irish Academic Press, 2013), p.124.

62. B. Simon and F. Redeker, *Praktisches Lehrbuch der Kindertuberkulose* (Leipzip: Curt Kabitzsch, 1930).

63. Medical Board, Royal City of Dublin Hospital to D. Price, 23 November 1932 (TCD, Price papers, MS 7534/28).

64. D. Coakley, *Baggot Street: A Short History of the Royal City of Dublin Hospital* (Dublin: Board of Governors, Royal City of Dublin Hospital, 1995), pp.75–6.

65. Price, *Dorothy Price*, pp.8–9.

66. Price, *Dorothy Price*, p.3, 9; also cited in Ó hÓgartaigh, 'Dr Dorothy', p.77. Peamount had been founded in 1912 by Lady Aberdeen and the Women's National Health Association.

67. Price, *Dorothy Price*, p.9.

68. Price, *Dorothy Price*, p.10; also cited in M. Ó hÓgartaigh, 'Dorothy Stopford-Price, p.115.

69. D. Price and T.G. Hardman, 'Report of a Tuberculin Survey amongst Children in Dublin Hospitals made by the Irish Paediatric Association', *IJMS*, 6, 187 (1941), pp.241–55.

70. Dorothy extended this work over an eleven-year period, publishing results that continued to support her thesis in 1939 and 1945.

71. D. Price, Text of Introduction for Dr Walter Pagel, 28 October 1937, Irish Paediatric Club (TCD, Price papers, MS 7534(190)).

72. Robert Collis (1900–75) was a paediatrician with extensive experience outside of Ireland, including a stint at the Hospital for Sick Children, Great Ormond Street, London and Johns Hopkins in Baltimore, USA. His Irish appointments included physician to the National Children's Hospital, Dublin and Director of Paediatrics in the Rotunda Hospital, Dublin.

73. J. Mowbray, 'Growth and Development of Paediatrics in Ireland', *Journal of the Irish Medical Association (JIMA)*, 60, 365 (1967), p.404.

74. Wallgren experimented with tuberculin testing and BCG vaccination in order to prevent tuberculosis in children. He was chief physician (1921–42) in the Gothenburg Children's Hospital which was Sweden's largest children's hospital. From 1942 to 1956, he held the Chair of Paediatrics at the Karolinska Institute, Stockholm and was also chief physician of the Norrtull's Children's Hospital which merged with the Karolinska in 1951.

75. Collis later became the English-language editor of Wallgren and Guidi Fanconi's book, *Lehrbuch der Pediatre*, republished in English as *Fanconi and Wallgren's Textbook of Paediatrics* (London: William Heinemann, 1952).

76. D. Price, The Diagnosis of Primary Tuberculosis of the Lungs in Childhood, MD thesis 1935 (TCD, Price papers, MS 7534 (66)).

Thursday, Dec 8th 1910.

We came up on deck early this morning, and directly after breakfast I went to Mrs Nakin's cabin, and told her our news, as we wanted her & the Murrays to know, so that they would not go on with the chaffing — She & Mrs Murray were both as kind as they could be & talkd to us so kindly, and Mr Murray gave us his address and extracted a promise that if he could do any thing to help us in any way, we would write, even down to borrowing money. We spent all the morning quietly on deck writing & avoiding people — We heard that we were going to get in an hour earlier to Bombay than we had hoped — The Captain for the gratification of the passengers, opened all the inwards parts of the ship for inspection — the store-rooms, pantry & kitchens; all very clean and quite inviting. After tea we were allowed in, two at a time, to see the Marconi operator at work. I went with Miss Ogilvie, who seemed to know a good deal about it — The operator used to be on the Mauretania — I had got the barber to wash my hair in the afternoon & dried it by hanging it out of the port in the wind — at about sun-down

1  Dorothy Stopford's diary, 8 December 1910. Courtesy of Sandra Lefroy.

2  Dorothy Stopford, clinical clerk at Meath Street Hospital, Dublin,
January 1920. Courtesy of Ida Milne.

3  Dorothy Stopford's graduation, Trinity
College Dublin, April 1921.
Reproduced by kind permission of the
Board of Trinity College Dublin.

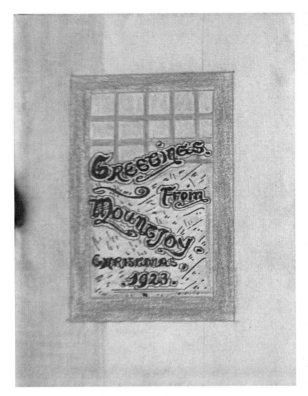

4 Christmas card (exterior) from
Liam Deasy, Mountjoy Gaol,
Dublin, to Dr Stopford, 1923.
Courtesy of the National Library
of Ireland.

5 Christmas card (interior) from
Liam Deasy, Mountjoy Gaol,
Dublin, to Dr Stopford, 1923.
Courtesy of the National Library
of Ireland.

FORM OF RESEARCH LICENCE.
-----------------------------------

THERAPEUTIC SUBSTANCES ACT, 1932.
------------------------------------

Licence No. 44 (R).

    The Minister for Local Government and Public Health in exercise of the powers conferred on him by the above mentioned Act, hereby licenses –

Dorothy Price, M.B., B.Ch.,
of
St. Ultan's Infant Hospital, Charlemont Street, Dublin,

being a person engaged in scientific research, to import for the purpose of scientific research at –

St. Ultan's Infant Hospital, Dublin,

or in such other place or places as the said Minister may from time to time authorise, the under-mentioned therapeutic substance from:

Dr. Wassen's Laboratory, Goteborg, Sweden,

namely:    B.C.G. Preventative Tuberculin Vaccine in single doses in sealed ampoules.

    This licence is granted subject to the conditions pertaining to the importation of therapeutic substances for the purpose of scientific research set out in any Regulations made under the said Act and for the time being in force and may be suspended or revoked by the said Minister if the licensee is convicted of an offence under the said Act.

    This licence will, unless previously suspended or revoked by the said Minister, continue in force for a period of two years from the date hereof.

    Given under the Official Seal of the Minister for Local Government and Public Health this 2½th day of December, in the year One Thousand Nine Hundred and Thirty-Six.

*Sean E. Meallay*

Minister for Local Government and Public Health.

6  First Research Licence granted to import BCG vaccine into Ireland, December 1936. Reproduced by kind permission of the Board of Trinity College Dublin.

7 Dorothy Price,
Undated. Courtesy of
the National Library of Ireland.

8 Liam Price, Undated.
Courtesy of the National
Library of Ireland.

9   Exterior of Dorothy Price's former home, 10 Fitzwilliam Place, Dublin.
    Courtesy of the Irish Medical Organisation. Photograph by Fiona Byrne, 2013.

10   Interior of Dorothy Price's former home, 10 Fitzwilliam Place, Dublin.
     Courtesy of the Irish Medical Organisation. Photograph by Fiona Byrne, 2013.

11   Drs Dorothy Price and Kathleen Lynn, St Ultan's Hospital, Dublin, April 1949.
Reproduced by kind permission of the Royal College of Physicians of Ireland.

12   Tuberculin testing in a teacher training college. National BCG Committee annual report 1955 (SU/2/6). Reproduced by kind permission of the Royal College of Physicians of Ireland.

13   Student nurses are given BCG vaccine. National BCG Committee annual report 1958 (SU/2/9). Reproduced by kind permission of the Royal College of Physicians of Ireland.

CHAPTER SIX

# PUSHING THE PLUNGER: BRINGING BCG TO IRELAND (1936–1941)

*Practical interest in BCG vaccination in Ireland dates from the mid-1930s. The energetic work of Dorothy Price in this field needs no comment here; in the future it may well be pointed to as a landmark in the history of Irish preventative medicine.[1]*

In the mid-1930s, Dorothy's interest in tuberculin testing for the diagnosis of tuberculosis came to be equalled, if not surpassed, by her interest in a new and somewhat controversial vaccine that could prevent tuberculosis. This vaccine was named *Bacillus Calmette-Guérin* (BCG) after the two French scientists Albert Calmette and Camille Guérin who developed it. It first became available for clinical use in the early 1920s but, at this time, it had not been tried in Ireland.[2] The Irish medical profession seemed to follow the English lead in rejecting the vaccine. BCG was controversial: Albert Calmette's statistics about the vaccine's efficacy were unreliable while, in a disastrous incident in Lübeck in Germany, in late 1929 and early 1930, seventy-seven infants died of tuberculosis following oral vaccination with a substance that purported to be BCG.[3] Issues such as nationalism, politics, the availability of hospital and sanitoria beds and the investment in public health infrastructure to deal with tuberculosis, seemed to influence the uptake or rejection of the vaccine in countries such as Britain, the United States, France, Norway and Sweden.[4] Scientific evidence came a poor second to all of these competing influences, or so it seemed to Dorothy.

Dorothy's enthusiasm for the vaccine was shared by very few of her Irish colleagues. A measure of the strength of the early opposition to the vaccine among the Irish medical profession is to be found in a letter written by Professor William Crofton of University College Dublin to *The Lancet* in 1932. He maintained that BCG was dangerous as the use of 'a living antigen' always caused the death of 'some abnormally susceptible individuals'.[5] Albert Calmette responded to Professor Crofton, reiterating that dead antigens do not immunise against tuberculosis. He compared BCG to Jenner's small-pox lymph and Pasteur's rabies and anthrax vaccine.[6] That same year another Irish doctor, M.H. O'Connor, wondered how the Irish medical profession might answer Calmette if:

he were to come to Dublin with the object of persuading us to introduce BCG vaccination. We might for example point out to him that all the recent work on the changes and mutations of organisms in cultures makes it almost impossible to believe that even an attenuated organism may not remain capable of recovering its virulence under certain circumstances ... But to my mind more forcible than all these objections (if perhaps more crude) would be to explain to him that at least 40 per cent of the cattle of this country are tuberculous and to suggest to him that when his remedy has reduced that percentage to zero without the loss of a single beast, then only would be the time to consider applying his remedy to human beings.[7]

The Irish State did not, however, forbid use of the vaccine and consented to Dorothy trying it out. The first use of the vaccine in Britain and Ireland seems to have been between 1928 and 1933, when an Irish doctor Lyle Cummins[8] and his colleagues, in Wales, used BCG on up to fifteen infants. This brief experiment was halted by the British Ministry of Health on the grounds that the vaccine was not standardised. Then, between 1937 and 1939, Dorothy experimented with it on five infants in Dublin. Two years after Dorothy began to work with BCG, the Second World War was declared and air travel restrictions rendered the vaccine unavailable. Throughout the

World War, Dorothy continued to promote the merits of the vaccine in the hopes that when the war ended she could introduce BCG on a large scale to Ireland. During the Emergency (as the Second World War was known in Ireland) she remained engaged with other research projects and continued her work with the Irish Red Cross as well as maintaining her clinical practice. She carried out tuberculin testing on a wide scale. She also identified a case of the very rare congenital form of tuberculosis and she wrote a book on childhood tuberculosis.

—  ............... .....•........  —

In August 1936, Dorothy and Liam went to Scandinavia: Liam was a delegate at an archaeology conference in Oslo and Dorothy intended to combine a holiday with the opportunity to visit various hospitals and clinics and to see BCG vaccine being used. The couple stayed in the Savoy Hotel initially and Liam used the hotel stationery to write to his mother – he seemed excited to be attending a large conference where the delegates were given badges and a 'sort of pin you stick in your coat lapel'. The King of Norway, Haakon VII, and the Norwegian foreign minister attended the opening of the conference. Liam and some of the other Irish delegates, including the archaeologists Sean O'Riordain and R.A.S. McAlister, gave a lunch party to about twenty of their Dutch, German and Norwegian colleagues. Dorothy wrote to Liam's mother that it went off in fine style: 'certainly Liam and Sean deserve great credit for doing it so well. McAlister made a short and excellent speech. The Free State is making a name for itself'.[9]

Dorothy and Liam were adventurous when it came to food, lunching on mushrooms and reindeer which they found delicious. Dorothy joined the archaeologists on a trip down Oslo Fjord – 350 people were conveyed in 12 buses. She sat next to Monsignor John Hynes, the head of Galway University. He was 'great fun, not at all clerical, more like a farmer, and at every stop he dashed out and got us bottles of beer or lemonade'.[10] Dorothy also went to the King's reception with Liam:

> I wore my green silk dress and Liam a stiff shirt and blue suit, we taxied to the palace and met the Irish crowd … we had to walk up a wide stairway and at the top the King and Queen

[Maud of Wales, the grand-daughter of Queen Victoria] stood, she covered with pearls, and we shook hands with both. I was the first of our batch and hadn't the faintest idea of what to do. Apparently, I should have said Price, Dublin. Instead I said How do you do? And gave a bobbish curtsey.[11]

Dorothy stayed away from the conference proper: instead, she put her energies into visiting fifteen hospitals with a local female doctor. Liam, signing himself as 'your loving son, Willie', reassured his mother that Dorothy's feet were 'wonderfully well, considering all she is doing'.[12] Addressing Liam's mother as 'Dearest Ma', Dorothy wrote that life had been so hectic that they hadn't found time to buy postcards yet. She told her mother-in-law that Liam was looking 'very smart and clean in his blue suit'.[13] She also sent on a diary of their various engagements. Evidently, Dorothy and her mother-in-law enjoyed a close relationship.

Dorothy was very keen to see BCG in action as Robert Collis who had visited Arvid Wallgren in Sweden had been enthusiastic about the vaccine.[14] The Scandinavian approach to BCG was particularly interesting to her. In France, BCG was developed as an oral vaccine and used extensively from the mid-1920s onwards. In 1926, in Norway, Johannes Heimbeck introduced BCG using subcutaneous vaccination. Then, in 1927, Arvid Wallgren introduced intradermal vaccination (that is, injecting the vaccine into the skin layers) to the city of Gothenburg in Sweden. Johannes Heimbeck and his co-workers gave up the subcutaneous methodology in favour of Arvid Wallgren's method which was the more superficial method of injection and thus less likely to cause abscesses.[15] By modifying the method of administration, the Scandinavians were responsible for pushing BCG into achieving its full potential.

However, in Oslo, where Dorothy first saw the vaccine being given, she heard that the immunity it conferred was short-lived. Dorothy was of the opinion that the immunity itself was less useful than naturally acquired immunity. This led her to think that BCG vaccination seemed like 'a lot of bother' although it appeared to be safe and could be of use for a child who had to return to a home where there was open tuberculosis present.[16] BCG seemed bothersome because in an area like Ireland, where tuberculosis was endemic, patients had to undergo a lengthy process, including tuberculin testing and isolation pre- and post-vaccination.[17]

The Prices journeyed on to Gothenburg, in Sweden, where Dorothy rapidly revised her unfavourable estimate of the vaccine and became convinced of the usefulness that BCG might have in an Irish setting. At the time of her visit Arvid Wallgren was not in Gothenburg, but she met with his assistants and toured the BCG manufacturing facilities in the city. Even at this early stage, Arvid Wallgren's experimental results were impressive. He had first introduced BCG to Gothenburg in 1926 and the tuberculosis death rate for infants in the city declined rapidly from 3.4 per thousand between 1921 and 1926 to 0.3 per thousand in 1933.[18] Arvid Wallgren was cautious, though, and stressed in his publications that it was not possible to 'establish how large a part BCG had played in the favourable results reported'.[19] Gothenburg had an active anti-tuberculosis campaign aside from BCG vaccination. There was no control group for comparison – only 10 of the 1,069 children and adults in the study did not receive the vaccine. These were children whose parents had refused vaccination. The follow-up in 1939 could only trace 85 per cent of participants.[20] These difficulties aside, those participants who were traced were all in good health and free from tuberculosis, suggesting the vaccine had been effective in providing immunity. At this stage, Anders Wassén conjectured, very conservatively, that the vaccine provided two years' protection.

Gothenburg's city physician, Karl Gezelius, whom Dorothy had met at the international hospitals' conference in Italy, told her about the vaccination experiments. He also introduced her to Anders Wassén, at Sahlgrenska Hospital Laboratory in Gothenburg which manufactured BCG vaccine.[21] Wassén's laboratory supplied BCG to Sweden and Norway, using BCG sub-cultured from a strain of bacilli he had obtained from Calmette in Paris in 1926. Anders Wassén showed Dorothy the laboratory and production methodology offering to send her the liquid vaccine, free, by air mail with the caveat that it had to be used within a week of arrival. In 1936, there were two state-licenced laboratories in Sweden making vaccine – a laboratory in Stockholm making oral vaccine for northern Sweden and the Gothenburg laboratory which made both oral vaccine and Arvid Wallgren's intradermal form. Dorothy was very impressed by the security arrangements at the Gothenburg laboratory as well as by the preparation methodology which followed Albert Calmette's methodology. She noted, approvingly, that the vaccine was kept under 'lock and key in a separate building which was intended for a plague lab'.[22] Dr Wassén, the sole key holder for the building, had instituted strict security in the wake of the Lübeck disaster which occurred in 1930 because of the laxity of laboratory arrangements.[23]

Dorothy and Liam completed their Scandinavian tour in Copenhagen where Dorothy met Dr Knud Winge, who was in charge of the Central Tuberculosis Station. In 1936, Knud Winge and his assistant, Dr Sigrid Holm, had been using BCG for nine months.[24] Dorothy also visited Dr K.A. Jensen of the State Serum Institute, who manufactured the BCG vaccine being used by Knud Winge. As they had been using the vaccine for less than a year, the Danish team had not yet evaluated its efficacy. Dorothy had hoped to return to Gothenburg to meet Arvid Wallgren but she contracted a flu-like illness and did not return to Sweden in this instance.[25] The illness was severe enough for Dorothy to be hospitalised. She wrote, from hospital, to 'Dearest Ma' that she was 'alright again. It is rather amusing being in hospital in the famous Finsen Institute which everyone has heard about'. So impressed was she with her experience that Dorothy penned another poem:

'Ode to Sister Lund Jensen'

When afflicted with pain, in the land of the Dane,
There's no reason for worry or fright.
Just step in a train, Barnegaard Noorgarden the name
And at Finsens you tell them your plight.

You are popped into bed, with hot bags to your head
And gelonida each hour four;
And if you have a temp, they will purge you with hemp
Till you run down to three seven four (C37.4)

The nurses are sweet, with quick running feet
That never sit down for a whiles;
Sister Lund you must meet, it's really a treat
With her most beguiling of smiles...

And so ladies all who would flee from your man,
Just land up in old Kobenhavan
Slip into Finsen (Med E if you can)
And you will surely find it a haven.[26]

In Finsen's, Dorothy was provided with 'queer meals' and 'queer medicines'. She had to swallow carroway seeds and reckoned she would end up chirping like a canary. However, she recovered well. By the time she returned to the Free State in the autumn of 1936 Dorothy had met almost all of the Scandinavian tuberculosis experts with the exception of the two pioneers, Arvid Wallgren and Johannes Heimbeck. Later, both Arvid Wallgren and Johannes Heimbeck were to become friends and correspondents of Dorothy.[27] On her return home, Dorothy immediately began to investigate the question of administering anti-tuberculosis vaccine to children in the Free State. It would be the first time BCG would be used in the Free State.[28] Her readiness to commence immediate experimentation may have been conditioned by her previous experience with experimental vaccines in St Ultan's. In September 1936, Dorothy contacted Dr Winslow Sterling Berry, the deputy chief medical adviser to the Department of Local Government and Public Health, to request that she be allowed to import BCG vaccine on an experimental basis. Dorothy stated that she would use the vaccine on a few selected babies from tubercular homes 'in order to test its efficacy under conditions existing in this country. The amount would be very small, and required only at intervals of two months'.[29] Dorothy justified her proposed experimentation with BCG by using her tuberculin testing results which had demonstrated Ireland's peculiar pattern of tuberculosis infection and immunity.[30] Her work had established that, in Ireland, only 11 per cent of 14-year-olds had been exposed to tuberculosis whereas there was a high rate of positive tuberculin reactions at age 14 in Paris (75 per cent) and in Denmark (56 per cent).[31] This meant that in Ireland in the 1930s, 89 per cent of the adolescent population did not have demonstrable immunity to tuberculosis and could, therefore, be considered susceptible to the disease.[32] Those who did contract tuberculosis later in life fared badly, with 16 per cent of young Irish adults dying of tuberculosis compared to 5 per cent in Denmark. Hence, Dorothy concluded that there was an urgent need for vaccination. The experience of Irish emigrants – in particular, young Irish women who went to England to train as nurses – provided further evidence for this theory. These largely tuberculin-negative nurses were particularly vulnerable to contracting tuberculosis once they began to work on the wards.[33]

Although BCG vaccination did not figure in the Department of Local Government and Public Health's plans, no objection was made to Dorothy's plans to experiment with the vaccine. Particulars of the manufacture of the vaccine and a guarantee that all precautions were being taken to isolate the cultures of BCG from other strains of tubercule bacilli were requested.[34] In response to Dorothy's queries, Anders Wassén sent a sheaf of documentation to the Swedish Consul in Dublin, including the Swedish law for preparation of BCG vaccine, quality control procedures and amounts of vaccine made to date.[35] While the Department of Local Government and Public Health expressed concerns about the storage and stability of the vaccine itself, it did not express any qualms about Dorothy's intentions to experiment on human subjects. On receipt of the documentation with respect to the preparation, a licence was granted to her on 5 December 1936.[36] This was a red letter day for Dorothy, who began to use the vaccine on suitable patients who presented themselves at her clinics or hospital.

Her approach was no different from most researchers working prior to 1948 when the first modern randomised controlled clinical trial was carried out. Most new treatments were introduced on the grounds that a professor or hospital consultant obtained comparatively better results with a new treatment given to a small series of patients.[37] The need for concurrent control groups, with random allocation of participants to the control and test groups, was not widely appreciated. However, Dorothy's epidemiological work with tuberculin meant that she appreciated the need for large numbers to achieve statistically significant results as well as the need for longitudinal follow-up of test results. Her tuberculin work was also begun on an ad hoc basis so, perhaps, she was of the opinion that a small informal start with BCG would allow her to test the methodology before expanding the numbers.

Dorothy received her first batch of vaccine in January 1937, two months after St Ultan's Hospital had opened an eight-bed dedicated tuberculosis unit.[38] She inoculated two infants with the first batch of vaccine. One of the infants – a month-old baby – died seven days after vaccination. Dorothy believed the death was due to gastroenteritis. She sought independent corroboration of this and asked the assistant state pathologist to carry out a post-mortem examination. This reliance on post-mortem results was typical of Dorothy's approach to medicine but her choice of the assistant state pathologist rather than the hospital pathologist was most unusual, demonstrating how critical it was for Dorothy to demonstrate that the death was unrelated to the vaccine.[39] In any event, no evidence of tuberculosis was found in the baby's tissues. The other baby, who was four days old at the time of vaccination, survived and became tuberculin positive three weeks after inoculation. This conversion from tuberculin negative to positive indicated that immunity to *Mycobacterium tuberculosis* had been acquired. Dorothy sent Anders Wassén an account of her first vaccinations along with slides of the tissues and glands taken at the post-mortem. She wrote that she wanted to continue with her work on BCG but was concerned about the very crowded conditions in St Ultan's Hospital.[40] She would not attempt another vaccination until the surviving child was out of hospital safely. She did not want to expose healthy babies to infections such as pneumonia and gastroenteritis which were rife in the hospital.

Although Dorothy was alone in using BCG in Ireland in the late 1930s, at least one other Irish doctor was open to its use. In June 1937, Dorothy received a letter from John Duffy of Dublin Corporation tuberculosis dispensary, informing her that the wives of two of his sputum-positive patients – their sputum had been shown to contain bacteria that cause tuberculosis – were expecting babies in the near future.[41] He told her that the maternity hospital authorities were willing to admit the women for confinement so that the babies would have no contact with their fathers. Duffy asked Dorothy if she would be interested in vaccinating the babies but she declined as details of a vaccination disaster in Ring, County Waterford were just becoming available.[42] (This case will be discussed more fully later.)

———————

The end of 1936 and the beginning of 1937 were extremely busy times for Dorothy with respect to tuberculosis research. Not only did she import BCG vaccine for the first time into Ireland, she also began a professional collaboration with Dr Walter Pagel, an eminent German pathologist and former lecturer in pathology in Heidelberg University, now based in England.[43] Initially, she consulted him about what she thought was a case of congenital tuberculosis and, from there, they continued to collaborate on various pathological issues. Inevitably, as time passed, they became friends: for Dorothy, the professional and personal always seemed to merge.

In November 1936, Dorothy wrote to Dr Pagel about a 'very interesting and remarkable case of an infant, Baby K., six weeks old, who died of congenital tuberculosis [tuberculosis was present at birth]'. She had removed the contents of the infant's thorax and abdomen at post mortem and St Ultan's pathologist Dr Farrington had prepared and interpreted sections for her. However, Dr Farrington had no special training in tuberculosis work. Dorothy had another difficulty: she told Walter Pagel that she could find very little in the English language literature: 'all is written in German papers to which I have no access'.[44] He sent her a relevant article by a German author, read through the draft of her paper which he found 'excellent' and he asked her to send on the specimens. Walter Pagel was very excited by the specimens as 'the large caseous portal gland, the dissemination in the liver and the spleen, by exceeding that in any other organ, points to the congenital nature of the disease'.[45] He took photographs, sent her copies and encouraged her to publish her findings in a high quality medical journal as the number of cases of congenital tuberculosis in the literature were very small and 'every such case deserves special attention and careful examination'.[46] In March 1937, Dorothy and her colleague Nora O'Leary spent a day with Walter Pagel in Papworth, 'talking and dissecting both pathological problems and specimens'.[47] With Walter's encouragement, in 1937, Dorothy published her findings on Baby K. who had died of a tuberculous infection at 49 days of life, in the *British Journal of Tuberculosis*.[48]

At this time, Walter Pagel was beginning to collaborate with two other clinicians on a textbook on tuberculosis that would become a standard English text. When the first edition was published in 1939, he reproduced the photograph of the liver which had illustrated Dorothy's article. Dorothy's work was referenced in a number of sections in the book. Baby K's liver continued to appear in the various reprints of the textbook.[49]

Walter Pagel was most encouraging to Dorothy and suggested to her, in 1937, that she might consider writing a book on childhood tuberculosis. She told him that she already had it in mind but wanted to collect more material. She had obtained permission from the Professor of Medicine in TCD to use and study any of his cases aged 6 to 14 while 'the younger ones abound in St Ultan's'.[50] Meanwhile, Dorothy invited Walter to come to Dublin to speak to the Irish Paediatric Club. He accepted the invitation and, along with his wife Magda, came to Dublin and stayed with the Prices. He gave a paper entitled 'The evolution of tuberculosis' which was subsequently published in the *Irish Journal of Medical Science*. Afterwards, Walter thanked Dorothy:

Dublin and Irish hospitality will be unforgettable to us and above all your and Mr Price's extreme kindness. We enjoyed everything thoroughly – the weather, your marvellous home and the undeserved attention we had did not allow 'the bad Pagel' to develop, neither the bad respiratory – nor the 'fully developed' bad luggage one ... Now I do hope: coolness, tidiness and quietness have returned to lofty Fitzwilliam place.[51]

Walter Pagel introduced Dorothy to Dr Stefan Engel, joint author of *Handbuch der Kindertuberkulose*.[52] Engel became one of her many correspondents, sending her several of his publications and helping her with various tuberculosis-related issues.

In November 1937, Dorothy expanded her clinical work when she was appointed as a consultant to the Royal Hospital for Consumption in Ireland (Newcastle Sanitorium).[53] In February 1938, Dorothy had a paper entitled 'Tuberculosis in Infants' published in the *British Medical Journal*.[53] This study of 78 cases of tuberculosis (with 60 deaths) in infants outlined her approach to childhood tuberculosis: healing could only be achieved in the primary stage, therefore early diagnosis by means of the tuberculin test, x-ray and history of contact was essential. A positive diagnosis was to be followed by immediate removal from the source of infection, and treatment with rest. Walter Pagel wrote immediately to congratulate Dorothy and to tell her that his colleague, Gregory Kayne, who had been appointed editor of the journal *Tubercle* was also impressed and would welcome a paper from Dorothy. Her research career was in full flight – these were prestigious journals. Her friendship with the Pagels – both Magda and Walter – continued, mostly via correspondence with occasional visits to their various homes in England.

— ·········· ···· ········ —

While Dorothy's working week was filled with worries and ideas about combating tuberculosis, she continued to enjoy an active social life. In July 1937, *The Irish Times* advised its readers that if they wanted to know what interesting visitors were passing through Dublin they would find them all in the foyer of the Abbey Theatre. Dorothy is mentioned for bringing Professor and Mrs Seth Thompson and Mrs Delargy to the Abbey. Professor Thompson, who held the Chair of English literature at the University of

Indiana, was an authority on folklore and a keen student of Irish drama. *The Irish Times* correspondent was keen to tell its readers that the Thompsons had just toured Connemara and Kerry with Mr James Delargy. The Abbey was packed and there was an 'air of animation' although this was not a first production by the Irish National Theatre of Blind Man's Buff, an adaption by Denis Johnston of Ernst Tollers's expressionist play *Die Blinde Göttin*.[54]

—— ............. ............ ——

Back at work in December 1937, Dorothy again inoculated an infant with BCG.[55] Her third attempt at vaccination was not successful as the two-month-old child did not become tuberculin positive and had to be revaccinated on 27 January 1938. A letter from Anders Wassén, accompanying a vial of vaccine, demonstrated the difficulties of working with a live vaccine: 'I hope you will have a better result with it. At least our experiences are better with the vaccine from the New Year because we now cultivate the bacilli for ten days in Sauton medium instead of twenty-one days'.[56] Dorothy received a further ampoule of vaccine in February 1938 which may have been used on the same baby. In April 1938, Dorothy vaccinated a fourth infant, a 5-year-old boy whose parents both had pulmonary tuberculosis.[57] In September and November 1938, Dorothy carried out two more BCG vaccinations. She records that she gave a total of five vaccinations to newborn infants of tubercular mothers in the years 1937 and 1938. By 1942, four were alive and well and had not developed tuberculosis, while she was unable to trace the last infant beyond 1940 as the family had disappeared.[58] She seems to have excluded the first baby who died of causes other than tuberculosis from her figures.

In August 1938, Dorothy and Liam returned to Scandinavia. Again, it seems to have been a visit with archaeological connotations. The couple began their tour in Aarhus in Denmark. They spent long lazy days on the beach. Dorothy wrote to her mother-in-law that they were:

> Covering ourselves from top to toe with nivea cream. We lie for a bit and then take bathe number one. The sea is gloriously clean and clear and green and salty. The beach is sandy and pebbly, not all sand but it can't be helped ... bathe number four about six and back to dinner at 6.30. Coffee about 7.30

and then we all go out and watch the sun setting out over the sea. It goes down like a great red globe.[59]

They spent a day with Harold Leask, the Inspector of National Monuments in Ireland, who joined them on the beach for the morning before they all went for a 'taxi ride in the afternoon, two hours, looking at ancient remains'.[60] There was news of minor catastrophes in Ireland: Liam's mother suffered a 'bit of a turn' and had to go to bed, while his sister Kathleen had an accident with the car. Luckily, Kathleen was unhurt, while both Mrs Price and the car recovered quickly. Then illness struck Dorothy and she remained in her hotel room in Denmark reading medical textbooks in German in preparation for going to Sweden.

On 22 August, Liam saw Dorothy off by train to Gothenburg to meet Arvid Wallgren. The next day, Liam got a card from her confirming that she had arrived safely. Unfortunately, Anders Wassén, whom she had met on her previous visit, was away on military service. Dorothy spent two days with Arvid visiting hospitals and sanatoria. She was hugely impressed by him: as well as becoming a lifelong disciple of his BCG doctrine, Dorothy became an admirer of his holistic approach to paediatric medicine.[61] He lent her a typescript of a forthcoming book on paediatrics that he was writing. She read it on the way home 'at odd moments in hotels, in wagon lits, & on the ferry'.[62] While the reading was 'rather superficial' she:

> got a general impression that a great wave of light & fresh air has been thrown on the subject of childhood tuberculosis, hitherto described in rather a stuffy manner by painfully conscientious German Pathological-Anatomists. From them one learns what a case should do according to rule and one tries to fit one's clinical picture into the most reasonable pigeonhole. Your point of view is from the child, or the multiple of the child, and what it does, to the pigeon-hole. As a result, the pigeon-holes must be more elastic & probably nearer the truth.[63]

Throughout the remainder of her professional life, Dorothy advocated intradermal BCG as she had first seen it carried out in the city of Gothenburg, Sweden.[64] She was unswerving in her loyalty to the Swedish vaccine, continuing to use it even when the Danish vaccine was selected by the World Health Organisation for its mass vaccination campaign after the Second World War.[65] Her two-year research licence, which allowed her to import BCG from Sweden into Ireland for experimental purposes, expired in December 1938 and she renewed it for the fee of £1. The issuing of a further two-year licence appears to have been a formality.

The early vaccinations carried out by Dorothy were experimental and limited in extent. In hindsight, Dorothy later suggested that if BCG had been given on a mass basis, 'the under twenty-five years tuberculosis death rates in 1941 [in Ireland], 2,260 in number, might have been one-fifth, or 452. Had Arvid Wallgren and his vaccine been at work, none would have died'. Dorothy's final sojourn on the continent prior to the Second World War was spent in Paris. There, in 1939, Dorothy watched BCG vaccinations being administered. She was not impressed and later wrote, without advancing any explicit reasons for her comments: 'Let us leave to Calmette and the French school due credit for their important laboratory discovery. With regard to the practical application of the vaccine, I have had opportunity to observe BCG inoculation of infants in Paris and found nothing in the process which recommends itself for imitation.'[66]

Meanwhile, the lack of awareness of BCG vaccination among the Irish medical profession and the resistance to vaccination on the part of the Irish public was highlighted by John Mowbray in an article in the *IJMS* in March 1939.[67] Deploring the lack of uptake of smallpox vaccination, he pointed to a 'slackness' on the part of the medical profession, an 'ingratitude' on the part of the public and 'criminal interference' by 'those who should know better'. Vaccination was compulsory but exemption was 'readily obtainable'. This boded ill for the 'reception of our immunisation activities in other diseases when this, the most brilliantly successful of them all, is treated with such ignorant contempt'. He pleaded for compulsion in diphtheria vaccination and while he noted that there was no satisfactory prophylaxis for measles and whooping cough, Mowbray did not even mention BCG and tuberculosis although tuberculosis was, at this time, killing far more Irish people than these other diseases.

— •••••••••••• •••••••••• —

Dorothy's job of convincing her peers, the Department of Local Government and Public Health, and the public that BCG would provide part of the solution to the problem of paediatric tuberculosis was rendered doubly difficult by an incident that occurred in the Free State just as she began her experimentation with the vaccine. In November 1936, twenty-four school children in Ring, County Waterford, were vaccinated against diphtheria with a preparation of diphtheria toxin antitoxin floccules (TAF), manufactured by Wellcome Borroughs in England. Subsequently, the children became ill with tuberculosis, many of them developing serious tubercular lesions. In April 1937, a 12-year-old girl died following her vaccination. The timing of this tragedy was to have serious implications for Dorothy's BCG plans. An inquest was held and the verdict of the jury read:

> ...we are of the opinion that the contents of one 25 cc bottle of prophylactic, labelled TAF Burroughs Wellcome, from which a portion of the material was extracted by Dr Daniel McCarthy for the purpose of the aforesaid inoculation contained tubercle bacilli, and that the inoculation was carried out by Dr McCarthy according to the most approved surgical technique. Every precaution was taken by him and those who assisted him to guard against infection arising from contaminated appliances and we exonerate them from any blame in this matter.[68]

This case was not concluded with the inquest as the girl's parents brought a case against Wellcome Burroughs, the manufacturers of the vaccine, and Dr Daniel McCarthy, the doctor who administered it. In 1939, the High Court trial was a *cause celebre* with extensive newspaper coverage.[69] There was also much interest in medical journals, including the *British Medical Journal* (*BMJ*) and *Journal of the Irish Free State Medical Union*.[70] Doctors, surgeons and medical students packed into the courtroom to hear the verdict. Dorothy was called as a witness on a minor point, and she followed the inquest and the trial diligently.[71] BCG, used to protect against tuberculosis, and TAF, used to protect against diphtheria, were very different substances but the evidence given at the trial by some experts led to confusion in the public mind. For instance, when Henry McAuley, an orthopaedic surgeon, was asked if he knew of a preparation that could produce symptoms similar to those observed in the case of the twenty-three children infected with tuberculosis following vaccination, he replied: 'It is a preparation called

BCG I think it is a possibility that they should consider – that tubercular germs were introduced of a virulence which was equivalent to that in BCG.'[72]

In support of his argument, he cited a paper written by Arvid Wallgren although he appeared to misunderstand the findings. The trial concluded in February 1939 with no blame being apportioned to the vaccinating doctor or the manufacturers of the vaccine due to a lack of evidence. BCG was not a virulent bacterium; however, according to Greta Jones, public confidence in BCG, which depended on correct vaccination procedures as well as a belief in the vaccine itself, was undermined.[73] The cause of the Ring disaster was never ascertained. A contemporaneous assessment in a leading article in *JMAE* found that 'every hypothesis put forward had innumerable difficulties in the way of its acceptance and the explanation of the occurrence must remain a mystery'.[74] Various versions of the event lingered in popular and medical memory.[75]

The Ring disaster, as it became known, highlighted many of the difficulties facing early vaccinators interested in using BCG. The perishable vaccine had a short shelf life so there were difficulties with storage and transportation as refrigeration was not commonly available. Syringes were not disposable and were used many times – they were usually dipped in alcohol or boiled in order to sterilise them between uses. There was a high level of active tuberculosis infection in the community so tuberculosis could be spread from one individual to another via the syringe. The disaster also highlighted the possibility for error or contamination at the manufacturing site – Wellcome Burroughs was carrying out research on live tubercle strains while producing vaccines at the same site.[76] The impact of the Ring disaster on public opinion was immediately evident to Dorothy. She was visited on 8 March 1939 by the father of one of the children she had vaccinated with BCG at St Ultan's Hospital. The father was concerned that an ulcer on the child's knee was the result of the vaccine. He said that he and some friends of his had read Dorothy's evidence in the Ring disaster and 'they say it's queer the leg hasn't healed'. He also claimed that he had not given permission for the vaccination. However, Dorothy countered that the child's mother had given permission.[77] The child's leg healed in time but the Ring disaster made Dorothy acutely aware that she had to record every detail 'in the event of her research work ever being subjected to public examination she could show that at every step of the way she had exercised all possible care'.[78]

Undeterred, Dorothy and her colleague Robert Collis continued their attempt to raise awareness among the Irish medical profession of the possibilities afforded by vaccination against tuberculosis. When they learned that Arvid Wallgren was going to speak at a conference in Windermere in England, they asked him to come to Dublin to speak to Irish doctors about his methods of dealing with tuberculosis. She wrote to him: 'Childhood tuberculosis is as yet untouched here by the Government, & when they start to do something I hope that it will be along the Göteborg lines & not on [the] English.'[79] Dorothy also asked Arvid to stay with herself and Liam in 10 Fitzwilliam Place, promising to show him some of the beauty spots by car on Sunday, trips to hospitals on Monday, a talk in the RCPI to which she would invite 'all the Professors & big-wigs' as well as a small informal meeting of the Paediatric Club.[80] He took up her invitation, modestly remarking that he hoped he would not bore her too much and that the trip would not be a failure for herself and Robert Collis. Dorothy was delighted to be able to introduce the great man to the Irish medical community and she put time and thought into how she would present him to her colleagues at the Irish Paediatric Club. A draft of her introduction reads:

> Our greatest ambition has been realised tonight in having Arvid Wallgren here amongst us. None in Europe or in the world is so well fitted to sh[o]w us how to eradicate tuberculosis in children. For 25 years he has studied and tonight he has summed up in 25 pages the result of his experience and his methods, both of which have culminated in such great success. The task of writing such a paper for a busy man is not light. He translated it himself from Swedish and this work that has laid at the disposal of our country is up to us to see what we can do with the problem. 1. [We] must recognise TB in children. 2. Must differentiate primary from other stages. Then [there will be] only early cases to deal with and advanced cases will become increasing rare. [We] are already feeling this in St Ultan's.

In May 1939, Arvid Wallgren spoke to the Irish Paediatric Club (which changed its name to the Irish Paediatric Association the following month) and guests at the RCPI, Dublin, on 'Combating tuberculosis in a Swedish city'. The Minister for Local Government and Public Health refused Dorothy's invitation to take the chair during this meeting.[81] As with Walter Pagel's visit, the *Irish Journal of Medical Science* published the talk. The timing of Arvid Wallgren's talk was unfortunate as it was preceded by the Ring disaster and almost immediately followed by the advent of the Second World War. Nonetheless, Dorothy was able to tell him that it had borne some fruit with individual doctors beginning routine tuberculin testing.

In June 1939, Dorothy was 'doubled up with rheumatism' and it continued into late that year. In October, she told Arvid that she had been

> ill in bed for six weeks with muscular rheumatism and a temperature. I am slightly better under autogenous vaccine therapy, but progress is very slow & I may still find myself in bed quite easily at the end of another six weeks. This answers the question of what I am doing – all tuberculosis activities have ceased for me, & I am even too sick to finish the book … so the anti-tuberculosis campaign must wait.[82]

In November 1939, Arvid's reply regretted that they would not meet as planned at an international conference in Boston. He wrote in his somewhat strained English:

> Probably neither you nor I can cross the Atlantic for the USA. If there is an international congress at all, which I cannot imagine, even if the war should stop for a day. It was twelve years after the late world war before paediatricians could meet at a common congress in a neutral country! Fortunately enough is the number of neutral states during this war very great and if the fighting peoples cannot meet, we neutral people ought to continue the co-operation for the benefit of mankind. Don't you think so?[84]

At Christmas 1939, Dorothy got dressed for the first time in months, putting on a frock and going down to the drawing room of their Dublin home for two hours. She had been miserable in bed for some sixteen weeks. She had a tonsillectomy but it took a further three weeks for her pains to recede. Dorothy wrote a long letter to Arvid on Christmas day, telling him the details of her illness. 'Only for Liam's care & encouragement & my nice doctors I would never have stuck it as I have no patience in a long illness,' she added.[85] While Dorothy was ill, her beloved mother Constance died. Dorothy's friend Annette Blondeau sympathised with her on being 'in bed and in pain for months. I felt terribly sorry for you and especially when your mother died and you were not able to go to her'.[86]

Dorothy and Liam were planning to go to a spa hotel in Cork for a fortnight and Dorothy told Arvid that she hoped to work on the final copy of her book again but she worried that it would be difficult to get it published. 'This war is awful. Closer to you than to us. I feel for your country & wonder when civilisation and progress will return to earth again. We spend so much on armies & things that I suppose there will be none left for tuberculosis – still the individuals who are keen will work on.'[87] She hoped to try to get an anti-tuberculosis league going in the spring, she told him.

——— ·········· ·····  ······· —

The impending war began to cast a long shadow over Dorothy's medical colleagues on the continent. In November 1938, Walter Pagel wrote to Dorothy asking if she knew of 'some working place and living' for three friends, exiles from CSR (Czechoslovak Republic), 'excellent men'. One was a neuropathologist, another was a tuberculosis clinician and sociologist, while the third was a 'brilliant worker in the physiological basis of thoracic surgery'. Then, the war moved even closer to Walter Pagel as his brother, a Jewish lawyer and former high official in the Berlin municipality, was arrested and taken to an unknown destination. Walter sought Dorothy's help in securing naturalisation in England. His brother was 'now arrested for 14 days. No-one knows where he is or how he is or whether he is at all. You can imagine how we are worried. I have, of course, guaranteed for him, but the visa has not yet been granted'.[88]

Walter asked Dorothy if she could approach the lawyer, Sir Andrew Lawrence, through her sister Edie. Sir Andrew was a relative of the Stopfords and Edie may also have come across him during her work. On 15 December

1938, Walter elaborated on his family's plight: he had just received a telegraph that his brother had been released but the remainder of Walter's fortune was still in Germany where it was supporting another brother and sister. They would be destitute if the monies were confiscated as he could not hope to support them on his salary alone. The German authorities would not confiscate the property of foreign subjects, only German Jews, so Walter was anxious to be naturalised as quickly as possible.[89] Evidently, Edie was able to help and Walter was very grateful. By April 1939, the Pagel household was full as Walter's brother and his wife had joined them and their daughter was being put up by a friend.

The war also began to impinge on Irish citizens, albeit not so dramatically. Although Ireland remained neutral, health service provision was adversely affected; there were difficulties in obtaining medical supplies and travel was restricted as petrol was rationed.[90] Food rationing, with concomitant nutritional deficits, had detrimental effects on the health of the population. Dorothy noted that 'frugality was becoming the rule, and children suffered greatly because of malnutrition or not getting food regularly'.[91] Morbidity and mortality from infectious diseases rose in Ireland during the Emergency.[92] Ireland consistently topped the mortality league for deaths from tuberculosis and for infant mortality when compared to its close neighbours.[93]

The severity of diseases such as tuberculosis also increased in many patients. From the middle of 1942, Dorothy noted that cases coming to St Ultan's Hospital had 'spreads and extensions of lesions, other than primary tuberculosis, such as we had not been seeing since about 1933-34'. In addition, the cases in the wards were beginning to show signs of spread and bone and spinal tuberculosis were developing. She believed the lack of healing was due to a problem with the type of brown bread now baked in Ireland as a result of the Emergency regulations with respect to wheat extraction. She felt vindicated when the addition of calcium to the diet resulted in a marked improvement.[94]

Another effect of the war was that Dorothy was unable to obtain a supply of BCG to continue her work.[95] Her interest in BCG intensified while the severity of tuberculosis rose. Although she could not travel to Europe during the war, Dorothy's web of correspondents kept her updated on the use of the vaccine at a time when there were difficulties accessing information about scientific developments on the continent.[96] In December 1941, Arvid

Wallgren wrote that Anders Wassén was continuing to make the vaccine and had vaccinated more than 4,000 children and young people (mainly school leavers and soldiers) in that year. He asserted: 'We have still the same astonishingly good results as before'.[97] Dorothy responded that she could see that BCG inoculation would be the solution to Ireland's tuberculosis problem but could not visualise its acceptance 'for many a day'.[98]

— ·········· ··········· —

By the end of 1940, Dorothy had put together a book on childhood tuberculosis. According to Dorothy, the book was 'written briefly in the manner of a textbook, with quotation of numerous cases to illustrate points. It is intended as a clinical guide for Tuberculosis Officers, Superintendents of Children's Sanatoria, Paediatricians and General Practitioners … no such book has yet been published in England or Ireland…'[99] She approached the Bristol publishing firm, Wrights, informing them that of the seven articles on Tuberculosis in Childhood which she had written in the last six years she was published one in the *BMJ*, one in the *British Journal of Tuberculosis* and five in the *Irish Journal of Medical Science*. Wrights was impressed with the content of her book but bemoaned the increased cost of printing during wartime. After some wrangling, Dorothy agreed to put up half the costs with any profits taking this into account. She had to ask her brother Robert, who was one of the trustees of her marriage settlement, to cable his approval from Washington for the transaction. Wrights' printing works were bombed twice during the gestation of the book, with inevitable delays but the book was salvaged and finally appeared in 1942. The book was reviewed widely in medical journals in Ireland, England and the United States. These reviews were mainly positive, however an anonymous review in the *BMJ* was critical. (Dorothy has pencilled 'Gregory Kayne' beside a copy of this review so presumably she attributed it to him.) Although it advised 'paediatricians and tuberculosis workers to read the book, not only because it contains useful and important matter, but also because it is based on a point of view fundamentally different from that current in this country'.[100] Dorothy's mentor, Walter Pagel, congratulated her: 'the book is splendid, an amazingly well produced practical guide'.[101]

— ·········· ··········· —

Meanwhile, Dorothy's championship of BCG was interlinked with her continuing use of tuberculin testing. Indeed, tuberculin testing in Ireland was, initially, largely a paediatric initiative spearheaded by Dorothy and her colleague Patricia Alston, who also worked in St Ultan's during the 1930s. The first published report of a tuberculin survey in the Irish Free State was in the *IJMS* in 1934, when Dorothy reported on tuberculin skin testing in 500 children, using Hamburger ointment, followed, if negative, by the more sensitive Mantoux test.[102] Dorothy compared her figures with studies done in Lund in Sweden and Helsingfors (now known as Helsinki) in Finland, where children who were considered to be 'non-tuberculous' were tested. Dorothy's Dublin study showed surprisingly low levels of exposure to tuberculosis compared to the Swedish and Finnish cohorts. As the possession of tuberculin sensitivity was linked to possession of immunity, Dorothy advocated a much larger study.

In 1938, the Irish Paediatric Association undertook a tuberculin survey among sick children attending hospitals in Dublin. In 1939, Dorothy was still the only Irish doctor publishing the results of trials with tuberculin although some other doctors were now using it. In 1941, Dorothy compiled and presented the results of 1,120 tests performed under the auspices of the Irish Paediatric Association.[103] Once again, these demonstrated that many cases of tuberculosis would have been misdiagnosed in the absence of a tuberculin test. In rural areas, a similar situation pertained. She published an extensive study of 1,500 adolescents in Dublin which bolstered her earlier findings of a low positivity rate.[104] The use of tuberculin became more widespread in Ireland and other studies began to be published, focusing on Irish adults as well as children.

In February 1942, Dorothy told Arvid Wallgren that she had reduced the mortality in St Ultan's tuberculosis unit from 77 per cent to 28 per cent over a five-year period. She was also researching the development of the tuberculous phlycten (an eye condition) and intended to investigate whether there is a vitamin C deficiency in primary tuberculosis. She was using sulphapyridine – an early sulphonamide with anti-bacterial activity; it is no longer used in humans – during 'initial fever in primary tuberculosis with I hope effect. For the first time, I have got a child under three months who was infected to live'.[105] She thanked him for the packet of reprints of medical papers as literature was very limited.

Throughout all of her work, Dorothy remained in close contact with her family. Her brother, Robert, was involved in the problem of international private debts in Austria and Hungary. This work came to an end under the Hitler regime and he remained in Budapest, helping the British Embassy to organise the escape of influential Jews to England. In 1939, he went to Washington as financial adviser to the British Embassy and, after the liberation of the Netherlands, he worked from England on the relief of distress in Holland and Belgium.[106] Dorothy's sister, Alice, remained in Dublin. Her daughter, Mary Wordsworth, married Jim Smith who worked as conservator of forests in Nigeria and Cameroon from 1929 to 1953 and Mary accompanied him on his travels. In time, Mary had two daughters – Penelope (Penny), born in Africa in 1941 and Alexandra (Sandra, later Sandra Lefroy) born in the Rotunda Hospital, Dublin in 1947. The children lived with their grandmother, Alice. According to Sandra Lefroy, their parents travelled 'to and fro on banana boats ... A colonial grand dowager had advised my mother [Mary Wordsworth] not to forget that there were "plenty of good women at home who will look after your children and only the bad women will look after your husband"'.[107]

Dorothy was now well after all the travails of her rheumatism and tonsillectomy and she rode her bicycle around her practice when it was dry, using the car on wet days. Liam and Dorothy bought a farm, in Castleruddery, County Wicklow, thirty-four miles from their Dublin home. They stayed there about twice a month and hoped to spend their holidays there. 'It is a sheep grazing farm, with the usual quota of tillage, and in a lovely and lonely mountainous district.'[108] They had plenty of wood and turf for fuel and all the farm produce they needed. She told Arvid Wallgren that Bob Collis was in his element, writing a new play (his previous play about Dublin's slums, *Marrowbone Lane*, was put on in the Gate Theatre in 1939), urging the 'claims of vitamins, and best of all feeding young school children out of the proceeds of his first play'.[109]

NOTES

1. J. St.P. Cowell, 'Experiences in the National BCG Scheme', *IJMS*, 6, 320 (1952), pp.358–71.

2. M. Girard, U. Fruth and M.P. Kieny, 'A Review of Vaccine Research and Development: Tuberculosis', *Vaccine*, no. 23 (2005), pp.5725–31.

3. L. Bryder, F. Condrau and M. Worboys, 'Tuberculosis and its Histories: Then and Now', in F. Condrau and M. Worboys (eds), *Tuberculosis Then and Now. Perspectives on the History of an Infectious Disease* (Montreal, Kingston, London and Ithica: McGill-Queen's University Press, 2010), p.15; L. Bryder, *Below the Magic Mountain. A Social History of Tuberculosis in Twentieth-Century Britain* (Oxford: Clarendon Press, 1988), p.139; Anonymous, 'The Lübeck Disaster. A General Review', *BMJ*, 1, 3674 (1931), pp.986–7.

4. See, for instance, F.B. Smith, *The Retreat of Tuberculosis 1850-1950* (London: Croom Helm, 1988), pp.194–203; L. Bryder, 'We shall not find Salvation in Inoculation: BCG Vaccination in Scandinavia, Britain and the U.S.A., 1921-1960', *Social Science and Medicine*, 49, 9 (1999), pp.1157–67; G.D. Feldberg, *Disease and Class. Tuberculosis and the Shaping of Modern North American Society* (New Brunswick: Rutgers University Press, 1995), pp.125–52.

5. W. Crofton, Correspondence, *Lancet*, 219, 5660 (1932), p.422.

6. A. Calmette, Correspondence, *Lancet*, 219, 5664 (1932), p.643.

7. M.H. O'Connor, *The Irish Journal of Medical Science*, 6, 74 (Feb 1932), pp.53–66.

8. Leading article, 'Immunisation against Tuberculosis', *BMJ*, 2, 4326 (1943), p.716; Smith, *The Retreat of Tuberculosis*, pp.199–200.

9. D. Price to Mrs Price (her mother-in-law), copy of letter, 8 August 1936 (TCD, Price papers, MS 7534(117)).

10. Ibid.

11. Ibid.

12. W. Price to Mrs Price, 3 August 1936 (TCD, Price papers, MS 7534(116)).

13. D. Price to Mrs Price (her mother-in-law), copy of letter, 8 August 1936 (TCD, Price papers, MS 7534(117)).

14. Professor R.A.Q. O'Meara, copy of speech, 22 October 1962 (NLI, MS 15342).

15. A. Wallgren and G. Dahlstrom, 'The Intradermal Method', in S.R. Rosenthal (ed.), *BCG Vaccine: Tuberculosis, Cancer* (Littleton: PSG Publishing, 1980), pp.146–8.

16. Price, notes, Norway, 1936 (TCD, Price papers, MS 7534(115-16)); Price, *Dorothy Price*, pp.14–16.

17. K.N. Irvine, *BCG & Vole Vaccination* (London: Edward Arnold, 1957), pp.87–97.

18. D. Price, notes on BCG manufacture, Gothenburg, 1936 (TCD, Price papers, MS 7534(119)).

19. A. Wallgren, 'BCG Vaccination: is it of any Value in Control of Tuberculosis?', *BMJ*, 1, 4562 (1948), p.1126.

20. M. Niemi, *Public Health and Municipal Policy Making: Britain and Sweden, 1900–1940* (Aldershott and Burlington: Ashgate Publishing, 2007), pp.136, 155.

21. Nieme, *Public Health*, p.57.

22. D. Price, notes (TCD, Price papers, MS 7534(118)).

23. BCG was a bacterium and it had to be maintained alive by the continuous provision of nutrients through sub-culture on to new media. Bacterial cultures, if improperly maintained, may become cross-contaminated with other laboratory cultures. It was never clear whether BCG cultures in Lübeck had become infected with virulent Mycobacterium tuberculosis or whether the cultures had simply been mixed up. In any case, the juxtaposition of the cultures should not have occurred.

24. D. Price, notes (TCD, Price papers, MS 7534(120)).

25. TCD, Price papers, MS 7534(119)). Price first met Wallgren two years later, in 1938, in Denmark.

26. Ode to Sister Lund Jensen, August 1935 (TCD, Price papers, MS 7537(125)).

27. See for instance: TCD, Price papers, MSS 7537(218/223/226/230/235)). Heimbeck visited St Ultan's Hospital in 1947.

28. D. Price to A. Wassén, draft letter, 31 October 1936 (TCD, Price papers, MS 7534(143)). 'This is the first time that such an application has been made for its use on the human subject; the formalities have taken some weeks.'

29. D. Price to W. Sterling Berry, copy of letter, 8 September 1936 (TCD, Price papers, MS7534(140)).

30. See Chapter One.

31. D. Price and G. T. Hardman, 'Report of Tuberculosis Skin tests with X-ray Findings', *Royal Academy of Medicine in Ireland, Communication to Medicine Section*, 23 March 1934; D. Price, notes (TCD, Price papers, MS 7535(6)).

32. *Irish Independent*, 1 July 1939.

33. *The Irish Times*, 3 September 1951; A. Mac Lellan, 'Victim or Vector: Tubercular Irish Nurses in England 1930-1960', in C. Cox and H. Marland (eds), *Migration, Health and Ethnicity in the Modern World* (Houndmills: Palgrave Macmillan, forthcoming 2014).

34. *Report of the Irish Chief Medical Adviser* (Wellcome Archives, Immunisation accidents: 19, Ring College, County Waterford, PP/JRH/A/75).

35. A. Wassén to D. Price, 31 October 1936 (TCD, Price papers, MS 7534(145)); Swedish Consulate to D. Price (TCD, Price papers, MS 7534(47)).

36. Letters regarding D. Price's application for BCG research licence (TCD, Price papers, MS 7534(140-56)).

37. S.J.L. Edwards, R.J. Lilford and J. Hewison, 'The Ethics of Randomised Controlled Trials from the Perspectives of Patients, the Public, and Healthcare Professionals', *BMJ*, 317, 7167 (1998), pp.1209–12; R. Doll, 'Controlled Trials: the 1948 Watershed', *BMJ*, 317, 7167 (1998), pp.1217–20; I. Chalmers, 'Unbiased, Relevant and Reliable Assessments in Health Care. Important Progress during the Past Century, but Plenty of Scope for doing Better', *BMJ*, 317, 7167 (1998), pp.1167–8; A. Yoshioka, 'Use of Randomisation in the MRC's Clinical Trial of Streptomycin in Pulmonary Tuberculosis in the 1940s', *BMJ*, 317, 7167 (1998), pp.1220–3.

38. Envelope that carried the first batch of BCG vaccine from Dr Wassén's laboratory, Goteborg, Sweden, Licence 44/R/batch 4/1937 (TCD, Price papers, MS 7534(158/2)).

39. L.Price, *Dorothy Price. An Account of Twenty Years' Fight against Tuberculosis in Ireland* (Oxford: Oxford University Press, 1957), p.8. For private circulation only.

40. D. Price to A. Wassén, draft letter, undated (TCD, Price papers, MS 7534(156)).

41. J. Duffy to D. Price, 8 June 1937 (TCD, Price papers, MS 7539(1)).

42. Price, *Dorothy Price*, p.22.

43. M. Winder and R. Burgess, 'Walter Pagel, Obituary', *Medical History*, 21, 42 (1983), pp.310–11.

44. D. Price to W. Pagel, undated (TCD, Price papers, MS 7534(148/1)).

45. W. Pagel to D. Price, 14 December 1939 (TCD, Price papers, MS 7534(134/1)).

46. W. Pagel to D. Price, undated (TCD, Price papers, MS 7534(136/1)).

47. M. and W. Pagel to D. Price, 10 March 1937 (TCD, Price papers, MS 7534(161)).

48. D. Price, 'A Case of Congenital Tuberculosis', *British Journal of Tuberculosis*, 31, 4 (1937), pp.264–70.

49. G. Kayne, W. Pagel and L. O'Shaughnessy (eds), *Pulmonary Tuberculosis: Pathology, Diagnosis, Management and Prevention* (Oxford: Oxford University Press, 1939). By 1964, all mention of Dorothy's work had vanished but Baby K's liver was once again included in the new edition of the textbook, this time with no attribution.

50. D. Price to W. Pagel, 3 June 1937 (TCD, Price papers, MS 7534 (174)).

51. W. Pagel and M. Pagel to D.Price, 4 November 1937 (TCD, Price papers, MS 7534 (196)).

52. S.Engel and C. von Pirquet, *Handbuch der Kindertuberkulose* (Leipzip: Thieme, 1930).

53. Price, *Dorothy Price*, p.24.

54. D. Price, 'Tuberculosis in Infants', *BMJ*, 1, 4022 (1938), pp.275–7.

55. *The Irish Times*, 16 July 1937.

56. D. Price to A. Wassén, draft letter, November 1937 (TCD, Price papers, MS 7534(214)); A. Wassén to D. Price, 8 December 1937(TCD, Price papers, MS 7534(216)). D. Price requested one ampoule containing one dose of BCG for injection of an infant in St Ultan's Hospital.

57. A. Wassén to D. Price, 25 January 1938 (TCD, Price papers, MS 7534(232)).

58. Price, *Dorothy Price*, pp.18–20. Together with the first two infants vaccinated in December 1936, this total of four would mean that only two new infants were vaccinated by April 1938 although by this time, six shipments of vaccine can be traced in the Price papers in TCD. It would seem that a two-month-old baby, J.D., had to be revaccinated twice. He was originally vaccinated in December 1937, then in January 1938 and, again, possibly, in February 1938. His name is recorded against the December and January vaccine delivery but no name is given for the February delivery.

59. D. Price, 'The Prevention of Tuberculosis in Infancy', *IJMS*, 6, 199 (1942), p.254.

60. D. Price to Mrs Price, 10 August 1938 (TCD, MS 7534 (265)).

61. L. Price to Mrs Price, 5 August 1938 (TCD, MS 7534 (264)).

62. G. Fanconi and S. Lobitz, 'Guido Fanconi (1892-1979)', *Nature Reviews Cancer*, 6 (2006), pp.893–8; In 1950, A. Wallgren and G. Fanconi co-edited *Lehrbuch der Pädiatrie* (Basel, 1950) which has been described as the 'most important European paediatric textbook for decades'. Fanconi's holistic patient-centred approach mirrored that of A. Wallgren and it was this approach that appealed to D. Price.

63. D. Price to A. Wallgren, 26 August 1938 (NLI, MS 15341 (11)).

64. Ibid.

65. A. Wallgren, 'The Intradermal Method', in S.R. Rosenthal (ed.), *B.C.G. Vaccine: Tuberculosis, Cancer*. (Littleton: PSG Publishing, 1980), p.148.

66. D. Price, *Tuberculosis in Childhood* (Bristol: Wrights, 1942,1st ed.), pp.141–4.

67. D. Price, 'The Role of BCG Vaccination in the Prevention of Tuberculosis', *IJMS*, 6, 220 (1944), pp.149–54.

68 J. Mowbray, 'Prophylaxis in Practice', *IJMS*, 6, 159 (1939), pp.97–114.

69. *Cork Examiner*, 14 June 1937; *Irish Independent*, 14 June 1937; *The Irish Times*, 14 June 1937.

70. Newspaper clippings (Wellcome Archives, Immunisation accidents: 19, Ring College, County Waterford, PP/JRH/A/75).

71. Anonymous, 'A Fatality after Immunisation', *BMJ*, 1, 3987 (1937), pp.1182–3; Anonymous,

'Fatality after Diphtheria Immunisation .Verdict of Coroner's Jury', *BMJ*, 1, 3990 (1937), pp.1344–5; Anonymous, 'The Dungarvan Inquest', *JIFSMU*, 1 (1939), no. 10, cited in *IMJ*, 80 (1987), p.101.

72. Newspaper clippings with respect to the Ring case, 1937 (TCD, Price papers, MS 7534(166-71)); Stenographers' transcripts of evidence given at the 1939 trial (TCD, Price papers, MS 7535(1-4)).

73. Transcript of evidence given by Mr Henry McAuley (surgeon) at 1939 High Court trial, Ring case (TCD, Price papers, MS 7535(3)); A. Wallgren, 'Intra-Dermal Vaccination with BCG virus', *Journal of the American Medical Association*, 91, 24 (1928), pp.1876–81.

74. G. Jones, *'Captain of all these Men of Death': The History of Tuberculosis in Nineteenth- and Twentieth-Century Ireland* (Amsterdam and New York: Rodopi, 2001), p.146.

75. Leading article, 'The Ring Case', *JMAÉ*, 20 (1939), p.31.

76. Deeny, notes (RCSI, Deeny papers, Dept. Health File 2, 19(1)); Parish, Victory with Vaccines, pp.100-1; L. Price, typewritten draft of Dorothy Price (TCD, Price papers, MS 7539(1)).

77. Evidence given by the State pathologist, Dr Patrick McGrath (TCD, Price papers, MS 7535(3)).

78. Price, *Dorothy Price*, pp.27–8; Price, notes (TCD, Price papers, MS 7535(15)).

79. Price, *Dorothy Price*, p.28.

80. D. Price to A. Wallgren, 23 March 1939 (NLI, MS 15341 (11)).

81. Ibid.

82. Secretary, Minister for Local Government and Public Health to D. Price, 4 May 1939 (TCD, Price papers, MS 7535(28)).

83. D. Price to A. Wallgren, 11 October 1939 (NLI, MS 15341 (11)).

84. A. Wallgren to D. Price, 28 November 1939 (TCD, Price papers, MS 7535(73)).

85. D. Price to A. Wallgren, 25 December 1939 (NLI, MS 15341 (11)).

86. A. Blondeau to D. Price, 21 May 1940 (TCD, Price papers, MS 7535 (123)).

87. D. Price to A. Wallgren, 25 December 1939 (NLI, MS 15341 (11)).

88. W. Pagel to D. Price, 25 November 1939 (TCD, Price papers, MS 7535(290)).

89. W. Pagel to D. Price, 15 December 1939 (TCD, Price papers, MS 7535(295)).

90. C. Wills, *That Neutral Island: A Cultural History of Ireland during World War Two* (London: Faber and Faber, 2007), p.49; J.F. Fleetwood, *The History of Medicine in Ireland* (Dublin: Skellig Press, 1983), p.276; T. Feeney, *Seán MacEntee. A Political Life* (Dublin: Irish Academic Press, 2009), p.132; M. Coleman, '"A Terrible Danger to the Morals of the Country": the Irish Hospital Sweepstakes in Great Britain, 1930–87', *Proceedings of the Royal Irish Academy*, 105C, 5 (2005)

p.217; B. Girvin, *The Emergency: Neutral Ireland 1939–45* (London: Pan Macmillan, 2006), pp.227–9; T. Gray, *The Lost Years. The Emergency in Ireland 1939–45* (London: Warner Futura, 1997), pp.183–90; R. Barrington, *Health, Medicine and Politics in Ireland 1900-1970* (Dublin: Institute of Public Administration, 1987), p.138.

91. *Irish Press*, 8 November 1940; D. Price, draft article for the National Association for the Prevention of Tuberculosis (British). (TCD, Price papers, MS 7536/243)); A. Sheehy Skeffington to Price,13 February 1943 (TCD, Price papers, MS 7536(239)); D. Price to A. Wallgren, draft letter, undated (TCD, Price papers, MS 7536(407)).

92. J.J. Lee, *Ireland, 1922–1985: Politics and Society* (Cambridge: Cambridge University Press, 1989), p.234; *Proposals for the Reform of the Health Services*, January 1946 (NAI, Dept. Taoiseach, S13444C).

93. J.E. Counihan and T.W.T. Dillon, 'Irish Tuberculosis Death Rates: a Statistical Study of their Reliability, with some Socio-Economic Conditions', *Journal of the Statistical and Social Inquiry Society of Ireland*, 17, 5 (1943/44), p.169. The death rate from tuberculosis rose from 109 per 100,000 in 1938 to 147 per 100,000 in 1941.

94. D. Price, draft memo, October 1943 (TCD, Price papers, MS 7536(419)); W. Sterling Berry to D. Price, 11 November 1943 (TCD, Price papers, MS 7536(418/1)); W. Sterling Berry gave a copy of Price's memo to the Parliamentary Secretary who was 'bucked no end' as Price's clinical findings confirmed his theory. 'You may go to the top of the class.'

95. Price, *Dorothy Price*, p.71; G. Hertzberg, 'Recent Experiences with BCG Vaccination in Norway', *Tubercle*, 28 (1947), p.1.

96. D. Price to G. Hansen, copy of letter, 13 June 1944 (TCD, Price papers, MS 7537(33)). Price asked Hansen to check a paper she wished to read to the RAMI, as she found it difficult to confirm references and statements, some of which were verbal communications before the war.

97. A. Wallgren to D. Price, 5 December 1941 (TCD, Price papers, MS 7535(211)).

98. D. Price to A. Wallgren, copy of letter, 17 February 1942 (NLI, MS 15342).

99. D. Price to J.S. Wright, 18 July 1940 (TCD, Price papers, MS 7571(1/2)).

100. Anonymous, 'Tuberculosis in Childhood', *BMJ*, 2, 4272 (1942), p.609.

101. W. Pagel to D. Price, 4 August 1942 (TCD, Price papers, MS 7571(1/135)).

102. D. Price, 'A Report of Tuberculin Skin Tests in Children', *IJMS*, 6, 103 (1934), pp.302–4.

103. D. Price, 'Report of a Tuberculin Survey amongst Children in Dublin Hospitals made by the Irish Paediatric Association', *IJMS*, 6, 187 (1941), pp.241–55.

104. Price, 'Tuberculosis in Adolescents', pp.124–9.

105. D. Price to A. Wallgren, 17 February 1942 (NLI, MS 15341 (11)).

106. L. Ó Broin, *Protestant Nationalists in Revolutionary Ireland: The Stopford Connection* (Dublin: Gill & Macmillan, 1985), pp.214–5.

107. Interview, Sandra Lefroy, December 2011.

108. D. Price to A. Wallgren, 17 February 1942 (NLI, MS 15341 (11)).

109. Ibid.

CHAPTER SEVEN

# 'A BRIEF EXCURSION INTO PUBLIC LIFE': PROPOSING A NATIONAL ANTI-TUBERCULOSIS LEAGUE (1942–1943)

*I'm hon Justice Conor Maguire[1]*
*I know the law and now aspire*
*To govern the Public Health of Éire*
*Now that I've learnt my A.B.C.*
*I'll teach the doctors about 'T.B.'*
*On which I'm a great authority.[2]*

A seed had been germinating for some time in Dorothy's mind: In 1939, Arvid Wallgren had suggested to her that she might consider setting up a national anti-tuberculosis league in Ireland. Ireland was unusual in that there was no such organisation in the country at the time although there were very high rates of tuberculosis infection. In many other European countries and in the United States, national leagues had been set up in the late 1800s soon after the German bacteriologist, Robert Koch, demonstrated that tuberculosis was caused by a bacterium. The leagues, which were usually charitable ventures run by the laity with some medical input, attempted to raise public awareness, and funds, and to instigate palliative, preventative and curative programmes.[3] Success was variable, with some leagues funding research, diagnostic interventions, vaccination programmes, sanatoria and preventoria as well as organising exhibitions and propaganda in order to educate the public and lobbying governments.[4] Prior to independence in 1922, the National Association for the Prevention of Tuberculosis (NAPT) and the Women's National Health Association (WNHA) had briefly attempted to educate the Irish public about tuberculosis. Following independence, the NAPT remained in operation in the six counties in Northern Ireland but ceased to function in the Free State. Meanwhile, the influence of the WNHA rapidly dwindled throughout the entire island.[5]

When, two decades later, in the 1940s, Dorothy decided to put together a league to attempt to focus interest in tackling tuberculosis, she little realised that she was about to stir up a sectarian storm. Dublin's formidable Catholic Archbishop reacted strongly to the idea of a league led by mainly Protestant doctors appropriating Ireland's tuberculosis problem. The very public spiking of Dorothy's guns was emblazoned in front-page headlines in Irish national newspapers. Ironically, the rather nasty battle served her purpose to some extent: the problem of tuberculosis became widely publicised, although not in the way she had imagined.

—•··········· ···•·······•—

Arvid Wallgren had written to Dorothy following his visit to Ireland in 1939. He was concerned at the continuing high rates of tuberculosis in Ireland and wanted to help her in her plans to tackle the disease. He wrote:

> … during the crossing [back from Ireland] and after my return I have focused my thoughts on the difficulties you have met with in Dublin when it has been a question of doing something against tuberculosis. I believe that I have suggested to you that you should try to start a national anti-tuberculosis league, similar to that they have in almost all countries … mix up Catholics and Protestants, physicians and laymen, republicans and people of other political inclinations … In collecting money you should start with Christmas stamps, May flowers and telegram forms … there are the Luxus telegram forms in Sweden which cost 75 ore extra, of which sum the telegraph office gets one third.[6]

Dorothy's response blended optimism with caution:

> you have seen our country men as they are – they talk too
> much, are very excitable, quick to take up a point, quick to
> drop it, excessively individualistic, team work difficult: we find
> it hard to make a sustained effort. But, the feeling spreads that
> there is a new approach to tuberculosis and that we are going
> to adopt it.[7]

She added that she would get together 'a small group of keen men, to discuss
it inside out ... perhaps a small medical association for a year might pave the
way before launching into a public campaign ... so many premature public
campaigns in this country have burst forth and withered away, I know them
only too well...'[8] Dorothy's attack of muscular rheumatism, which lasted for
such an extended period in 1939, had initially put it out of her mind. Then
she became pre-occupied with preparing the first edition of her book on
childhood tuberculosis. So it was 1942 before she got around to organising
a planning group to put together the structure of such a league.[9] Two years
earlier an attempt along these lines had been made by some of Dorothy's
colleagues in the Royal Academy of Medicine in Ireland (RAMI). They
met with the Minister for Local Government and Public Health and the
municipal authorities but although they were received with 'great courtesy',
they 'could not report that they had attained their objectives' of increasing
bed accommodation, dispensary staff, and financial supports for families.[10]
Dorothy's interest in forming a league in 1942 may have been rekindled
following the failed RAMI attempt. Three of the doctors on the RAMI
committee – T.W.T. Dillon, R.J. Rowlette and John Duffy – became
members of the executive committee of Dorothy's planning group.

In March 1942, Dorothy told John Duffy as well as Dr Brendan
O'Brien, of Newcastle Sanatorium, County Dublin and Baggot Street
Hospital, Dublin (where she held a weekly children's dispensary), about
Arvid Wallgren's suggestion.[11] She also composed a draft letter to Dr
Gustaf Neander in Stockholm, asking for details of the Swedish league.[12]
There were significant difficulties in founding a national league in Ireland
during the Emergency as travel was curtailed due to petrol rationing and
communication was largely by letter.[13] Dorothy brushed the difficulties aside
and spread her net nationally, writing to Dr J.C. Saunders, the Medical

Officer of Health (MOH) in Cork city, in the south of Ireland, that as no-one else was 'making a move' she wanted to convene a small group. She told him that:

> So far I have only spoken to Dr Duffy, Theo Dillon and Brendan O'Brien. It may come to nothing but I think we should explore possibilities. I thought if we got four to six enthusiasts first and then call in others as we went along to give it weight. Will you talk over the need etc for such a national league with Dr Fitzpatrick [MOH Cork City] and let me know if you think it is wanted. If you will be in town soon I would get Dr Duffy and call a small meeting. If anyone else strikes you as particularly keen let us know. It means a frightful lot of work, I fear, but every county MOH and tuberculosis expert says it is badly wanted. The idea is that it should first be medical and later call in big employers of labour, labour people etc. I think each county should work out its own details.[14]

The first meeting of the planning group was held on 19 March 1942, in the Price's home, 10 Fitzwilliam Place, Dublin. (This house had also hosted the inaugural meeting of the Irish Paediatric Club.) Drs J.C. Saunders, John Duffy, Brendan O'Brien, and, of course, Dorothy, were present. They were all outward looking and at least three of the four members of this nuclear group had studied abroad. Brendan O'Brien had spent two years in Switzerland with tuberculosis expert Dr Gustav Maurer, while John Duffy had studied in Wales, Switzerland and the United States. Dorothy, as we know, had studied in Germany and visited hospitals and clinics in Paris, England and Scandinavia.[15] The views of this group with respect to tuberculosis were probably more radical than their colleagues.[16]

John Duffy was also a committed Catholic. He informed John Charles McQuaid, Catholic Archbishop of Dublin, of the founding of the planning group and assured him there was nothing in it contrary to Catholic teaching.[17] There was nothing particularly unusual in John Duffy writing to the Archbishop – the voluminous correspondence in the Archbishop McQuaid's papers testifies to the number of Catholics who informed him of such developments. The Archbishop has attracted a huge amount of attention from historians and has been variously cast and recast as reactionary, progressive, oppressive, hardworking, authoritarian, charitable, and, as the decades passed, increasingly irrelevant.[18] In April 1941, Archbishop McQuaid founded the Catholic Social Service Conference to co-ordinate the welfare work being done on an ad hoc basis by various Catholic groups. He was very interested in developments in health and social welfare. At the time of the attempted foundation of the national anti-tuberculosis league, Archbishop McQuaid was probably at his most relevant with respect to public health. He was aware of the problems and gaps in the welfare and charitable services and of the difficulties endured by tuberculosis sufferers, particularly those in the lower income brackets.

At this stage, he does not seem to have been unduly perturbed by the group's plans and the planning group expanded rapidly. On 26 June 1942, at a national meeting of the County Medical Officers of Health (CMOHs), the planning group expanded further and the executive committee that was formed included R.J. Rowlette, president of the RCPI, nine CMOHs, several Dublin doctors, Brice Clarke, chief TO at Whiteabbey and Graymount Sanatoria Section, County Antrim, Cork-based Professor J.M. O'Donovan and Professor Walter Fallon from Galway.[19] R.J. Rowlette was appointed as chairman, with Dorothy and John Duffy as honorary secretaries. The Provisional Executive Committee, with Dorothy as its driving force, was a very active group, meeting twenty-three times between 19 March 1942 and 9 March 1943. While they got a largely positive response there were those who disagreed with their approach. For instance, the Kilkenny CMOH wrote to the League at Dorothy's address:

> A Chara,
>
> I received a circular from you yesterday, with no signature about the formation of an Anti-Tuberculosis League in Ireland. I beg to state that before I take part in the formation of a Tuberculosis League, my public health nurses will have to get petrol to enable them to carry on their TB visiting, as I consider the only people to deal with tuberculosis are those trained for the job.[20]

The planning work took up a large amount of Dorothy's time (a small standing committee met weekly and she attended almost all meetings) but she was eager and enthusiastic, believing that the formation of a national anti-tuberculosis league would make a huge difference to the tuberculosis epidemic in Ireland. While there was no effective treatment, patients could be helped towards health by improved diets, rest and perhaps some surgical procedures; diagnosis could be achieved earlier and patients with infective disease could be isolated or cautioned as to how to avoid spreading infected droplets when coughing or spitting. At this time, spitting was an accepted social habit and many public places provided spittoons for the use of their patrons. People who had not come into contact with tuberculosis might be offered the preventive BCG vaccine if it became available again after the Emergency.

Initially, the main aims of the planning group included the use of tuberculin testing and X-rays to aid in early and accurate diagnosis of tuberculosis and the prevention of the spread of disease, with particular emphasis on young adults and children. After-care and rehabilitation of discharged patients was also considered. Care of patients in their homes, including help with food and beddings, was mooted. In order to counteract the social stigma still associated with tuberculosis, the use of propaganda including lectures, films and leaflets was proposed. A demand for increased sanatorium beds was also to be forwarded.[21]

In Ireland at the time there seemed to be a lack of urgency in the government's approach to tuberculosis, while the people, themselves seemed to accept the high infection, sickness and death rates as normal. James Dillon, the brother of Professor T.W.T. Dillon, informed the Dáil that tuberculosis 'is one of these problems in respect of which a sort of universal lethargy descends on us, not for the want of good will, but because there does not seem to be anybody to kick up a row about it.'[22] Under Dorothy's guidance, the number of doctors willing to 'kick up a row' grew. The planning group invited the eight professors of medicine in Ireland to become vice presidents of the league. The following month, July 1942, the *Irish Journal of Medical Science* devoted an entire issue to tuberculosis.[23] In her contribution, Dorothy made a strong case for BCG vaccination. A letter, signed by Dorothy, R.J. Rowlette and John Duffy, was published in the Irish medical journals stating the objects of the league and inviting members to join. General interest in a league grew. In August 1942, the *Irish Press* carried a report that the proposed league 'could do enormous good'.[24] The planning group was an all-Ireland organisation with Brice Clarke acting as liaison with colleagues in Northern Ireland. While all-Ireland co-operation was important, it was intended that the group would look beyond the island of Ireland and liaise with similar bodies in other countries. However, the Second World War made international collaboration difficult. When Dorothy wrote to Dr Harley Williams, secretary of the British NAPT, his reply in April 1942, summarised the wartime problems:

> ...*L'Union Internationale contre le Tuberculose* had its headquarters in Paris. We have not heard anything for nearly two years, although the secretary (whose name, unfortunately is Dr Alice Churchill, and who is a British subject) is safe. For the time being, therefore, all international functions are in abeyance.
> We ourselves are in touch with the United States and Canada, and are hoping to hold the international field together until peace returns. It has been agreed between the National Tuberculosis Association of America and ourselves that I shall be a kind of agent for collecting information regarding other bodies outside the German sphere of influence. It would be most convenient, therefore, if you would let me know when your association is established...[25]

Although 'international functions' had ceased for anti-tuberculosis leagues, Dorothy received co-operation, help and advice from the British NAPT, including nutrition survey forms, questionnaires, and posters. She also received documentation from the Swedish and American leagues.[26] In November 1942, the group began to recruit veterinarians whose co-operation was important as bovine tuberculosis, which was mainly transmitted through unpasteurised milk, remained a significant issue.[27] More physicians were also required and a leaflet was widely circulated among the medical profession, stressing that tuberculosis was 'both a preventable and a curable disease'. The three essential features of a successful anti-tuberculosis campaign were put forward as 'early diagnosis with X-ray control of very suspicious cases, isolation and intensive treatment of the infected person, and economic assistance to the patient and his family'. According to the leaflet, a campaign along these lines could halve the death rate within twenty years. Wherever a strong anti-tuberculosis league was in existence, the death rate declined according to the leaflet which ended with an emotive appeal:

In Ireland, we have insufficient information, a sporadic interest which needs constant stimulation and little, if any, system of after-care or rehabilitation. Is it any wonder that fifty per cent of all those who die between the ages of fifteen and thirty-five die of tuberculosis? This fearful wastage can be ended, and therefore it must. We appeal to the medical men and women of Ireland to help in founding such a League.[28]

On 19 November 1942, Dorothy and her colleagues convened a meeting in the RCPI, open to all interested physicians and veterinarians.[29] They must have been pleased as the meeting was attended by ninety-five doctors and the *Journal of the Medical Association of Éire* subsequently published a very positive leading article re-iterating that Ireland was very much behind in 'our activities against tuberculosis and in our results'. It pointed out that the 'natural conditions' in Scotland and Northern Ireland were similar so their reduction in mortality had to be due to 'greater activity'.[30] The *Irish Press* said the league had to deal with a problem of national importance and 'one of which we have right to be ashamed'.

Non-medical members were now solicited: the interests of invitees spanned a spectrum of views, experience, religious, professional and political affiliations. Many of these were personally known to Dorothy through her Republican, medical, social and family networks. The group widened to include General Richard Mulcahy, a conservative Catholic and a Knight of Columbanus, who was also a former IRA chief of staff – he had occasionally taken refuge in Dorothy's sister Alice's house; he had also smuggled a file into Robert Barton in gaol – and Minister for Defence and Minister for Local Government and Public Health.[31] Another notable recruit was Erskine Childers, a friend of the Stopfords, a Protestant and Fianna Fáil back bench TD who subsequently became parliamentary secretary to the Minister for Local Government and Public Health (1944–7). Later, he became Minister for Health (1969–73) and President of Ireland (1973–4).[32] Senator Thomas Foran, a Catholic trade unionist and friend of the late James Connolly, was also invited to join the group.[33] Owen Sheehy Skeffington, atheist and Trinity College Dublin (TCD) lecturer who subsequently became a Senator for the college, joined.[34] There were also representatives of professional groups including Rory Henderson, the secretary of the National Health Insurance Society, R.J. Kidney, the secretary of the Irish Drug Association, and Lieutenant Colonel Doherty, the president of the veterinary association. Miss M.T. Brennan, an almoner in Sir Patrick Dun's Hospital, Dublin, represented a professional group that was acutely aware of the inter-relationship between poverty and tuberculosis. Dorothy's own experience would have predisposed her to the inclusion of an almoner.[35] While the religious affiliation of all of the members of the Provisional Executive Committee could not be determined, there was a Catholic majority.[36] The newly-expanded committee first met on 12 January 1943.

This eclectic group should have been able to make some impact on the national consciousness and effect political change. Dorothy, herself, with her heterogeneity of social and professional contacts, and her understanding of the value of publicity provided various valuable access points to power and influence. She had Republican credentials that stood her in good stead with the Fianna Fáil government.[37] She was also well connected socially, part of a wealthy elite.[38] Her position as secretary of the medical board of St Ultan's Hospital enhanced her professional profile as the hospital continuously sought and received publicity. Dorothy's philanthropic associations with various organisations such as the Sunshine Home for children with rickets, the Cottage Hospital for Little Children, Kingstown, the Protestant Orphan Society and the National Society for the Prevention of Cruelty to Children had also raised her media profile. Her good working relationship with E.J.T. McWeeney, the tuberculosis inspector in the Department of Local Government and Public Health, provided her with some understanding of and access to the internal workings of the department. Meanwhile, others on the committee also had public, professional and social influence and contacts. As noted by *The Irish Times*, the planning group was 'thoroughly representative, including, *inter alia*, prominent members of all three political parties'.[39] Dorothy and her colleagues had good reason to suppose that they could begin to turn the tide on the Irish tuberculosis epidemic. Indeed, although the group did not survive sufficiently long for its potential to be tested, it did achieve a certain iconic significance.[40]

By the end of 1942, according to Dorothy, the group now numbered: 'twenty members (nine medical, two veterinary and nine lay) with up to 100 people to constitute a central committee (40 doctors already, with remainder to be chosen), the eight professors of medicine on board as vice presidents'.[41] As the league expanded, John Duffy kept Archbishop McQuaid informed of developments. In a letter dated 8 November 1942, he had reassured the Archbishop that the Catholic interest was being looked after:

> To secure a Catholic representation I have succeeded, as I had planned, in having the county branches of the League placed under the guidance of the County Medical Officers of Health, practically all of whom are Catholics, and many of them leading Catholic activists. Consequently, there is little to fear in this regard. For Your Grace's information, I enclose a copy of our programme aims (drawn up by Dr Kevin Malley and myself) for submission to the meeting. I trust there is nothing in it which is not in keeping with Catholic ideals, nevertheless I should be very grateful for any criticism, advice or guidance which Your Grace might be pleased to offer me. May I also humbly beg Your Grace's blessing on my efforts in this project?[42]

A handwritten sentence in the Archbishop's writing, on the top of a copy of the letter, stated: 'I approve and assure you in advance of support of Catholic Social Service Conference.' The committee's later reliance on this assurance was to prove fatal for the league. Meanwhile, the planning group invited representatives of diverse organisations to attend the public meeting on 15 February 1943, in the Hibernian Hotel, Dublin. Dorothy drew up lists of people who might be interested and useful: the Catholic and Protestant hierarchy, employers and trade unions were included among the invitees.[43] A total of 276 invitations were sent, followed by the same number of reminder postcards. These included 129 letters sent to organisations, 33 letters to firms, 110 personal copies (including hospital matrons, almoners and Garda representatives) and some 'separate' letters.[44] The general invitation letter, dated 1 February 1943, contained the following plea:

> Dear Sir, the Provisional Executive Committee have been empowered by the medical and veterinary professions in Ireland to proceed in the formation of a National Anti-Tuberculosis League. We invite the interest of your organisation in the project. For the success of such an effort, the help and co-operation of every citizen is required in order to make it a

nation-wide movement ... we hope that you can attend, for it is only by the support of influential bodies such as yours that the movement can hope to succeed in checking this wastage of young life ... signed on behalf of the Provisional Executive Committee, Dorothy Price, John Duffy, acting honorary secretaries.[45]

Individual letters were sent to the Catholic and Protestant Archbishops of Dublin, Dr McQuaid and Dr Barton, also to Dr Dignan, the Bishop of Clonfert, and to the Minister for Local Government and Public Health, Seán MacEntee.[46]

The agenda for the first public meeting of the planning group was short but seemingly well-choreographed. It seems that Dorothy and John Duffy made a strategic decision to remain in the background. The chair was to be taken by R.J. Rowlette who would give the opening address.[47] The first resolution 'That the Irish National Anti-Tuberculosis League be formed' was to be proposed by Professor Theo Dillon and seconded by Owen Sheehy Skeffington. The second resolution was to be 'That the Provisional Executive Committee be empowered to act for one year.'[48] The invitees turned out in substantial numbers. Doctors, social workers and public representatives crowded into the room at the Royal Hibernian Hotel, Dublin, on 15 February 1943. However, before the opening address was even delivered, Monsignor Daniel Molony, on behalf of Archbishop McQuaid, insisted on reading out a letter expressing the His Grace's 'definite opinion' that a national anti-tuberculosis campaign should be 'carried on in Éire' however this should be under the guidance of the Red Cross Society rather than the proposed league.[49] The letter elaborated that the Irish Red Cross Society enjoyed Government patronage and was a nation-wide organisation. It had a large membership of trained workers, 'who, at the end of the war, would have ample opportunity to devote their trained energies to an anti-tuberculosis campaign with undistracted attention'.[50] When the letter had been read, the Chairman of the Central Council of the Irish Red Cross, Mr Justice Conor Maguire said that while the suggestion was not made at the instance of the society, they would be prepared to take charge of the campaign against tuberculosis.[51]

The meeting fell into disarray. There was 'universal consternation' among the 'distinguished Dubliners' gathered in the Hibernian Hotel when

Archbishop McQuaid's statement was read out.[52] There were a number of objections to the proposed subsuming of the anti-tuberculosis league by the Red Cross but no one, including Dorothy, seemed to consider it possible to ignore Archbishop McQuaid's opinion and carry on with the meeting establishing the league.[53] The resolution to form a league was not put to the floor. Bizarrely, the second resolution, which allowed the Provisional Executive Committee to function for a year, was passed and a Provisional Executive Committee was duly empowered to continue functioning. The events were reported prominently in the media. The proposed national league was effectively 'torpedoed', making front page news in the following day's *Irish Times* which was unsympathetic towards the Catholic intervention.[54]

It appears from the committee's disorganised response that Archbishop McQuaid's broadside took them by surprise. To Dorothy, the intervention came as a 'bombshell': neither she nor the committee had any intimation that the Archbishop or the Red Cross society was going to intervene in the proceedings.[55] In fact, they had confidently expected the Archbishop's representative to publicly support the motion to form the association that was to have been proposed by Theo Dillon and seconded by Skeffington. Prior to the meeting, the planning group had received two letters from Archbishop McQuaid. Although positively interpreted, there were hints in the correspondence that all was not well. It seems Dorothy may have missed these as she was reading the letters in the light of Archbishop McQuaid's earlier written promise of support for the league. The Archbishop's response to the planning group's invitation to attend the public meeting read as follows:

> Dear Dr Duffy,
> I have received the letter in which you and your acting joint secretary have kindly invited me to attend a meeting at which the need for an Irish National Anti-Tuberculosis League and the immediate aims of such a league will be explained. May I be allowed to say – and you, I feel, will understand me – that I appreciate already the need for Anti-Tuberculosis measures in Ireland.

While I thank you, and through you, the Provisional
Executive Committee, for having the courtesy to invite me, I
regret I do not find it possible to attend, but I hope to send a
representative,
I am, yours faithfully, John C. McQuaid, Archbishop of Dublin
etc.[56]

This was dated 6 February 1943. Dorothy and the committee did not
question why it was not possible for Archbishop McQuaid to attend. Instead,
John Duffy's fulsome reply conveyed 'deep appreciation and grateful thanks'
to His Grace for his preceding letter, with its intimation of interest in the
project. He thanked the Archbishop for his offer to send a representative
and made the following request:

The Provisional Committee would be most grateful if your
Grace would consent to allow your Representative to become
a member of, and act on the working Executive which will
be formally proposed at the meeting, and thus authorized
and empowered to proceed with the organisation and work
of the League. The present committee feel that the addition
to it of Your Grace's representative would not only in itself
be an invaluable help, but would also go a very long way
towards making the League a success. Again thanking Your
Grace for your kind interest, and adding, on my own behalf,
kind regards, I have the honour to remain, Your Grace's most
obedient servant, Acting Joint Secretary.[57]

His Grace became terser and replied: 'Dear Dr Duffy, I have received your
message asking for the name of my Representative. I should prefer no
publicity, for your committee is in such a provisionally inchoate stage, that
the use of my name would be very importune, I am, yours sincerely, John
C. McQuaid.'[58] Perhaps, if Dorothy and the committee had been more
seasoned political operators, the phrase 'provisonally inchoate' might have
alerted them and they might have wondered why the use of Archbishop
McQuaid's name would be so 'importune', and been better prepared for
events. In contrast to the hints afforded by a close reading of Archbishop
McQuaid's letters, the correspondence with the Irish Red Cross prior to the

public meeting did not convey any hint of what was actually being planned. Indeed, the organisation had proffered useful co-operation, should the planning group be inclined to accept this service.[59]

It has been suggested that Archbishop McQuaid's intervention may not have come as a surprise to John Duffy and that he was the person who alerted Archbishop McQuaid to developments as he was 'alarmed by what he perceived as the ascendancy domination of its central committee'.[60] The Archbishop, himself, was 'fully aware of the looming importance of welfare and determined to oil the wheels of the Catholic welfare machine'.[61] While the planning group was orchestrating its public debut, the Archbishop was endeavouring to secure a leading role in the anti-tuberculosis campaign for the Irish Red Cross which was essentially under Catholic control.[62] Archbishop McQuaid was skilled at persuading State authorities to finance social and educational initiatives which were then run by clergy or lay Catholic organisations.[63] In order to secure his preferred option of the Red Cross running the prominent public health campaign to combat tuberculosis that appeared to be in the offing, Archbishop McQuaid enlisted the help of a number of his close supporters as well as seeking the support of the Irish Medical Association, the president of the Irish Red Cross, and the approval of various members of the Government.[64]

However, Archbishop McQuaid did not plan to engage in direct confrontation in public. By 9 February 1942, Archbishop McQuaid had appointed Monsignor Daniel Molony to attend the public planning group meeting in his stead. On 11 February, at 10.15 a.m., he telephoned Dr Conn Ward, parliamentary secretary at the Department of Local Government and Public Health, and explained his views about the proposed league.[65] Conn Ward agreed he would see the Minister, Seán MacEntee, on the matter. Archbishop McQuaid then sent a letter by hand to the Minister explaining that 'the purpose of my interest in the affair is precisely, to obtain, as far as I can secure, that such a movement (the NATL) will be directed on the right lines'.[66] In his view, the right lines were for the campaign against tuberculosis to be subsumed by the Red Cross, which was 'under a Minister'. Archbishop McQuaid's direct appeal to Seán MacEntee was something of a gamble.[67] In this instance, he was happy to support Archbishop McQuaid's viewpoint. At 3.15 p.m., the Minister telephoned the Archbishop, pledging that he would send a representative to the public meeting giving 'a headline of direction rather than a blessing'.[68]

A letter sent from Seán MacEntee's secretary to the planning group the next day conveyed the Minister's disposition to send a representative to the meeting. It did not mention Archbishop McQuaid's opposition to the proposed league but raised the objection that, in the Ministers' view, 'the incidence of this disease cannot be countered in any revolutionary manner without devising a system that will ensure the notification of every possible case while the disease is in its early stages'.[69] Dorothy's response was that compulsory notification was also desired by the league but her hope that the Minister for Local Government and Public Health would take a 'personal interest' in the league was to prove misplaced.[70]

On 11 February, Archbishop McQuaid spoke to Frank Aiken, Minister for Co-Ordination of Defensive Measures – whom Rosamond Jacob recalls meeting socially in Dorothy and Liam's home – and asked him to 'call up'. By 4 p.m., Frank Aiken said he would see Mr Justice Maguire, who was president of the Irish Red Cross. This meeting evidently took place immediately for barely an hour had elapsed when Justice Maguire called Archbishop McQuaid and expressed 'pain and surprise at a movement apart from the Red Cross'.[71] This pain was rather sudden as the organisation was aware of the proposed league, and, indeed, had previously offered its assistance to the league's founders. Justice Maguire's response has been described as 'disingenuous' as he had 'secretly and enthusiastically co-operated to frustrate the ambitions of the multi-denominational group'.[72] Following the public meeting of 15 February, where his letter caused consternation, Archbishop McQuaid's informants provided him with a wealth of detail on the response from various parties. Dr Conor Martin complained of being 'rudely told to sit down when he was anxious to defend the Red Cross'.[73] Monsignor Molony wrote that the meeting appeared to him to be 'packed by the opposition' and he referred to an attack by Owen Sheehy Skeffington on the Red Cross's handling of the North Strand bombings in April 1941.[74] Archbishop McQuaid's notes record details of the behaviour of what he terms the 'opposition' with 'Sheehy Skeffington cold and venomous. Dr Dillon boomed. Dr Malley opposed Red Cross and proposed a committee on which Molony was not named…'. The Archbishop's use of the term 'the opposition' was a clear reflection of his sectarian reading of this skirmish. Archbishop McQuaid conferred with Catholic stalwarts Brother Cleary, Dr Stafford Johnson and Dr Lea Wilson and 'agreed Red Cross should go ahead'.[75]

In the days following the 15 February meeting, representatives of the Red Cross and the planning group met and Archbishop McQuaid continued to monitor the situation, and intervene as he saw fit. On 17 February, he wrote to Conor Maguire that 'the attitude towards the Red Cross – a body of proven worth – is truly painful. It is besides a strange logic that rejects a body like yours in favour of a non-existent league, not merely of an unproved league.'[76] On 20 February, he recorded that he saw the Taoiseach, Éamon de Valera, who had also used Dorothy's sister Alice's home for meetings and for refuge during the War of Independence, and 'again explained need of Government patronage for Anti T.B. especially in local areas where only government intervention could reach'.[77] The Taoiseach did not side with Dorothy and her proposed league. As a staunch supporter of de Valera and republicanism, Dorothy must have been dismayed by his dismissal of her efforts. Instead of supporting her, he promised to inform John Duffy that 'as the Archbishop had suggested the Red Cross, the provisional committee ought at once to see what they could do to work under the Red Cross'. While there is no record of John Duffy's response, this intervention must have increased the pressure on the planning group to be reconstituted as part of the Irish Red Cross. By 6 March, Molony reported to Archbishop McQuaid on a meeting of twenty-two members of the Red Cross with nineteen members of the planning group. His letter reads like a parish football match report: 'net result eight from the Red Cross and seven from Anti TB but all Catholics except for two, Dr Rowlette and Dr Price. In addition, doctors elected from Cork, Limerick, Waterford and Galway all Red Cross people...'[78]

On 8 March, Archbishop McQuaid received a copy of a letter from Dr Ward to Conor Maguire, the President of the Red Cross – it contained the final stamp of approval from the Government.

> A chara, the Minister for Local Government and Health has asked me to write to you personally to say how greatly he welcomes the announcement that a campaign to combat tuberculosis, a work which is so vitally important to the health and well-being of our people, is to be conducted under the aegis and with the help of the Irish Red Cross Society.[79]

On 5 April 1943, the first meeting of the Red Cross Anti-Tuberculosis committee was held. It was a large unwieldy committee – thirty-nine members, including Dorothy, attended and there were ten apologies. A standing committee was appointed and, once again, Dorothy and John Duffy were appointed as honorary secretaries.[80] Two days later, a triumphant Archbishop McQuaid again wrote to Conor Maguire, congratulating him on his 'courage and firmness' and consoling him that if he had 'received some scars in the combat, you will have the comfort of knowing that throughout Ireland, not merely in Dublin, your attitude is known and profoundly respected. You have but to follow up this initial success and within a year the Red Cross will have firmly gripped the situation'.[81]

Archbishop McQuaid put a good deal of time and energy into making sure that Dorothy's proposed anti-tuberculosis campaign was wrested from the control of her committee and carried out by the Red Cross. When the historian John Whyte put the matter directly to the Archbishop, his reply was evasive. Archbishop McQuaid claimed that it had not been his intention to put pressure on anyone. He had merely wished to express what he considered 'well-founded objections'.[82] This is clearly an understatement in light of the surviving memoranda written by Archbishop McQuaid which were not available to John Whyte but which can now be read in the Dublin Diocesan Archives. The language used in the memos and letters neatly written by Archbishop McQuaid and Monsignor Molony would seem to suggest that the motivation for intervention was largely anxiety about Protestant usurpation of the anti-tuberculosis campaign, as tuberculosis had become such a prominent social and medical problem.

Archbishop McQuaid's intervention may be contrasted unfavourably with his predecessor Dr William Walsh's generous response, in 1907, to the founding of the WHNA, which was led by the Protestant Lady Aberdeen.[83] The reason behind the radically different responses of Walsh and Archbishop McQuaid to proposed voluntary attempts to tackle tuberculosis would seem to lie in the changed attitude of the Catholic Church towards social issues as well as the increased power the Church enjoyed in independent Ireland as opposed to its position prior to independence. According to John Whyte, the best date to choose for marking the beginnings of the Catholic social movement is 1931, as Pope Pius XI's encyclical *Quadragesimo Anno*, which promoted vocationalism, was published in that year.[84] Hence, Archbishop McQuaid's assurance to the planning group that it would enjoy the support of the CSSC was not in keeping with his wish to 'ensure complete control of social work'.[85] His later *volte face*, as the league prepared to go public, was more in character. In 1943, in addition to wanting to support the Red Cross, he was deeply suspicious of the leaders of the proposed league and their associations with TCD.

Some of the committee members, including Dorothy, had crossed paths with the Archbishop in the past. Dorothy was a member of the medical board at St Ultan's Hospital where Archbishop McQuaid had opposed plans for an amalgamated children's hospital, as it would 'for generations to come, hand over Catholic children to an almost exclusively non-Catholic control'.[86] In addition, St Ultan's Hospital had publicly championed *Marrowbone Lane*, a play written by Robert Collis containing what Archbishop McQuaid considered offensive allusions to Dublin tenements.[87] Dorothy's progress was monitored by Dr Lea Wilson, a defender of Catholic interests in the medical sphere and one of Archbishop McQuaid's regular informants. Wilson had previously written to him about the undesirability of Dorothy, a Protestant, running a dispensary in the Royal City of Dublin hospital: 'mostly RC [Roman Catholic] babies and children; knowing the boards of this hospital are all C of I [Church of Ireland] and some FM [Free Mason] surely this is not advisable'.[88] Equally undesirable to Lea Wilson, as she informed Archbishop McQuaid, was the foundation of the Irish Paediatric Club, which she had refused to join, on the grounds that it was founded by Drs Collis, Ella Webb and Dorothy Price and that meetings were usually attended by seven Church of Ireland members and two Catholic members. R.J. Rowlette was also unacceptable to the Archbishop as he had opposed the section of the Criminal Law Amendment Act of 1935 that forbade the manufacture or import of contraceptives into the Free State.[89] Although Archbishop McQuaid was concerned about Protestant leadership, the majority of the Provisional Executive Committee of the planning group was Catholic. In hindsight, Dorothy's husband, Liam Price, opined that they would have put themselves 'in a false position' if they had opposed the Archbishop, although many of them disagreed with his actions.[90] If all of the above reasons are not enough, there may have been other external pressures on Archbishop McQuaid – for instance, the British Beveridge Report had just been published, and may have afforded McQuaid a glimpse of an unwelcome future across the water. The plan laid down in this report did not include health services but it was predicated on the establishment of a national health service that would be paid for out of general taxation.[91]

Dorothy noted that, under the Red Cross, the campaign would be confined to the twenty-six counties, would exclude Northern Ireland, and they could not join the International Union against Tuberculosis as they operated separately to the Red Cross. Seven days after Archbishop McQuaid's letter was read out at the public meeting, the Provisional Executive Committee, which had been mandated to continue for a year, reconvened with all members present.[92] Dorothy was anxious to salvage as much independence as possible and, in particular, to retain the right to make what she called 'friendly criticism' of the Government.[93] She was overruled by R.J. Rowlette and Theo Dillon, who were of the opinion that the success of further co-operation would depend on good will and not on 'formulae'.[94] Meanwhile, amidst all of the reconstruction and remonstration, Dorothy misread the situation and believed that the Red Cross had influenced the Archbishop rather the other way around. Her immediate belief was that if the planning group could 'get his ear', Archbishop McQuaid might accommodate their position. Noting the support of Dr Sterling Berry, the Department's chief medical adviser, she also considered having someone approach Seán MacEntee.[95] She exhorted herself to 'keep cool, don't be in a hurry. We are in a very strong position with all the best medical people behind us. Have courage'. In the end, the league did not approach the Archbishop or the Minister and, indeed, any such direct approach would have proved fruitless. Dorothy 'fired off' a letter to Harley Williams, secretary of the British NAPT, telling him the league had not been formed as the Archbishop of Dublin had insisted that this should be the work of the Red Cross.[96] William's prompt reply sympathised with her:

> It seems unfortunate that a high clerical dignitary should express such an opinion on what is, after all, primarily a question of medicine, but I suppose you will tell me I am speaking without knowledge of conditions in Ireland, where ecclesiastical opinion always has great weight. I do not know of any other country in which the Red Cross do anti-tuberculosis work. In all the countries attached to the International Union there are special anti-tuberculosis leagues...[97]

Dorothy corresponded with various Irish doctors and veterinarians – there were letters, some marked confidential, lamenting the intervention by Archbishop McQuaid and speculating as to its cause. With the benefit of hindsight, the University College Galway Professor, Walter Fallon wrote to Dorothy that if he had been in the chair he would have ruled 'out of order'.[98] J.C. Saunders and Colonel Doherty questioned the motivation and abilities of the Red Cross with respect to combating tuberculosis in humans and animals.[99] J.M. O'Donovan, Professor of Medicine at University College Cork, wrote that he would postpone telling Dorothy his 'full opinion of the last move until I see you because ordinary paper might not convey my ideas properly without being scorched'.[100] From Northern Ireland, Brice Clarke, sounded a more optimistic note:

> I hope you have all recovered your equilibrium after the recent 'torpedo attack'. It is so clear that an ad hoc body is required to deal with urgent tuberculosis problems in Ireland that I am sure the reasonable view will prevail. I hope that it will be possible to have an inaugural meeting of the Belfast branch within the next few weeks.[101]

A little later, Brice Clarke seemed to realise that there would be no Belfast branch, and that any organisation under the auspices of the Irish Red Cross would be unable to function on a cross-border basis. He sympathised with Dorothy: 'indeed you and your colleagues have been badly treated and I have no doubt that this rash and impertinent interference will in the end do more harm to the powers that instigated it than to our national struggle against tuberculosis'. The coverage in *The Irish Times* on 16 and 17 February inspired him to pen the following piece of doggerel which Dorothy kept among her medical papers (now in TCD Manuscripts Room):

> I'm hon Justice Conor Maguire
> I know the law and now aspire
> To govern the Public Health of Éire
> Now that I've learnt my A.B.C.
> I'll teach the doctors about 'T.B.'
> On which I'm a great authority.[102]

As a writer of doggerel herself, she must, despite her annoyance, have been amused. On 21 February 1943, an article in the *Sunday Independent* again raised questions about the suitability of the Red Cross to take over the anti-tuberculosis drive.[103] Newspaper coverage became more muted, with the planning group nursing its grievances in private. *The Irish Times*, with its Protestant leanings, had suggested in a leading article that the league should continue but a subsequent letter written by R.J. Rowlette, and published in the newspaper without consultation with the committee, indicated that negotiation with the Irish Red Cross was on the cards.[104] By 27 February, the day after a private meeting of the central council of the Red Cross, *The Irish Times*, which had continued to favour the establishment of Dorothy's proposed league over the Red Cross, published a report headlined: 'Concerted Anti-T.B. Action'. This article concluded: 'It is believed that the decision of the Central Council of the Red Cross yesterday will leave the way open for concerted action against the ravages of TB. The Anti TB League, which began its work last year, already has done a considerable amount of research into the question.'[105]

A hurt and disappointed Dorothy was clear that the planning group had lost out, and she was about to become a member of a 'committee of the Red Cross society for twenty-six counties' burdened with a 'terrible weight of ignorance and lack of interest in the subject of tuberculosis'.[106] The planning group held a further official meeting on 5 March with the newly-convened Anti-Tuberculosis Committee of the Red Cross. At the final meeting of the planning group's Provisional Executive Committee on 9 March 1943, it was agreed that the Red Cross Anti-Tuberculosis Committee would co-opt all members of the Provisional Executive Committee; it would be left to this committee to draw up its own rules, appoint its own officers and staff and it would be provided with funds. A press statement was agreed, bringing an end to the acrimonious public airing of differences: 'At a meeting of the Anti-Tuberculosis committee of the Irish Red Cross and the Provisional Executive Committee of the proposed Anti-Tuberculosis League complete agreement was reached for the fusion of the two bodies to conduct an anti-tuberculosis campaign under the aegis of the Irish Red Cross Society.'[107] Dorothy, T.W.T. Dillon and R.J. Rowlette were present on behalf of the planning group, while there were eight members of the Red Cross present, including Justices Maguire and Wylie.

Dorothy dryly summed up events in a letter to Arvid Wallgren, noting she had 'an interesting year', and was now back at clinical work after a 'brief excursion into public life'. A group of the 'best tuberculosis doctors' worked for a year to form an anti-tuberculosis league on international lines. She retold the story of 'what amounted to a royal command' that the campaign be conducted by the Red Cross. 'The reception which the Anti-Tuberculosis League got would lead one to suppose that we were naughty children caught (just in time) in the act of doing something disgraceful.' She concluded: 'we shall achieve something, rather emaciated in contrast with what we had anticipated; we are not badly off for money which is one thing. However, the embryo country must be led step by step in accordance with its awakening mentality…'.[108]

——————— •••••• •••• •••• ••••••• ———

While forming this league, Dorothy continued to promote the use of the BCG vaccine. In 1943, Dorothy informed Arvid that she hoped to read a paper on BCG to the Academy of Medicine but it would take 'much hard work' to get the doctors to accept the idea; individual parents would be more easily convinced.'[109] Arvid Wallgren told Dorothy that the situation was otherwise in Sweden where some 18,000 soldiers had been vaccinated in the first six months of 1942, while in Gothenburg, more than 5,000 children were vaccinated.[110] Here, 'all physicians are now convinced of the effect'.[111] In 1943, Dorothy's membership of the American Trudeau Society, the medical section of the National Tuberculosis Association (American, NTA) opened up access to a new source of medical literature and to tuberculosis experts in North America and Canada.[112] The society sent her about a dozen papers on BCG published in the United States, which did not espouse mass vaccination, and Canada, where French Canada was enthusiastic about the 'French' vaccine, between 1935 and 1940. Dorothy began to correspond with R.G. Ferguson, in Saskatchewan, Canada, who had vaccinated 1,800 tuberculin negative nurses with BCG. She synthesised and disseminated the information she had garnered from her various correspondents in an attempt to convince Irish physicians to consider BCG.[113] The Chief Medical Adviser James Deeny commented, somewhat derisively, that 'At each meeting, more or less, Dorothy made a speech about BCG.'[114] In addition to disseminating information, Dorothy was frequently consulted for advice on vaccination.[115]

Dorothy's work with tuberculin had also been interrupted with the advent of the Second World War when supplies of Hamburger's percutaneous tuberculin ointment became unavailable. After trying various alternatives, her solution was to manufacture an ointment in the laboratory of St Ultan's Hospital. In early 1943, Dorothy combined two parts of old tuberculin and one part of wool fat ointment to make an ointment which she called Dublin Moro. She used this as a painless screening test in children. Then, if it was negative, a Mantoux test, which involved an injection, was carried out. She believed that a two-tier tuberculin test was justified as a child who had a painless first test was more likely to return for a second test.[116] The Dublin Moro test proved reliable.[117] Dorothy began to supply the ointment to her colleagues. There were difficulties with obtaining tubes so the ointment was made up in three cubic centimetre (cc) or five cc syringes and single doses expelled. She informed the Department of Local Government and Public Health of this project, explaining that she was giving it, free of charge, to those who asked her for it, mainly assistant CMOHs and doctors dealing with children.[118] The demand was such that she began to charge the cost price of the materials. She requested and received confirmation from the Department that the 1932 Therapeutic Substances Act, which governed standards in specified medicines, did not apply so she did not require a licence.[119] The cost price was less than one penny per test, provided the material was kept in a syringe and there was no waste. Precise directions for use were supplied with the ointment.[120]

The year 1943 proved to be a busy one for Dorothy: she and Walter Pagel once again collaborated on an unusual tuberculosis case which Dorothy had come across. At this time, there were only three published reports of an early tuberculous lung focus. In the case described by Dorothy and Walter, a four-week-old lung focus was present in an infant aged two months old. Sadly, the child died: she had been born into a home where her mother and elder sister had advanced pulmonary tuberculosis. The joint paper authored by Dorothy and Walter describing the lung focus was published in 1943 in the *American Review of Tuberculosis*.[121] This paper, and the manufacture of the Moro ointment, may have provided some solace to Dorothy in a year marred by the 'torpedoing' of the proposed anti-tuberculosis league. Her family life, too, was a tremendous support. Liam was well and driving around in a 'gas-producer car'. Dorothy had a little petrol and rode a bicycle when it ran out. The couple spent the summer on their farm in Wicklow and enjoyed working in the fields and orchard.[122]

NOTES

1.    Justice Conor Maguire was chairman of the Central Council of the Irish Red Cross.

2.    B. Clarke to D. Price, 6 March 1943 (TCD, Price papers, MS 7536(343)).

3.    L.Bryder, *Below the Magic Mountain: A Social History of Tuberculosis in Twentieth-Century Britain* (Oxford: Oxford University Press, 1988), pp.15–17.

4.    T. Dormandy, *The White Death: A History of Tuberculosis* (London: the Hambledon Press, 1999), pp.297–303.

5.    G. Jones, '*Captain of all these Men of Death*'. *The History of Tuberculosis in Nineteenth- and Twentieth-Century Ireland* (Amsterdam and New York: Editions Rodopi, 2001), p.13, 135.

6.    A. Wallgren to D. Price, 30 May 1939 (TCD, Price papers, MS 7534/43).

7.    D. Price to A. Wallgren, draft letter, June 1939 (TCD, Price papers, MS 7534/57).

8.    Ibid.

9.    L. Price, *Dorothy Price. An Account of Twenty Years' Fight against Tuberculosis in Ireland* (Oxford: Oxford University Press, 1957), pp.35–6.

10.   C.S. Breatnach and J.B. Moynihan, 'The Academy's Foray into the Politics of Phthisis (Tuberculosis) 1940-1946', *IJMS*, 173, 1 (2004), pp.48–52.

11.   Price, *Dorothy Price*, p.46; John Duffy (RCPI, ACC/1954/1, TPCK/7, Kirkpatrick Archive, newspaper cuttings); D. Price to M. Naughten, CMO. Tipperary South Riding, draft letter, undated (TCD, Price papers, MS 7535/219).

12.   D. Price to G. Neander, Stockholm, draft letter, and Price to Saunders, Cork, draft letter (marked private), 10 March 1942 (TCD, Price papers, MS 7535(214)).

13.   D. Price to J.C. Saunders, draft letter, 10 March 1942 (TCD, Price papers, MS 7535/214); Price and Saunders correspondence, (TCD, Price papers, MS 7534 (200/228/294)), MS 7535(5/20/31/35/135)).

14.   D. Price to J.C. Saunders, draft letter, 10 March 1942 (TCD, Price papers MS 7535(214)).

15.   D. Price to M. Naughten, CMOH Tipperary South Riding, draft letter, 21 March 1942 (TCD, Price papers MS 7535(219)).

16.   J. Duffy to D. Price, letter, 8 June 1937 (TCD, Price papers, MS 7534(175)).

17.   J. Duffy to J.C. McQuaid, letter, 8 November 1942 (DDA, McQuaid papers, AB8/B, Govt.

box 4, XVIII); see M. Ó hÓgartaigh, *Kathleen Lynn. Irishwoman, Patriot, Doctor* (Dublin and Portland: Irish Academic Press, 2006), pp.120–3.

18.  D. Ferriter, 'Sex and the Archbishop: John Charles McQuaid and Social Change in 1960s Ireland', in T.E. Hachey (ed.), *Turning Points in Twentieth-Century Irish History* (Dublin: Irish Academic Press, 2011), pp.13–154; E. McKee, 'Church-State Relations and the Development of Irish Health Policy. The Mother-and-Child Scheme 1944–53', *Irish Historical Studies*, 25, 98 (1986), pp.159–94; C. Cullen and M. Ó hÓgarthaigh (eds), *His Grace is Displeased: Selected Correspondence of John Charles McQuaid* (Dublin: Irish Academic Press, 2012).

19.  Price, *Dorothy Price*, p.48.

20.  K.G. McColgan, Kilkenny CMOH to D. Price, 26 September 1942 (TCD, Price papers, MS 7536(9)).

21.  Price, *Dorothy Price*, pp.46–7.

22.  Dáil Debates, vol. 87, no. 9, col. 1058, 16 June 1942; Breatnach and Moynihan, 'The Academy's Foray', pp.49–50.

23.  *IJMS*, 6, 199 (July 1942). Entire issue was dedicated to tuberculosis.

24.  *Irish Press*, 14 August 1942; *The Irish Times*, 8 November 1940.

25.  H. Williams, NAPT, London, to Price, letter, 24 April 1942 (TCD, Price papers, MS 7536(225)).

26.  NAPT documentation, 1942 (TCD, Price papers, MS 7536(247)).

27.  F.B. Smith, *The Retreat of Tuberculosis, 1850–1950* (London, New York and Sydney: Croom Helm, 1988), pp.192–3; Dormandy, *The White Death*, p.240.

28.  Bundle of thirty-five leaflets, some hand annotated (TCD, Price papers, MS 7536(29)).

29.  Planning Group minute book (TCD, Price papers, MS 7536(280)).

30.  Leading article, 'The Tuberculosis Campaign', *JMAÉ*, 11, 66 (1942), p.61.

31.  R. Fanning, 'Mulcahy, Richard', in *Dictionary of Irish Biography* online, (accessed 28 July 2010).

32.  P.J. Dempsey and L.W. White, 'Childers, Erskine Hamilton', in *Dictionary of Irish Biography* online, (accessed 28 July 2010).

33.  A. Murphy, 'Foran, Thomas', in *Dictionary of Irish Biography* online, (accessed 28 July 2010).

34.  C.E.J. Caldicott, 'Skeffington, Owen Lancelot Sheehy', in *Dictionary of Irish Biography* online, (accessed 28 July 2010); D. Lowry, 'Kettle, Thomas Michael ('Tom')', in *Dictionary of Irish Biography* online, (accessed 20 October 2010).

35. M.T. Brennan, Almoner's Report, Sir Patrick Dun's Hospital Annual Report 1940 (RCPI, PDH/1/1/11), p.9; M.T. Brennan and C. Alexander, Almoner's Report, Sir Patrick Dun's Hospital Annual Report 1941 (RCPI, PDH/1/1/11), p.8.

36. Price, *Dorothy Price*, pp.52–7.

37. D. Price, notes (TCD, Price papers, MS 7539(119)).

38. See for instance: *The Irish Times*, 14 April 1931; *The Irish Times*, 12 August 1932; *The Irish Times*, 27 July 1933; *The Irish Times*, 16 July 1937; *The Irish Times*, 29 August 1941.

39. Leading article, *The Irish Times*, 17 February 1943.

40. This was evidenced in the desire by Noël Browne, a subsequent Minister for Health with a penchant for publicity, to be 'remembered' as a member of the group although he was in England at the time. N. Browne, *Against the Tide* (Dublin: Gill & Macmillan, 1986), pp.85–6; J. Horgan, *Noël Browne: Passionate Outsider* (Dublin, Gill & Macmillan, 2004), pp.35–7.

41. D. Price, 'Organisation pro-tem', undated memo (TCD, Price papers, MS 7535(301)).

42. J. Duffy to J. C. McQuaid, 8 November 1942 (DDA, McQuaid papers, AB8/B, Govt. Box 4, XVIII).

43. Lists of possible invitees in Price's handwriting (TCD, Price papers, MS 7536(288/289)); lists with names of organisations or individuals, presumably for lobbying with respect to the proposed NATL (TCD, Price papers, MS 7536/288/292/293/297/298/299).

44. D. Price, notes (TCD, Price papers, MS 7536 (255)).

45. Letter headed Irish National Anti-Tuberculosis League, RCPI, Kildare Street, Dublin, 1 February 1943 (TCD, Price papers, MS 7536 (288)).

46. Price, *Dorothy Price*, p.54.

47. Planning Group Minute Book, 25 January 1943 (TCD, Price papers, MS 7536(280)).

48. Leaflets with agenda of first public meeting of National Anti-Tuberculosis League, 15 February 1943 (TCD, Price papers, MS 271/1/2/3/4).

49. *The Irish Times*, 16 February 1943; *Irish Independent*, 16 February 1943; J. Cooney, *John Charles McQuaid: Ruler of Catholic Ireland* (Dublin: O'Brien Press, 1999), p.164.

50. TCD, Price papers, MS 7530(6).

51. *Irish Independent*, 16 February 1943.

52. J. Whyte, *Church & State in Modern Ireland 1923–1979* (Dublin: Gill & Macmillan, 1980), p.79.

53. Leading article, *The Irish Times*, 17 February 1943; Notebook entitled 'D. Price' (TCD, Price papers, MS 7536(281)).

54. *The Irish Times*, 16 February 1943; Price, *Dorothy Price*, pp.56–7.

55. Price, *Dorothy Price*, pp.55–6.

56.   J.C. McQuaid to J. Duffy, 6 February 1943 (TCD, Price papers, MS 7526(13)).

57.   J. Duffy to J.C. McQuaid, unsigned copy of letter, 8 February 1943 (TCD, Price papers, MS 7536(214)).

58.   J.C. McQuaid to J. Duffy, 11 February 1943 (TCD, Price papers, MS 7536(215)).

59.   C. McNamara to R.J. Rowlette, 27 November 1942 (TCD, Price papers, MS 7536(94)).

60.   Breatnach and Moynihan, 'The Academy's Foray', p.51.

61.   L. Earner-Byrne, 'Managing Motherhood. Negotiating a Maternity Service for Catholic Mothers in Dublin 1930-1954', *SHM*, 19, 2 (2006), p.266.

62.   Walsh to C. J. McQuaid, 26 February 1942 (DDA, McQuaid papers, AB8/B/XV/a). Cited in Cooney, *McQuaid*, p.164.

63.   Cooney, *McQuaid*, p.140.

64.   R. Barrington, *Health, Medicine and Politics in Ireland 1900–1970* (Dublin: Institute of Public Administration, 1987), p.162.

65.   McQuaid, memo, 11 February 1943 (DDA, McQuaid papers, AB8/B, Govt. Box 4, XVIII); D. Ferriter, *Occasions of Sin: Sex & Society in Modern Ireland* (London: Profile Books, 2009), p.265. Ferriter has shown that Ward was a frequent and sympathetic correspondent of McQuaid's, keeping him updated on public health developments.

66.   C. McQuaid to S.T. MacEntee, copy of letter, 11 February 1943 (DDA, McQuaid papers, AB8/B, Govt. Box 4, XVIII).

67.   T. Feeney, *Seán MacEntee. A Political Life* (Dublin: Irish Academic Press, 2009), pp.228–9. Feeney has opined that while MacEntee's Catholicism should 'not be discounted', his approach to public policy making was often secular.

68.   McQuaid, notes, 11 February 1943 (DDA, McQuaid papers, AB8/B, Govt. Box 4, XVIII).

69.   Secretary, Department Local Government and Public Health to Price, letter, 12 February 1943 (TCD MS 7536/237).

70.   D. Price to S.T. MacEntee, letter, 13 February 1943 (TCD MS 7536/238).

71.   McQuaid, notes, 11 February 1943 (DDA, McQuaid papers, AB8/B, Govt. Box 4, XVIII).

72.   Horgan, *Noël Browne*, pp.36–7; Jones, '*Captain of all these Men of Death*', p.213.

73.   McQuaid, notes, 16 February 1943 (DDA, McQuaid papers, AB8/B, Govt. Box 4, XVIII).

74.   Dáil Debates, vol. 85, no. 14, col. 2008-12, 19 February 1942; Seanad Debates, vol. 25, no. 25, col. 2046-484, 13 August 1941.

75.   McQuaid, notes, 16 February 1943 (DDA, McQuaid papers, AB8/B, Govt. Box 4, XVIII).

76.   McQuaid to Maguire, copy of letter, 17 February 1942 (DDA, McQuaid papers, AB8/B, Govt. Box 4, XVIII).

77.  McQuaid, notes, 20 February 1943 (DDA, McQuaid papers, AB8/B, Govt. Box 4, XVIII).

78.  D. Molony to J.C. McQuaid, 6 March 1943, letter (DDA, McQuaid papers, AB8/B, Govt. Box 4, XVIII).

79.  Ward to Maguire, copy of letter, 8 March 1943 (DDA, McQuaid papers, AB8/B, Govt. Box 4, XVIII).

80.  Minutes of Red Cross Anti-Tuberculosis Committee, 5 April 1943 (TCD, Price papers, MS 7536(366)).

81.  J.C. McQuaid to C. Maguire, letter, 7 April 1943 (DDA, McQuaid papers, AB8/B, Govt. Box 4, XVIII).

82.  Whyte, *Church & State*, p.79.

83.  M. Keane, *Ishbel. Lady Aberdeen in Ireland* (Newtownards: Colourpoint Books, 1999), p.130.

84.  Whyte, *Church & State*, pp.65–9.

85.  Ferriter, *Occasions of Sin*, p.228.

86.  For a full account of this episode, see Ó hÓgartaigh, *Kathleen Lynn*, pp.96–105; J.C. McQuaid to E. de Valera, 11 May 1935 (UCD, DVA 1440/2), cited in Cooney, *McQuaid*, p.89; Memorandum of the Irish Medical Guild of St Luke, S.S. Cosmos and Damien, *The Proposed Re-Organisation of Irish Hospitals. Grave Problem for Catholics*, 1934 (Thomas Finlay papers, Irish Jesuit Archives, J9/26 (1-11)). With thanks to Declan O'Keeffe for drawing this to my attention.

87.  R. Collis, *Marrowbone Lane* (Dublin: Runa Press, 1943). The play was first put on in the Gate Theatre, Dublin, in 1939. Ferriter, *Occasions of Sin*, pp.300–1; C. Clear, *Women of the House. Women's Household Work in Ireland 1926–1961* (Dublin: Irish Academic Press, 2000), pp.58–9; F. Clarke, 'Collis, (William) Robert Fitzgerald', in *Dictionary of Irish Biography* online, (accessed 10 December 2010).

88.  Lea Wilson, undated memo (DDA, Lea Wilson papers, AB8/A/IV).

89.  Jones, '*Captain of all these Men of Death*', p.213.

90.  Price, *Dorothy Price*, p.57.

91.  McKee, 'Church-State Relations', p.193. McKee suggests that 'vulnerability to a possible charge of negligence was the key factor motivating the hierarchy and fuelling its anxieties'; Jones, '*Captain of all these Men of Death*', pp.196–7. Jones suggests that the Catholic Church may have been concerned that the league would act as a Trojan Horse for expanding the powers of the state, as one of their objectives was to lobby governments for it in December 1942, two months prior to the first public meeting.

92.  Minutes of meeting, 22 increased funding to provide additional hospital beds, outpatient facilities and increased financial supports for tuberculosis sufferers and their dependents;

Whyte, *Church & State*, pp.126–7. The Beveridge Report was published in February 1943 (TCD, Price papers, MS 7536(280)).

93. D. Price to R.J. Rowlette, copy of letter, 15 March 1943 (TCD, Price papers, MS 7536(354/1)).

94. Minutes of meeting attended by Provisional Executive Committee of Planning group and the Red Cross Anti-Tuberculosis Committee, 21 St Stephen's Green, Dublin, 5 March 1943 (TCD, Price papers, MS 7536(354/2)); Rowlette to Price, letter, 20 March 1943 (TCD, Price papers, MS 7536(357)).

95. D. Price, notes, undated, 1943 (TCD, Price papers, MS 7536(278)).

96. D. Price to H. Williams, copy of letter, 16 February 1943 (TCD, Price papers, MS (7536(297)).

97. H. Williams to D. Price, letter, 22 February 1943 (TCD, Price papers, MS 7536(302)).

98. W. Fallon to D. Price, letter, 1 March 1943 (TCD, Price papers, MS 7536(325)).

99. Saunders to Price, letter (marked confidential), 18 February 1943 (TCD, Price papers, MS 7536(314)); A.G. Doherty to Price, letter, 26 February 1943 (TCD, Price papers, MS 7536(315)).

100. J.M. O'Donovan to Price, letter, 22 February 1943 (TCD, Price papers, MS 7536(304)).

101. B.R. Clarke to Price, letter, 25 February 1943 (TCD, Price papers, MS 7536(312)).

102. B. Clarke to D. Price, letter, 6 March 1943 (TCD, Price papers, MS 7536(343)).

103. *Sunday Independent*, 21 February 1943.

104. Rowlette, Correspondence, *The Irish Times*, 18 February 1943; Price, *Dorothy Price*, pp.57–8.

105. *The Irish Times*, 17 February 1943.

106. D. Price to J.M. O'Donovan, copy of letter, 6 March 1943 (TCD, Price papers, MS 7536(342)); Price, *Dorothy Price*, p.60.

107. Planning Group Minute Book, 9 February 1943 (TCD, Price papers, MS 7536(280)).

108. D. Price to A. Wallgren, copy of letter, 13 October 1943 (TCD, Price papers, MS 7536(407)).

109. D. Price to A. Wallgren, draft letter, 13 October 1942 (TCD, Price papers, MS 7536(407)).

110. D. Price to A. Wallgren, copy of letter, 13 October 1943 (NLI, MS 15342); A. Wallgren to D. Price, 10 October 1943 (TCD, Price papers, MS 7536(16)). The article was published in *Archiv für Kinderheitkunde*, 1941.

111. A. Wallgren to D. Price, 23 December 1944 (TCD, Price papers, MS 7537(45)).

112. Certificate from American Trudeau Association confirming Price's election to membership, 23 December 1943 (TCD, Price papers, MS 7536(421)).

113. See, for instance, D. Price, 'The Prognosis of Primary Tuberculosis of the Lung', *Tubercule*,

28, 2 (1947), pp.27–31; D. Price, 'Report of a Tuberculin Survey amongst Children in Dublin Hospitals made by the Irish Paediatric Association', *IJMS*, 6, 187 (1941), pp.241–55; J.M. Coolican to Price, 24 October 1941 (TCD, Price papers, MS 7535 (191)); Fitzpatrick, CMOH Cork City to Price, 12 September 1941 (TCD MS 7535 (189)); TCD, Price papers, MS 7536 (392)); D. Price, 'The Prevention of Tuberculosis in Infancy', *IJMS*, 6, 199 (1942), pp.252–5; Price, *Dorothy Price*, p.68; Price, Lecture to Cork Clinical Society (TCD, Price papers, MS 7536(434)); D. Price, 'The Role of BCG Vaccination in the Prevention of Tuberculosis', *IJMS*, 6, 221 (1944), pp.150, 156–7; TCD, Price papers, MS 7537 (193-5); D. Price, 'Tuberculosis in Infancy', *Irish Medical Directory* (1945), pp.43–7. Deaths from Tubercular Meningitis in Éire: 1930: 252, 1931: 269, 1932: 269, 1935: 300, 1941: 297, 1942: 356.

114. J. Deeny, notes (RCSI, Deeny papers, Dept. Health File 2, 19/1). J. Deeny gives credit for the introduction of BCG to Ireland to Mairead Dunlevy, rather than Dorothy Price.

115. See, for instance, R. Martin to Price, 22 November 1942 (TCD, Price papers, MS 7536(18)); Puce to Price, 1944 (TCD, Price papers, MS 7537(9)); Chief TO, Worchestershire County Council, England to Price, 1944 (TCD, Price papers, MS 7537(13)); Dr S.G. Tippett, Guildford to Price, 4 June 1943 (TCD, Price papers, MS 7536(396)).

116. D. Price, P. Alston and K. Murphy, 'The Dublin Moro Tuberculin Test', *Journal of the Medical Association of Éire (JMAÉ)*, 18, 105 (1946), p.40.

117. Price, Alston and Murphy, 'The Dublin Moro', p.41.

118. D. Price to The Secretary, Department of Local Government and Public Health, copy of letter, 24 Sept. 1943 (TCD, Price papers, MS 7536/404).

119. Secretary, Department Local Government and Public Health to Dorothy Price, letter, 6 Oct. 1943 (TCD, Price papers, MS 7536(406)).

120. Dublin Moro ointment instructions (TCD, Price papers, MS 7536(429)).

121. W. Pagel and D.S. Price, 'An Early Primary Tuberculosis Pulmonary Focus about Four to Eight Weeks Old', *American Review of Tuberculosis*, 6, 47 (1943), p.614.

122. D. Price to A. Wallgren, 13 October 1943 (NLI, MS 15341(11)).

CHAPTER EIGHT

# 'Moving on the Right lines': Tackling Ireland's Tuberculosis Epidemic (1943–1949)

From 1943 to 1949, Dorothy struggled against illness to try and complete all the professional goals she had set for herself. Towards the end of the Second World War, she worked, somewhat reluctantly, with the Irish Red Cross which had superseded her proposed national anti-tuberculosis league. She continued to carry out tuberculin studies. When the war ended, Dorothy immediately imported BCG vaccine into Ireland and began to use it on a much wider scale than she had previously done. A second edition of her textbook was published in 1948 when Dorothy was 58 years old.[1] At national level, in 1949, she became the first chairperson of a new body, the National BCG Committee, marking the high point of her fight against tuberculosis.

— ·····''···· ····'······ —

Despite Dorothy's misgivings, the initial energy displayed by the Anti-Tuberculosis section of the Red Cross, of which she was a member from March 1943 to June 1944, was impressive. Work was divided into six committees: Dorothy was a member of one of the most active committees – the survey committee – which compiled and sent a questionnaire about tuberculosis diagnosis and treatment to County Medical Officers of Health (CMOHs) and Tuberculosis Officers (TOs) throughout Ireland.[2] Much useful information was gleaned and the responses to the questionnaire formed the basis of a detailed long-term anti-tuberculosis plan, compiled by the Red Cross, which the Department was to view favourably. Dorothy's contribution to the plan focused on her speciality – children's tuberculosis.[3] Her objectives included tuberculin testing of all children, to be carried out at school medical visits, baby clubs, or any other point of contact with the healthcare system as well as an exploration of the possibility of preventative inoculations. The Departmental Inspector, Theo McWeeney concluded that the Red Cross plan provided a 'more efficient solution of our institutional problem' than the proposals offered by the Hospitals Commission, which was the official planning and advisory organisation.[4] When the Red Cross formed a public health committee to devise a community-based pilot scheme to combat tuberculosis in Dun Laoghaire, Dorothy inevitably became a member. This scheme, which never came to fruition, was intended to serve as a model for combating tuberculosis in suburban areas.[5]

Dorothy became impatient with the Red Cross's rate of progress and, in February 1944, one year after her proposed league was stopped by Archbishop McQuaid, she wrote to Professor O'Donovan in Cork, remarking that he would be first in the field at undertaking a tuberculin-based survey of tuberculosis infection rates in the general population, as 'in Dublin, we are still talking and building castles in the air'.[6] Later, in 1944, Dorothy and her colleagues at St Ultan's used tuberculin testing to trace contacts in an outbreak in an unnamed institution and this led directly to the Red Cross funding a preventorium at Ballyroan.[7] Dorothy became one of six doctors on the 'selection bureau' for Ballyroan, which determined whether children should be admitted.[8]

Dorothy's association with the Irish Red Cross Society proved to be brief. As the Archbishop had intended, Catholic rhetoric and control became part of the anti-tuberculosis campaign. The committee was top heavy with clergy and religious representatives. One of the key initiatives, a preventorium established in Ballyroan, was run by the Catholic Sisters of Mercy, at the instigation of Archbishop McQuaid. In addition, Monsignor Molony continued to act as Archbishop McQuaid's informant, keeping him informed of decisions made at meetings, and assuring him that Dorothy was the only Protestant attendee at most committees. In June 1944, Dorothy's membership of the Red Cross Anti-Tuberculosis Committee came to an abrupt end when a ruling was made that all members of the committee must also be members of the Red Cross. Dorothy protested to the secretary of the Red Cross that such a ruling would limit greatly the amount of expert help available. She added that 'tuberculosis' should be first on the agenda and 'Red Cross' second, and she pointed out that such a ruling would be a breach of previous arrangements.[9] The reply from Conor Maguire was uncompromising: 'I regret very much that we should lose expert advice through insisting on the members of the committee being members of the society. If this should happen, I do not feel the society is at fault. There was no support for your point of view at the meeting. The view which I put forward was unanimously endorsed.'[10] At a meeting held on 23 June 1944, the chairman read out Dorothy's letter and commented that 'certain members of the society felt reluctance in appealing for subscriptions and recruits, while some members of the largest spending section of the Society had not joined the Society'.[11]

Although she was no longer a member of the Anti-Tuberculosis section of the Red Cross, Dorothy continued to do 'her share of the work' for the Red Cross: she remained a member of the Ballyroan selection bureau until 17 September 1945 when she was replaced by Dr Mairead Dunlevy. She wrote a propaganda pamphlet for the society entitled 'A long term plan for prevention'.[12] This was one of a series of six leaflets produced by the Red Cross and up to 70,000 copies of these leaflets were distributed.[13] The Red Cross enjoyed other successes. For instance, attendances at a tuberculosis exhibition which had been scheduled to run for a fortnight in the Mansion House, Dublin, were so large that it was retained for a third week. Dorothy gave a lecture at the exhibition on childhood tuberculosis.[14] In addition to educational activities and political planning, the Red Cross funded some scientific research.[15]

In November 1944, Dr P.F. Fitzpatrick, Medical Officer of Health (MOH) at Cork Corporation, wrote to Dorothy stating that the great attention which tuberculosis was now getting was a 'monument to her labours. There is no doubt that this is the direct outcome of the trail blazed by you and the unique group who had this work at heart'.[16] In July 1945, Dorothy informed Arvid Wallgren that there was a big change in the Irish attitude towards tuberculosis. There had been 'some terrible setbacks' in 1942, when her proposed league first began to 'push' its views publicly.[17]

At national level, by the end of 1944, various bodies – the Hospitals Commission, the Royal Irish Academy of Medicine and the Red Cross – had put forward proposals to tackle tuberculosis.[18] The Department's

Chief Medical Adviser, James Deeny found himself 'in the midst of a situation of conflicting reports, proposals and pressure groups'. He was also conscious of 'mounting public indignation'. He believed that combating tuberculosis 'could not be handled by any purely voluntary body, without an organisation, staff or knowledge. T.B. was far too serious an issue to play games with. It had to be faced'.[19] His exasperation with voluntary groups came to a head in 1945 over the Red Cross's proposals for the Dun Laoghaire pilot community scheme. Deeny later recalled that 'in a heated argument with Professor Dillon, I let go and more or less committed the Government to ending tuberculosis. This rash promise was leaked to the paper'.[20] The programme Deeny drew up that year was published as the White Paper, *Tuberculosis*, in January 1946.[21] The Red Cross had received substantial State funding in the form of £135,389 from the Irish Hospitals' Sweepstake between 1940 and 1944. However, a Red Cross fund-raising campaign, 'the half million drive' was a very public failure[22] and the anti-tuberculosis drive by the Red Cross began to founder.

In 1947, Conor McNamara, the Irish Red Cross secretary wrote to the secretary of the Department of Health that 'pending the provision of adequate bed accommodation we have slowed up somewhat on propaganda, with the result that there has been a noticeable decline in interest in the problem throughout the country, and particularly among our branches'. In March 1948, James Deeny commented that 'They [the Red Cross] began this work, carried out a short program and then folded up.' In 1949, the Department took over responsibility for anti-tuberculosis propaganda. So, how different might the anti-tuberculosis campaign have been if it had been run under the auspices of Dorothy's proposed league rather than the Red Cross? Certainly, her approach was more radical in its espousal of tuberculin testing, X-rays and BCG vaccination. This radicalism was lost for a time but it would be overly simplistic to agree entirely with Dorothy's later analysis, published in *The Irish Times*:

> But, why are we in Ireland so behind other nations in this matter [tackling tuberculosis]? For one thing, we have no National Anti-Tuberculosis Association, which would spread knowledge and co-ordinate voluntary efforts with public health work. A spontaneous and promising effort on these lines a decade ago was thwarted, thus thrusting the entire onus of combating

tuberculosis on the Department of Health. The Department rose to the challenge but is hemmed in by involved restrictions and regulations and much responsibility devolves on local authorities.[23]

— •••••••••••• ••••••••••• —

Although Dorothy's Red Cross work was time consuming, it was largely accomplished outside the working day, and, during the 1940s, she continued on with her clinical and research work. The 'Dublin Moro' ointment, made up in St Ultan's and used in the diagnosis of tuberculosis, continued to prove popular with the medical profession. In 1944, Professor J.M. O'Donovan, in Cork, asked for 'some ointment if you can let me have some at any price'.[24] Price duly sent him two cc of Moro, which would have done nearly 100 tests, at a cost of four shillings. Requests came from doctors variously wishing to use the ointment in diagnosis in their practice or an institution or in tuberculin surveys. Price recorded the despatch of forty-six batches of Moro ointment between October 1943 and February 1946 in a small red notebook which is among her papers in TCD.[25] In 1945, official approval of the ointment was signified when Theo McWeeney directed the Galway CMOH to request ointment from Dorothy to carry out a survey of the Aran Islands.[26] That year, Patricia "Pat" Alston, with the approval of the Department of Local Government and Public Health, carried out a further study comparing various tuberculin skin tests.[27] The study found that the Dublin Moro ointment was the best first test but that it would have to be followed up by the more sensitive Mantoux which required an injection. The Chief Medical Adviser, James Deeny, who was not an admirer of Dorothy, nonetheless wrote to her that 'the results obtained with your Dublin tuberculin ointment must have been very gratifying to you'.[28] Dorothy continued to receive requests for the ointment throughout 1946 and Theo McWeeney informed her that he wanted to discuss getting the Moro ointment made up commercially as, backed by the more sensitive Mantoux test, it was going to be 'the method of choice'. The Dublin Moro ointment was later made up by the National Vaccine Institute, Dublin.[29] Dublin Moro was used as an initial screening test in most of the tuberculin studies carried out in Ireland in the 1940s as well as by the National BCG Committee in the 1950s. As such, it played an integral part of the introduction of tuberculin testing in Ireland.

Despite the increasing use of tuberculin for epidemiological and research studies, it still did not seem to have become part of standard paediatric practice. In 1945, Robert Collis upset his colleagues by alleging that 50 per cent of diagnosis of childhood diseases was wrong. He clarified that he was speaking in respect of tuberculosis where it was 'necessary to correlate the history of the case and the clinical findings with a tuberculin test, a sedimentation time and an x-ray'. Unfortunately, this was rarely done; in some 50 per cent of cases referred to his clinic an incorrect diagnosis had been made. The tuberculosis officers in the Dublin area rarely used tuberculin tests according to Collis. This was due to 'lack of proper paediatric training of students in our medical schools'.[30] However, in 1945, diagnosis of tuberculosis within the public health service began to change when the Dublin Corporation Primary Tuberculosis Clinic was established, providing a clinical diagnostic and treatment service for Dublin's children. According to the clinic director, Dr Mairead (also known as Pearl) Dunlevy, this was the 'first attempt by any local authority in these islands to set up a medical centre for the special study and control of primary tuberculosis in children'.[31] Mairead Dunlevy began to conduct various epidemiological studies which she published in medical journals. Her approach to childhood tuberculosis was remarkably similar to Dorothy's although she championed the Danish tuberculin and BCG vaccine while Dorothy remained loyal to the Swedish products. Mairead may have been attempting to establish her independence as she was younger than Dorothy and a later entrant into the field of childhood tuberculosis – in any event, they were destined to clash although they also respected each other's work.[32]

Alongside her work with tuberculin for diagnosis of tuberculosis, Dorothy became increasingly determined to introduce BCG vaccine into Ireland in order to prevent the disease. In 1944, Dorothy repositioned her stance on BCG vaccine, removing it from the realm of experimental science and placing it into the 'tried and tested' category.[33] She stated: 'If you work with an untried vaccine you experiment; if you work with a known weapon in a trained hand, you start with an advantage of 16 years' experience. There is no need for us to experiment with BCG; we may start with Sweden as our model.' Dorothy pointed out that, as the majority of young people died after a short illness, three years prior to their death they would have been tuberculin negative and could have been protected by BCG. In addition to the deaths, she highlighted the 'years of crippling ill-health' associated with tuberculosis. She wondered 'why should the Irish medical profession shut out from their minds something which is unfamiliar, and, therefore, alarming to us?' Her endorsement of BCG was occasionally echoed by other Irish doctors.[34] In addition to targeting a medical audience, Dorothy preached BCG vaccination to the public. On 7 May 1945, the day before the end of the war in Europe, VE day, Dorothy used the opening of a new extension to St Ultan's Hospital tuberculosis unit to promote BCG. She told of the success to date and stressed that prevention by means of BCG must be the next objective.[35] By this time, it was claimed that the immunity lasted from five to ten years rather than the earlier projection of two years.

In July 1945, an optimistic Dorothy wrote to Arvid Wallgren:

> Our Public Health Department are waking up, a very good doctor has been appointed to a key position [presumably James Deeny] and three sanatoria are to be built before 1947, containing 2,100 beds ... after some terrible set-backs I think things are moving, and what is so important they are moving on the right lines: the preventive aspect is I think correctly approached. I heard that your Dublin lecture is going to be reprinted and I also hear that they will in due course follow my advice and send a man over to you to learn all about BCG.[36]

Dorothy's propaganda appeared to be paying off, although she tempered her enthusiasm by expressing the fear that 'they might make mistakes and try to make the vaccine here in our national enthusiasm [James Deeny suggested this]'.[37] Dorothy's advocacy of BCG vaccine, during and immediately following the Second World War, was set against a rapidly changing political and public health canvas and these changes facilitated the eventual introduction of a mass BCG vaccination programme. However, there were competing views on how to tackle tuberculosis. With limited resources, BCG was seen by at least one sanatorium doctor as an unwelcome development which would consume resources that might be better spent on bed provision.[38] The official response of the Department of

Health remained fixated on cure rather than prevention.[39]

When the Second World War ended, Dorothy began to import BCG again, informing Dr Wassén that she would begin again in 'a very small way; every eight weeks I would vaccinate four to six newborns'.[40] The prophylactic BCG service offered by St Ultan's Hospital to infants at risk of contracting tuberculosis expanded slowly. In May 1945, Parliamentary secretary Dr Conn Ward opened a new wing in St Ultan's Hospital.[41] The new thirty-bed unit was intended for the treatment of tubercular children under the age of 5 years, and replaced the older nine-cot accommodation. Six of the cots were reserved for recipients of BCG who required isolation from tubercular family members until the vaccine worked. In addition to inpatient services, the hospital had a tuberculosis clinic that offered outpatient treatment and vaccination. In 1946, Dorothy became ill but she was eager to continue BCG vaccination. Her research licence only allowed her to vaccinate and she wrote to James Deeny to ask if her assistant Pat Alston could vaccinate on her behalf. There were six doses of BCG vaccine already in Ireland – five destined for patients in St Ultan's Hospital and one for the Rotunda Hospital.[42] Permission was granted and Pat Alston became the second person to vaccinate with BCG in Ireland. Patricia was devoted to Dorothy and Harry E. Counihan, a colleague of Dorothy's, has suggested that if Dorothy had asked Pat to stand on her head, she would have done so.[43] 'She was years younger than Dorothy and was her junior. She followed Dorothy's instructions but she was good at her job,' he added.

Even with its new wing, St Ultan's still had a waiting list for cots for treatment of children infected with tuberculosis. Difficult choices had to be made. Assigning cots to children for BCG meant that healthy children of tubercular parents were being favoured over sick children. Dorothy sought a new unit dedicated to BCG only. James Deeny advised against it as he (correctly) foresaw the proposed unit as the forerunner of a bid by Dorothy to control the national implementation of the vaccine.[44]

Despite her illness, Dorothy delivered a strident speech at the St Ultan's Hospital 1946 Annual General Meeting, urging the benefits of BCG. The hospital was now receiving three shipments per week of BCG and Dorothy used the opportunity to stake her claim to expertise with the vaccine:

> Like everything else in this world, it must be done just right
> to succeed in its purpose, namely the protection of the child

against tuberculosis in all its forms. And I say emphatically that interference by amateurs or incomplete co-operation on the part of the parents will disturb the proper development of immunity, an immunity which logically follows vaccination, according to the knowledge of the sequence of events revealed by science.[45]

The reference to 'amateurs' was a clear indication that she did not approve of the Department of Public Health and Local Government's suggestions that the vaccine could be administered by CMOHs, TOs or nurses.[46] Dorothy, at this stage, was the sole importer of BCG into Ireland and the vaccine was still being supplied free by Anders Wassén in Sweden. In her speech, which was widely reported in the daily and evening newspapers, she issued an open invitation to the parents of Dublin to bring their children to St Ultan's Hospital outpatients to avail of BCG vaccination.[47] She urged parents who were suffering from tuberculosis not to allow 'selfish reasons' to interfere with vaccination, which would necessitate some weeks away from home. Kathleen Lynn, vice chairwoman of St Ultan's Hospital, was appreciative of the interest Dorothy had stirred up, telling her she had 'put St Ultan's Hospital on the map'.[48]

Dorothy's reputation had spread beyond Ireland and in 1946, she was asked by the Tuberculosis Association of India to be a corresponding member. Her name had been suggested to them by Sir Wilson Jameson, Chief Medical Officer to the Ministry of Health, London.[49] Dorothy agreed to act as corresponding member for Ireland. During 1946, her networking once again brought a tuberculosis expert, Stefan Engel, to Ireland to speak to the Irish Paediatric Association. As was usual, Engel stayed with the Price's during his visit to Dublin.

In September 1946, in order to concentrate solely on tuberculosis, Dorothy resigned the position she had held in the Royal City of Dublin Hospital, Baggot Street since 1932. At the end of the year, she gave up her private practice.[50] By December 1946, Dorothy and Pat had vaccinated thirty-five children – thirty in St Ultan's Hospital and five in the Rotunda Hospital.[51] All had become tuberculin positive after vaccination and contact cases were kept in isolation in the hospital for six weeks before vaccination and for as long as it took afterwards – on average forty-four days – to become positive post-vaccination. Three children developed tuberculosis pre-vaccination, which Dorothy said demonstrated the importance of isolation. A follow-up of the five cases vaccinated between 1937 and 1938 showed they were all healthy and well.

— •••••••••••• ••••••••••••• —

Amongst Dorothy's copious medical papers in TCD Manuscripts room there is an incongruous treasure: a diary entitled 'Castleruddery'.[52] This diary, which opens on New Year's Day in 1946 and closes on 31 December of that year, provides a counterpoint to Dorothy's increasingly busy research and clinical schedule. In it, Dorothy chronicles a year's worth of visits to their holiday home in Castleruddery, County Wicklow. It is the diary of a serious gardener with each entry beginning with a weather report usually including the wind direction and strength. Dorothy and Liam competed in respect to fruit growing and jam making, with each of them claiming their own patches of garden. In addition to gardening, Liam used Castleruddery as a base for hillwalking and for his antiquarian studies, while Dorothy took advantage of the quietness to revise her childhood tuberculosis book for a second edition.

On 1 January 1946, a strong wind was blowing from the southeast. Liam and Robert (presumably Dorothy's brother or, possibly, Robert Collis) went back to Dublin at midday while Dorothy stayed on. She spent the day cutting back the pear tree at the bottom of the orchard, cleaning and laying laurels against the cowshed and drying nettles after tea. Liam had tidied up his loganberry patch before he left for town. There were wild geraniums out on the front avenue and Dorothy added turf dust to the azaleas. The next day, in a white frost, Dorothy tied up her loganberries and cut ivy back. She went back to town on 6 January.

In February, when Dorothy and Liam visited Castleruddery, the snowdrops were blooming on the front lawn 'tall and open and at their best' while the green shoots of daffodils were peeking up. Dorothy was ill from 3 March until 18 April and didn't visit Wicklow. When she arrived back on a lovely April day, with a north wind, she noted the scallions in the upper garden were well up while the cherries and plums were in full bloom. Liam planted lettuce and two rows of kidney beans. On the day they returned to town, Dorothy picked three dozen narcissi in bud and they lasted at Number 10 Fitzwilliam Place, their Dublin home, until 5 May.

In May, Dorothy's sister Alice and her granddaughter Penelope (Penny) came to stay and when Liam came down for a day he took Penny on a tadpole hunt. As the year went on, the profusion of produce that cropped in the garden was astonishing: carrots, potatoes, damsons, pears, plums, apples, lettuce, broadbeans, raspberries, loganberries, parsley, peas, spinach… They gave away windfalls to the local Garda station and sold some of the produce.

In July 1946, Dr Cullen, the Resident Medical Superintendent of Newcastle Sanitorium and Dr Noël Browne, the Assistant Medical Superintendent, called to Dorothy to discuss the inaugural meeting of the Irish Tuberculosis Society (ITS), a professional society for doctors. She suggested that she would ask Dr Frederick Heaf, the Chief Medical Officer to the London County Council, to speak. The meeting was duly arranged for October. (Heaf stayed with the Prices in Dublin during his visit; Dorothy also spoke at the first ITS meeting on the subject of BCG vaccination.)

Meanwhile, Dorothy seemed to spend some of her time destroying birds' eggs and nests – she gave short shrift to a thrushes' nest in a damson tree while a blackbird's nest in the shrubbery was also raided for eggs. But still the jackdaws and rats got some of the new potatoes while caterpillars feasted on the cabbage. In September, when Walter and Magda Pagel holidayed in Glendalough, County Wicklow – Dorothy had recommended the place to them – Dorothy and Liam motored over to spend an occasional day with them.

The diary closes at Christmas 1946 when, on 21 December, they arrived at Castleruddery in torrents of rain. That night, Liam became ill and stayed in bed all the next day 'on Bovril'. Dorothy, too, stayed in out of the unending rain. She noted that four pink roses were out on the arch – 'one polyanthus rose and a few jaded yellow ones'. The following day, Liam was feeling better but still in bed. 'Hoar frost, everything including the trees white, with fernlike pattern inside all the windows,' wrote Dorothy. On Christmas day, she got the fires going in the sitting and bedrooms before she went to church. Liam stayed in bed late – they dined at 2.30 p.m. and then spent the afternoon dozing.

Gardening resumed once the Christmas fare was digested – in the days following Christmas, Dorothy tied up loganberries, nailed up wall fruit trees, pruned apple trees, clipped laurels and cut up sticks. The last entry in the diary provides an account of produce picked during each month in

1946, the jam that was made, which room it was made in – sitting room or kitchen – and whether Liam or Dorothy made it. There are also records of sales of produce with prices recorded.

At this time, Dorothy was 56 years of age. Her work, her gardening, family and friends were consuming interests and she never regained her early interest in fashion and her appearance. Harry Counihan remembers that she was 'never well dressed. She was not smart. She wore an awful old hat. She had no feminine instinct for clothes. By the time I met her, she was well into her 50s. She was very settled – fanatical about her work'.[53] Castleruddery provided a haven for Dorothy and Liam, somewhere they could relax and spend time in the outdoors which they both loved. Dorothy was a fond great-aunt. In 1948, she wrote:

> I have my sister Mrs Wordsworth living quite close to me. She has a house and the two grandchildren and a nurse whilst Mary is away in West Africa with her husband Jim Smith. The children are very nice. Penelope aged seven who is absolutely full of life and tricks and very sturdy and Sandra aged one and a half who tries to be in the middle of everything. They are very nice children, rather like Mary in face, but very much more strong in body as they take after Jim who is a very square strong Scotsman. They have, however, got decidedly Irish accents now! It is great fun for me to have them so close.[54]

Dorothy loved to entertain young people in their holiday home. Sandra Lefroy remembers that the house was sparsely furnished: 'I went there with friends. It was an adventure sleeping in camp beds. Not much in the way of creature comforts. It was part of the family canon – a lot of picnics, climbing Lug [Lugnaquilla]. County Wicklow was very much part of the scene. Dorothy was very keen on fishing.' The holidays there were always hilarious, according to Sandra, with jokes and pranks such as putting the sharp-edged pieces of a monkey puzzle tree between the bed sheets of unwary guests.

In 1947, Dorothy reiterated the statement she had made three years earlier that BCG was tried and tested:

> It would be a mistake to introduce BCG vaccination into this country as an experimental procedure. The pioneer work has been done elsewhere, and, indeed, some of it has been done in Dublin. From the very beginning it should be employed as a weapon against tuberculosis but with very special care for the purpose of gaining lay and medical confidence for a procedure new here...[55]

Despite Dorothy's espousal of the vaccine, St Ultan's board decided to take back the six cots allocated to the BCG patients and re-assign them for treatment of tubercular children. This meant a curtailment of the BCG programme for children exposed to infection at home unless they could be otherwise isolated. Nevertheless, the outpatients BCG programme at St Ultan's continued. In September 1947, the eminent Norwegian Dr Johannes Heimbeck lectured in Dublin, at the invitation of the Medical Research Council, on 'Vaccination against tuberculosis'. He visited the tuberculosis unit at St Ultan's Hospital and vaccinated some children there. Dorothy subsequently introduced his three-puncture method, and, in turn, he became a supporter of Dorothy's bid for a separate BCG unit.[56] Heimbeck suggested he would source a wooden hut in Norway, which the hospital could import. Encouraged by the Departmental inspector, Theo McWeeney, Dorothy immediately wrote to the Department, once again requesting a BCG unit. She based the 'claim to consideration' for the BCG hut on her track record: success with seventy-three vaccinations, the fact that she was vaccinating 'ten years before BCG was thought of either in Ireland or England' and the reduction in death rate achieved to date in the hospital. In addition, she claimed the approach to childhood tuberculosis in St Ultan's Hospital was now 'the basis for the present methods of TOs throughout Ireland. Logically, the BCG unit is the final requisite for fulfilment of this work'.[57]

A flurry of correspondence between Johannes Heimbeck and Dorothy ensued, with Johannes Heimbeck asserting that 'It [the BCG unit] must be arranged'.[58] He even provided the name of a suitable architect.[59] Kathleen Lynn, the vice chairwoman of St Ultan's Hospital, noted that Dorothy was 'agitated' and 'impetuous'.[60] Lynn worried that Dorothy would 'rush things'. In the end, the Department refused to sanction the proposal largely on the grounds that the trade unions would not work with the hut, which was a prefabricated structure.[61] With no funds of its own, and a reliance on the Hospitals Commission, which allocated the Hospital Sweepstakes money, St Ultan's Hospital could not go ahead with a separate BCG unit. A temporarily defeated Dorothy wrote to Johannes Heimbeck: 'I have never put in a more warlike two months. I got Herpes Opthalmicus out of it, and went down to a conference with a red scarf over one eye, looking as Dr McWeeney put it like a sinister female pirate. I am sure your government departments are not so stupid'.[62]

Even though the hut did not cross the seas, Johannes Heimbeck's championship of the proposed BCG unit at St Ultan's Hospital, coupled with his offer, gave Dorothy considerable bargaining power with the Department of Health, which subsequently offered her a one-storey building. Dorothy promptly rejected this and demanded the two-storey building she had looked for in 1946. She wrote to Johannes Heimbeck:

> We are in a very strong position on account of your recommendation and cheap offer. It is a great battle, and without your help we should have got nothing. It is a bitter disappointment to me that we shall not have the Heimbeck Norwegian house, for many reasons. But, if we get our original request granted, we are content that the BCG work will now proceed, which is the important point.[63]

In January 1948, the Minister for Health sanctioned the two-storey BCG unit. This sanction came with the proviso that 'subject to the reservation of a small proportion of the cots for the use of the hospital's own patients, the remainder might be reserved for cases sent to the hospital for vaccination by the corporation'.[64]

Although Dorothy's single-minded anti-tuberculosis crusade, with its concomitant publicity for St Ultan's Hospital was a source of pride to Kathleen Lynn, and provided the hospital with excellent media coverage, it was also a source of difficulty.[65] There was some hostility to Dorothy's apparent desire to take over the entire hospital to treat tubercular children – in effect, turning what was intended to be a general infants' hospital into a tuberculosis hospital for advanced cases, with an annex for preventative work. In 1946, Rose Doherty, a member of the medical board and future chairwoman of the hospital, pointed out that doctors working in the tuberculosis unit had access to many more beds than those on the general staff.[66] On 7 April 1948, Dorothy asked for yet more beds for tuberculosis cases.[67] In June 1948, a special meeting of the medical committee was held, and Rose Doherty pointed out that even if seventy-eight beds were filled with cases of tuberculosis, the waiting list problem would not be solved. It was agreed that no more cases of tuberculosis would be admitted to the general wards.[68] Rose Doherty also contacted Kathleen Lynn with regard to what she interpreted as threatening behaviour by Dorothy and her assistant Pat Alston.[69] The discontent continued and, the following year it was Dorothy's turn to complain. She asserted that the tuberculosis unit had fewer trained nurses than the general hospital.[70]

The new BCG unit at St Ultan's Hospital, the first such unit in the country, finally opened on 20 June 1949. It comprised offices and committee rooms on the ground floor, together with outpatients and tuberculosis clinics and a new radiological department.[71] On the upper floor, there were twelve cots and an isolation cubicle. The unit was said to be 'the best designed clinic in these islands'.[72] The unit was designed as a sun trap with balconies sheltered by an overhanging roof. An article in a nursing magazine enthused: 'The colours of the walls are all pastel and are very beautiful. One gets an extraordinary impression of light and space and complete transparency'.[73] St Ultan's Hospital had grown from a two-cot hospital in 1919 to a ninety-bed hospital for children up to five years of age. In effect, the hospital dealt with as many tuberculosis as it did general cases. There were forty-seven cots for general medical cases up to two years; thirty cots for tubercular cases up to five years and thirteen cots for BCG vaccination up to five years.[74]

— •••••••••••• •••••••••• —

In 1946, as Dorothy was battling to get a new BCG unit at St Ultan's Hospital, the Irish Government began, for the first time, to consider the use of BCG as a mass measure to protect the health of the population. It is unclear as to what exactly motivated this turnaround. In January of that year, the White Paper *Tuberculosis* had been more concerned with bed provision but, in September, a committee was formed under the auspices of the MRC to consider the use of the vaccine. Dorothy's continuous advocacy of BCG during the Second World War, coupled with the availability of the vaccine once the war had ended, may have contributed to this new openness. There was also a sudden surge in BCG use worldwide, spearheaded by the Scandinavians.[75]

In August 1946, during a trip to the United States, James Deeny met the Danish Professor Jenner and said he changed his views about BCG after meeting him. In a comprehensive memorandum, he stated that the bulk of deaths in Ireland were among young people and, hence, BCG offered a solution. Although he was reiterating Dorothy's long held conviction, he attributed his newfound faith in BCG solely to Professor Jenner. He went on to explain that he had previously refrained from advocating BCG as he 'did not see his way clear as regards the best technique of approach and how most benefit could be derived from its use'. He also expressed a sense of 'uneasy responsibility' in recommending such a method due to 'insufficient knowledge'.[76] However, with the end of the war and availability of information about the Scandinavian use of BCG, the time was right.[77] In 1941, the use of the vaccine, which had been pioneered in Sweden by Arvid Wallgren, had become 'universal' in that country.[78] In a dismissal of Dorothy's efforts to date, James Deeny wrote that in order to reduce mortality, 'much more than tinkering with it on a small scale' was required.[79]

The Minister for Local Government and Public Health, Seán MacEntee suggested setting up a committee under the auspices of the Medical Research Council (MRC). The committee comprised eleven doctors, including both Dorothy and James Deeny, and was chaired by Professor J.M. O'Connor, dean of the Medical School in University College Dublin (UCD). O'Connor had to deal with at least two radically opposed ideas of how a national BCG scheme might be implemented. James Deeny wanted BCG integrated into the existing tuberculosis services, while Dorothy wanted a separate autonomous body under her control.

On 1 September 1946, the day after the Minister wrote to the MRC, Theo McWeeney departed for Copenhagen in a rushed development orchestrated by James Deeny, who was so keen for Theo McWeeney to go that he drove through the night to collect the inspector who was on holiday in Glenbeigh in County Kerry.[80] James Deeny briefed him: 'Now the important thing is to secure all the available information in a way that is completely documented, exact and defined. This gang (Price, Bigger,

Moore etc) will tear you to bits if everything isn't absolutely concrete'.[81] James Deeny hoped this fact-finding trip would undermine Dorothy's authority. Instead, Theo McWeeney, acknowledging Dorothy's network of Scandinavian contacts, turned to her for information and introductions to the various experts. He brought back figures from Johannes Heimbeck in Norway and his subsequent statement to the committee summed up the current state of knowledge of BCG in the Scandinavian countries. Theo McWeeney noted that reliable vaccine could be obtained from the State Serum Institute in Copenhagen or the laboratory in Gothenburg, Sweden. In line with the thinking in the Department of Local Government and Public Health, McWeeney suggested vaccination be carried out by TOs who should be certified as competent, following a course of instruction. He pointed out that Dorothy already had considerable experience in this technique. Dorothy, who did not agree with the suggestion about the role of TOs, presented the committee with a summary of the literature on BCG. James Deeny's version of events was that it was Theo McWeeney's 'knowledge and first-hand experience' which was the guiding influence in making a decision although he acknowledged that McWeeney had received 'valuable support from Dr Price'.[82] The Department's version of events was publicly aired and McWeeney's visit to Scandinavia was presented as the event which prompted the entire MRC committee investigation, although it happened after the fact.[83]

On 18 October 1946, Dorothy rather bizarrely vaccinated herself. She injected BCG into her arm in order to 'test the reaction'. She was tuberculin positive so was immune to tuberculosis and was not a candidate for the vaccine. Perhaps, she wanted to see what would happen if a tuberculin positive individual got the vaccine in error. In her case, an initial itchy oozing swelling subsided into a small permanent scar 'which caused no discomfort or trouble'. This type of experimentation by doctors on themselves was, at this time, reasonably common.[84]

Meanwhile, the MRC committee met nine times and submitted its final recommendations to the MRC in May 1947. The committee, including Dorothy, unanimously agreed: 'That a good case had been established for the use of BCG vaccination in this country as a means of increasing resistance to tubercle infection, provided very great care is exercised in the organisation, and administration of any scheme of BCG vaccination'.[85]

Although agreement about the introduction of BCG to Ireland was now reached in principle, there were still contentious issues to be debated. Dorothy was adamant that the Swedish vaccine was preferable. She said the Gothenburg vaccine had been kept constant for twenty years and that it appeared to be the standard vaccine to which others resorted in times of difficulty. Theo McWeeney, representing the view of the Department of Public Health and Local Government, was firmly in favour of using the Danish vaccine from the State Serum Institute. This vaccine had been chosen by the Danish Red Cross after the war and Dr Holm of the State Serum Institute was already preparing to scale up preparation of the vaccine to supply what became a mass vaccination programme under the Joint Enterprise Programme in the late 1940s.[86]

The other major argument centred ostensibly around the choice of vaccinators. Dorothy wanted vaccinators to operate outside the tuberculosis service while the Departmental officials wanted to train CMOHs and TOs, thereby integrating BCG into an extant service. This disagreement was about more than vaccinators – the main issue was control of the programme. The pending rows were temporarily averted by an agreed statement that the vaccine would be imported from either Sweden or Denmark and that vaccination should only be carried out by a limited number of trained vaccinators but did not specify who these vaccinators would be. Finally, the vaccine was to be designated a therapeutic rather than an experimental substance.[87] In November 1947, the newly-formed Department of Health formally signalled its support of a mass BCG campaign.[88] A small committee was set up to advise the Minister Dr James Ryan on 'the detailed working of the scheme' and Dorothy was invited to become a member of this committee in November 1947.[89]

In January 1948, the second BCG committee, called the BCG Advisory Committee, was set up by Ministerial order. Its brief was to advise the Minister for Health on the detailed working of BCG vaccination schemes.[90] Dorothy duly attended meetings every Monday from 2 February to 22 March 1948 in the department's headquarters in the Custom House in Dublin. Dublin Corporation had devised a BCG scheme for Dublin and this was put for consideration to this committee.[91] The scheme was accepted in principle by the BCG advisory committee. Mairead Dunlevy's choice of Danish vaccine was agreed and tuberculin for diagnostic purposes was also to be imported from the State Serum Institute in Denmark.[92] Dorothy was unhappy with this choice but she was overruled. Meanwhile, she and Pat Alston continued to use the Swedish vaccine in St Ultan's Hospital and the Rotunda Hospital.

Nine months after the use of BCG on a national basis had been agreed, a new Minister for Health, Noël Browne – the doctor from Newcastle Sanitorium who had collaborated with Dorothy on the formation of the ITS – was appointed on 18 February 1948. The Minister was a strong advocate of mass immunisation.[93] He was also a 'great admirer' of Dorothy.[94] For Dorothy, he represented renewed hopes that her desired autonomous BCG service would come into being. She had collaborated with him when he was secretary of the Irish Tuberculosis Society (ITS), a professional association of medical doctors, set up in 1946.[95] Over the next two years, Dorothy had continued to correspond with Noël Browne on matters tubercular.[96] On his appointment as Minister for Health, she sent him a letter of congratulation. His reply expressed the wish that 'we can all now work for the achievement of a tuberculosis service of which we can all be very proud indeed'. Very soon after he wrote this letter, he received the first report of the BCG advisory committee, which was submitted on 7 April 1948. This was also its last report as the workings of this committee were superseded when, a few weeks later, Browne announced his intention of setting up a National Consultative Council on Tuberculosis to 'advise him on matters relating to the prevention and treatment of tuberculosis'.[97] He appointed Dorothy as chairwoman of this council. This appointment was vital in that it allowed her to achieve her aims in the face of opposition from officials of the Department of Health.

— •••••••••• •••••••••• —

Dorothy had an opportunity to meet Arvid Wallgren again when he came to Belfast to give a paper at the British National Association for the Prevention of Tuberculosis conference at the end of June 1948. Dorothy also spoke. She invited Arvid and Bob Collis to come and stay in Dublin and then to go down to their farm. Liam would be on leave and they could all enjoy a holiday. Arvid brought his daughter Gudrun with him, and after the meeting Dorothy drove them to Dublin. On the following Sunday, she took Arvid and Gudrun to Glendalough, Glenmalure and the Glen of Imaal, both very scenic areas of County Wicklow. They also walked the farm at

Castleruddery, switching the heads off thistles. When the Wallgrens left, Dorothy and Liam made blackcurrant jam and weeded. A flycatcher had made a nest in the raspberries and they were careful not to disturb her. It was 'peaceful and monotonous and certainly very different from New York' where Arvid was attending another conference.[98]

—⋯⋯⋯⋯ ⋯⋯⋯⋯—

Dorothy took up her duties as chairman of the National Consultative Council on Tuberculosis on 15 June 1948.[99] Its diverse membership made it a difficult council to chair and, on a number of occasions when agreement could not be reached, Dorothy resorted to the methodology of compiling a main report with separate dissenting minority reports appended. The council had a wide brief, considering matters such as the control of the use of streptomycin which was in scarce supply, the role to be undertaken by regional sanitoria, the provision of accommodation for children with tuberculosis, as well as the possibility of re-organising the tuberculosis services under a central body. However, the issue that concerned Dorothy most was that of BCG vaccine. She was very pleased when Noël Browne referred the issue of a national BCG scheme to the Council. Dorothy quickly circulated a draft scheme, sited in St Ultan's Hospital, to the council members in November 1948, noting that the MRC committee had already approved a national scheme. Dorothy was adamant that 'success in BCG schemes would depend for some years on their being run under central control, with the responsibility undertaken by persons who had first-hand experience in matters relating to BCG'.[100] The obvious subtext was that she would run the scheme, which would set up its headquarters in 'her' hospital. She wanted the scheme to be funded by the Hospitals Commission but to be independent of the Department of Health. Ultimate control would rest with her and she intended to oversee every detail. In 1989, James Deeny later recalled that the basic objection of the Departmental officials to Dorothy's proposals was that 'we had enough of these independent groups floating around, each doing their own thing; for this job we wanted a close-knit integrated organisation'. He was also 'horrified' at the idea of placing the BCG unit in St Ultan's Hospital, which was already 'a hospital for advanced tubercular children' and where there might be a risk of cross-infection and contamination of the vaccine'.[101] While the local authority and Departmental officials wrangled with Dorothy about control of the proposed scheme, another committee member, Dr T.F. McNamara, vociferously disagreed with most of the committee's work, usually citing moral or Christian objections and the right of doctors to autonomous decision-making. As far as he was concerned, BCG could 'not be recommended as a State policy. It is still under investigation and it would be rash to describe it as a standard accepted medical practice'.[102] Dorothy viewed McNamara as a 'crank' and later stated that he was 'the bane of our existence on the Tuberculosis Consultative Council'.[103]

Unsurprisingly, the council meetings were acrimonious. They were also often long: many of the meetings of the council and its subcommittees were held in the Price's home, sometimes going on until after 11 p.m. In a letter to Arvid Wallgren, Dorothy was not optimistic about getting a national BCG scheme started on her terms:

> I am making one great effort next week to get my plan for extension of BCG work in Ireland adopted. It is a simple and workable plan, but oh! The difficulties – the legacy of British rule remains in our Departmental machinery and red tape; my only hope lies in our big-minded Minister for Health but he is having his appendix out. If I fail, I will withdraw to St Ultan's again.[104]

Dorothy added that her own health was beginning to fail. Her committee work, which was all voluntary and unpaid, was extending into the late hours and her doctor had restricted her to stopping work at 5 p.m.[105] In the end, Dorothy's powers of persuasion prevailed and the final majority report of the National Tuberculosis Consultative Council recommended that a central body direct the introduction of mass BCG vaccination, with the scheme operated through St Ultan's Hospital and an annual grant paid to the board from the Hospitals' Trust Fund. At the insistence of the Departmental officials, a concluding paragraph was appended: 'It should be understood that the recommendations contained herein regarding the establishment of a BCG Control Organisation are a temporary measure until such time as health authorities are in a position to assume control of

BCG vaccination as part of their tuberculosis service.'[106]

This final paragraph in the report of the National Consultative Council on Tuberculosis was to cause disputes for years to come, with the Department and the BCG Committee disagreeing over whether the time had come for health authorities to assume control of vaccination. Dorothy's need for control was partly motivated by her knowledge of the slowness of Departmental machinery, which could stymie planning and decision-making, and by the fact that many local authority doctors were already overworked and unlikely to have the time or enthusiasm to add BCG to their myriad duties.[107] However, from the Department's point of view, a BCG committee that operated outside its auspices would be difficult to integrate into the already extant tuberculosis service. They would be required to fund a service that they would not control.

In the midst of all the voluntary committees and clinical work, family life and friendships continued. Dorothy's correspondence with Cissie and Birdie Crowley of Kilbrittain continued throughout Dorothy's life, gradually dwindling to the usual catch-up at Christmas correspondence of old friends who no longer see each other. For Christmas 1948, Birdie sent her a 'beautiful turkey … we enjoyed the creature very much, it was succulent, evidently killed at just the right moment and tasted good old Kilbrittain flavour'. Dorothy was behind with her shopping as she had to write a paper on tuberculosis but she went to Mrs Twomey's 'magnificent shop' in O'Connell Street and told them that they must catch a post for Christmas. When they heard it was for Kilbrittain, they said: 'Kilbrittain will get it, the Crowleys will get it'. She told Birdie that she met Peter Kearney there – it was a great place for running into old friends. In Cork for the opening of Lesley Barry's St Raphael's tuberculosis preventorium, she had caught a glimpse of other past friends – 'Tom [presumably Tom Barry] is a tall hat!! Just the same as ever. Also got a glimpse of Denis Lordan and the Robert Langfords.'

The second edition of Dorothy's book *Childhood Tuberculosis* was published in 1948. She immediately began to plan a third edition as she was galled that a twelve-month delay at the binders meant the book was out of date almost as soon as it was printed. She was annoyed that the publishers changed the date of the preface from September 1947 to December 1947. 'That was very wrong of them because I never saw the book after September, and in those three months I have had something to say about streptomycin [she had begun to use it in St Ultan's in November 1947], calciferol, [the] three-injection method of BCG, and would have brought the bibliography up to date,' she grumbled.[108]

Nonetheless, she sent a copy of the book to Dr J.B. McDougall of the Tuberculosis Section of the World Health Organisation.[109] He responded that he knew her book well and he had the 'highest admiration for it'. Dorothy must have been further gratified when he added that she might like to know that it had been included in the 'official list of publications which are being recommended to Governments by the World Health Organisation. That I believe expresses my own high opinion of its contents.'[110]

It seemed 1949 would be a busy year for Dorothy – in addition to heading up the new committee, she would be assisting Liam, who was president of the Irish Society of Antiquaries and which was celebrating its centenary in July. Dorothy and Liam expected 'foreign visitors and a week of tremendous activities'. Liam's presidential address was entitled 'four thousand years of Irish history'.[111]

NOTES

1.  D. Price, *Tuberculosis in Childhood* (Bristol: Wrights, 1948).

2.  Minutes, 12 April 1943 (Irish Red Cross (IRC), Minute Book of the Anti-Tuberculosis Standing Committee).

3.  Draft plan of campaign with respect to childhood tuberculosis (TCD, Price papers, MS 7536 (387/392/393)).

4.  Memo, E.J.T. McWeeney, 17 July 1944 (NAI, Dept. Health D102/5); M. Coleman, *The Irish Sweep: A History of the Irish Hospital Sweepstake, 1930–87* (Dublin: UCD Press, 2009), p.xv.

5.  C. Maguire to Dr C. Ward, 20 September 1944 (NAI, Dept. Health D102(16)); W.B. Kannel and D. Levy, 'Commentary: Medical Aspects of the Framingham Community Health and Tuberculosis Demonstration', *International Journal of Epidemiology*, 34, 6 (2005), pp.1187–8.

6.  D. Price to O'Donovan, 26 February 1944 (TCD, Price papers, MS 7537(11)); 'Nationwide T.B. Surveys Advocated', *Irish Press*, 8 March 1944.

7.  'Thirteen Children Saved by Red Cross', *The Irish Times*, 3 October 1944.

8. Minutes, 21 June 1942 (IRC, Minutebook of the Anti-Tuberculosis standing committee); Minutes, 7 January 1944 (IRC, Minutebook of the Ballyroan Selection Committee).

9. D. Price to C. Maguire, 10 June 1944 (TCD, Price papers, MS 7537(2)).

10. C. Maguire to D. Price, 25 June 1944 (TCD, Price papers, MS 7537(27)).

11. Minutes of general meeting of IRC Anti-Tuberculosis section, 21 St Stephen's Green, Dublin, 23 June 1944 (TCD, Price papers, MS 7537(28)).

12. L. Price, *Dorothy Price: An Account of Twenty Years' Fight Against Tuberculosis in Ireland* (Oxford: Oxford University Press, 1957), p.73.

13. Anti-Tuberculosis section of Irish Red Cross Society, *Tuberculosis Exhibition Handbook* (TCD, Price papers, MS 7537(86)).

14. *Tuberculosis Exhibition Handbook*, 1945 (TCD, Price papers, MS 7537(86)); Poster advertising Tuberculosis Exhibition, May to June 1945 (TCD, Price papers, MS 7537(58)); Anonymous, 'The Exhibition', *The Irish Red Cross Monthly Bulletin* (May 1945), pp.137–40.

15. W.C. Kidney, 'Tuberculosis: a Social Survey', *Journal of the Statistical and Social Inquiry Society of Ireland (JSSISI)* 17 (1943/44), pp.642–70; Anonymous, 'Anti-Tuberculosis Section', *The Irish Red Cross Monthly Bulletin* (June 1946), pp.158–60.

16. P.F. Fitzpatrick to D. Price, 30 November 1944 (TCD, Price papers, MS 7537(43)).

17. D. Price to A. Wallgren, draft letter, 27 July 1945 (TCD, Price papers, MS 7537(68)). 18.

18. R. Barrington, 'Introduction' in J. Deeny (ed.), *The End of an Epidemic: Essays in Irish Public Health 1935–65* (Dublin: Farmar, 1995), pp.1–7.

19. J. Deeny, *To Cure and to Care: Memoirs of a Chief Medical Officer* (Dun Laoghaire: Glendale Press, 1989), pp.127–8.

20. Report of conference held in Department of Local Government and Public Health, 20 October 1944 (NAI, Dept. Health D102 (16)).

21. Deeny, *To Cure and to Care*, p.128.

22. *The Irish Times*, 29 March 1944.

23. D. Price, 'Tuberculosis and BCG Vaccination', *The Irish Times*, 8 July 1952.

24. Professor J.M. O'Donovan to Price, 22 February1944 (TCD, Price papers, MS 7537(11); Price to O'Donovan, draft letter, 26 February1944 (TCD, Price papers, MS 7537(11); P. Liddy, County Wexford to Price, 4 May 1944 (TCD, Price papers, MS 7537(20)).

25. Price, red notebook (TCD, Price papers, MS 7537(266).

26. Galway CMOH to Price, undated (TCD, Price papers, MS 7537(53).

27. P. Alston, 'Tuberculin Survey in an Industrial School, County Dublin. January–March 1945', *IJMS*, 6, 244 (1946), pp.130–3.

28. J. Deeny to D. Price, 27 April 1945 (TCD, Price papers, MS 7537(57).

29. D. Price, *Tuberculosis in Childhood* (Bristol: Wrights, 1942, 1st edn; Anonymous, Review of *Tuberculosis in Childhood* (1st edn), *BMJ*, 2, 4272 (1942), p.609.

30. R. Collis, Correspondence, *JMAÉ*, 16, 91 (1945), p.11.

31. M. Dunlevy, 'Medical and Social Problems of Childhood Tuberculosis in Dublin', *JMAÉ*, 23, 134 (1948), pp.19–20.

32. H.E. Counihan, Interview 2008.

33. D. Price, 'The Role of BCG Vaccination in the Prevention of Tuberculosis', *IJMS* 6, 221 (1944), pp.150, 156–7.

34. J.T. Daniels,'The Trend in Tuberculosis', *IJMS* 6, 227 (1944), pp.568–80.

35. Price, *Dorothy Price*, p.76.

36. D. Price to A. Wallgren, 27 July 1945 (NLI, MS 15342).

37. Ibid.

38. Dr R. McCaully, Correspondence, *Irish Independent*, 25 November 1947.

39. J. Deeny to Dr N. Horner, *BMJ* editor, 31 January 1946 (RCSI, Deeny papers, Tuberculosis box).

40. D. Price to A. Wassén, 8 October 1945 (TCD, Price papers, MS 7537(73)).

41. St Ultan's Annual Report 1946, p.15 (RCPI, SU/1/3).

42. D. Price to J. Deeny, 18 April 1946 (TCD, Price papers, MS 7537(124)).

43. Interview Dr H.E. Counihan, 9 June 2008.

44. J. Deeny, memo, 19 August 1946 (NAI, Dept. Health, D113(1)).

45. D. Price's speech, St. Ultan's Hospital AGM, 30 May 1946 (TCD, Price papers, MS 7537(135)).

46. D. Price to A. Wallgren, draft letter, 12 December 1950 (TCD, Price papers, MS 7539(101)).

47. *Evening Herald*, 30 June 1946; *Irish Independent*, 31 June 1946; *Irish Press*, 31 June 1946; *The Irish Times*, 31 June 1946.

48. K. Lynn to D. Price, 2 June 1946 (TCD, Price papers, MS 7537(141)).

49. Price, *Dorothy Price*, p.80.

50. Ibid., p.87.

51. D. Price, *Report of BCG vaccinations 1937 to 1946 St Ultan's Hospital*, TCD, Price papers, MS 7537(251(2)).

52. D. Price, Castleruddery diary, 1946 (TCD, Price papers, MS 7537 (191)).

53.  Interview, H.E. Counihan.

54.  D. Price to B. Crowley, 27 December 1948 (NLI, Crowley family papers, ACC 4767).

55.  D. Price, memo, 10 February1947 (TCD, Price papers, MS 7537(192)).

56.  D. Price to J. Heimbeck, 9 January 1948 (TCD, Price papers, MS 7538(223)).

57.  D. Price to T. McWeeney, memo, 14 November 1947 (TCD, Price papers, MS 7537(225)).

58.  TCD, Price papers, MS 7537(226/229/230/232/233).

59.  J. Heimbeck to D. Price, 24 November 1947 (TCD, Price papers, MS 7537(230)).

60.  Kathleen Lynn diaries, 4 December 1947, 16 December 1947, 18 December 1947 (RCPI, KL/1/3).

61.  Memo, 1 December 1947 (NAI, Dept. Taoiseach, S16225).

62.  D. Price to J. Heimbeck, 21 December 1947 (TCD, Price papers, MS 7537(235)).

63.  Ibid.

64.  Letter to Dublin City Manager, 15 November1947 (NAI, Dept. Health, D113(1)).

65.  See for instance: *The Irish Times*, 1 June 1945; *The Irish Press*, 2 June 1945, *The Irish Times* and *Evening Mail*, 31 May 1946; Kathleen Lynn diaries, 4 May 1949, 19 June 1949 (RCPI, KL/1/3).

66.  *St Ultan's Medical Committee Reports 1948–1963*, 4 September 1946 (RCPI, SU/3/2/3).

67.  *St Ultan's Medical Committee Reports 1948–1963*, 7 April 1948 (RCPI, SU/3/2/3).

68.  *St Ultan's Medical Committee Reports 1948–1963*, 23 June 1948 (RCPI, SU/3/2/3).

69.  Kathleen Lynn diaries, 17, 18 and 21 June 1948 (RCPI, KL/1/3).

70.  *St Ultan's Medical Committee Reports 1948–1963*, 6 April 1949 (RCPI, SU/3/2/3).

71.  *St Ultan's Annual Report 1949* (RCPI, SU/1/3).

72.  *St Ultan's Annual Report 1950* (RCPI, SU/1/4).

73.  M.R. Canon, *Irish Nursing World*, December 1950 (TCD, Price papers, MS 539(118)).

74.  Departmental Secretary to the Taoiseach, 25 May 1957 (NAI, Dept. Taoiseach, S16555).

75.  *The Conference on European BCG Programmes conducted with the Assistance of the Joint Enterprise, Copenhagen, Denmark, 8–12 September 1949* (London, 1951), p.13.

76.  J. Deeny, memo, 19 August 1946 (NAI, Dept. Local Govt. and Public Health, D113/1).

77.  J.A.D. Deeny, 'Aspects of the Problem in Éire', *IJMS* 6, 252 (1946), pp.774–8.

78.  A.W. Dickie, 'BCG Vaccination in Stockholm', *UMJ* 19, 1 (1950), p.37.

79.  J. Deeny, memo, 19 August 1946 (NAI, Dept. Local Govt. and Public Health, D113/1).

80. E.J.T. McWeeney to D. Price, 2 September 1946 (TCD, Price papers, MS 7535(153)); T. McWeeney to D. Price, 18 September 1946 (TCD, Price papers, MS 7535(158)); J. Deeny, notes (RCSI, Deeny papers, Dept. Health File 2, 19/1).

81. J. Deeny to E.J.T. McWeeney, 11 September 1946 (RCSI, Deeny papers, Tuberculosis box).

82. J. Deeny, notes (RCSI, Deeny papers, Dept. Health File 2, 19/1).

83. *Irish Independent*, 24 September 1947.

84. Price, *Dorothy Price*, p.92; T.D. Brock, *Robert Koch: A Life in Medicine and Bacteriology* (Washington: ASM Press, 1999), p.200.

85. *Report of the BCG Committee of the MRC of Ireland* (TCD, Price papers, MS 7537(256)).

86. Review and digest of selected publications by D. Price (TCD, Price papers, MS 7537(263)).

87. *Report of the BCG Committee of the MRC of Ireland* (TCD, Price papers, MS 7537(256)).

88. *Irish Independent*, 15 November 1947.

89. E.M. Kane, secretary of the MRC, to D. Price, 21 November 1947 (TCD, Price papers, MS 7537(210)).

90. Carbon copy Ministerial Order, 12 January 1948 (TCD, Price papers, MS 7538(10/2)).

91. M. Crowe, acting MOH Dublin city, to P.J. Hernon, city manager, 17 December 1947 (TCD, Price papers, MS 7537(220 )).

92. *The report of the BCG Advisory Committee*, 7 April 1948 (TCD, Price papers, MS 7538(27)).

93. Dáil Debates, vol. 111, 16, col. 2263, 6 July 1948.

94. H.E. Counihan, interview.

95. *The Irish Times*, October 10 1946; F. Heaf to D. Price, 12 December 1947 (TCD, Price papers, MS 7537 ( 234/1)); Dorothy Price, 'Is BCG Vaccination a Practical Proposition in Éire?', *IJMS* 6, 252 (1946), pp.779–86.

96. D. Price, diary, Castleruddery, 1946 (TCD, Price papers, MS 7538(191)); Browne to Price, 29 November 1946 (TCD, Price papers, MS 7538(182)); Browne to Price, 23 July 1947 (TCD, Price papers, MS 7537(212)).

97. Department of Health to D. Price, DOH Ref PH35/267, 23 April 1948 (TCD, Price papers, MS 7538(36)).

98. D. Price to A. Wallgren, 13 July 1948 (NLI, MS 15341 (11)).

99. Copy of Ministerial Order, Establishment of the Consultative Council on Tuberculosis, 27 May 1948 (TCD, Price papers, MS 7538(123)).

100. Price, *Dorothy Price*, p.116.

101. Deeny, *To Cure and to Care*, p.168.

102. See, for instance, T.C.J. O'Connor and T.F. McNamara, minority report on streptomycin use (TCD, Price papers, MS 7538(184)); T.F. McNamara, memo (TCD, Price papers, MS 7538(153/2)).

103. D. Price to J. Cowell, 7 October 1950 (TCD, Price papers, MS 7538(84)).

104. D. Price to A. Wallgren, draft letter, January 1949 (TCD, Price papers, MS 7538(236)).

105. Dáil Debates, vol. 122, 7, col. 1216, 11 July 1950.

106. Consultative Council on Tuberculosis report on BCG (TCD, Price papers, MS 7538(190/2)).

107. See, for instance, J.C. Saunders to D. Price, 18 February 1943 (TCD, Price papers, MS 7536(314)).

108. D. Price to A. Wallgren, 2 September 1948 (NLI MS 15341 (11)).

109. D. Price to J.B. McDougall, 23 May 1949 (TCD, Price papers, MS 7539 (6)).

110. J.B. McDougall to D. Price, 18 May 1949 (TCD, Price papers, MS 7539 (7)).

111. D. Price to A. Wallgren, 18 May 1949 (NLI MS 15341 (11))

CHAPTER NINE

# 'The Capacity to Say "No"': Rolling out a Mass Vaccination Campaign (1949–1954)

'I personally would not be responsible for the appointment of any doctor as a vaccinator unless I had with my own eyes seen him perform (with sterile saline) a BCG-type of intradermal injection on my own arm and on the arm of an infant.'[1]

Dorothy's immediate family, especially Liam, provided a bulwark of support as she spent most of 1949 engaged in bitter battles centring around the control of the BCG vaccination campaign. In 1950, she had a stroke and retired from the National BCG Committee and her remaining clinical work. However, she retained her interest in and frequently advised on the rollout of the national BCG vaccination campaign. She also collated and published the findings of the National BCG Committee in various medical journals. When Dorothy could no longer travel abroad, letters from far flung friends, relatives and colleagues continued to pour in to the Price home and were diligently answered. Dorothy and Liam moved from 10 Fitzwilliam Place to 8 Herbert Park, Donnybrook, in Dublin when Dorothy's illness required a more manageable house. Their new home was opposite Alice's house so Dorothy was close to her sister and her great-nieces, Penny and Sandra, who lived with her. Liam and Dorothy remained devoted to each other and continued to visit their farm in Wicklow at regular intervals – this was always a welcome respite from the busyness of town and professional life.

— .....·..··.. ....·.··....· —

The report of the National Tuberculosis Consultative Council with respect to the national BCG scheme was sent to the Minister for Health on 21 February 1949, provoking a flurry of largely hostile memos and notes between Departmental officials. It is noteworthy that there was no opposition expressed to BCG vaccination *per se*. The hostility centred on control and administrative issues.[2] In April, Noël Browne put an end to the various discussions and asked Dorothy to establish a BCG committee that would operate through St Ultan's Hospital. It seemed he had induced the Hospital's Trust Fund to add the National BCG scheme to its over-committed agenda. Dorothy was optimistic the new committee should 'run smoothly' as the seven doctors '...will all, I hope, be allies of BCG and friends of mine. Better late than never, although I think we shall be the last nation in Europe to form a BCG scheme – our Ultan's vaccinations total 411 and Dr Dunlevy in Dublin Tuberculosis Service has done over 200'.[3] Her optimism about the makeup of the new committee was somewhat misplaced and there were some further stormy times ahead. Yet, Dorothy, with the vital backing of Noël Browne, had achieved her goal and was about to chair a National BCG Committee as it rolled out a mass vaccination programme in Ireland. Dorothy was delighted but regretted the time taken for Ireland's Department of Health to introduce this national scheme.[4] BCG had become a mainstay of the post-war public health programme on the continent. More than eight million people worldwide were vaccinated with BCG under the Joint Enterprise programme which was established following the Second World War.[5] Great Britain had still not introduced mass BCG vaccination but the Irish medical profession now seemed to have developed the confidence to forge ahead.

The effort of securing a committee had, however, exhausted Dorothy. 'I got a tired heart but it has got quite well since the BCG plans went the right way, so I suppose it was largely boredom and frustration.'[6]

— .....·..··.. ....·.··....· —

Dorothy's committee was not solely composed of her allies as Noël Browne appointed a further three doctors to the scheme. The inclusion of Mairead Dunlevy 'greatly annoyed' Dorothy, however Mairead was an obvious candidate for membership as she, Pat Alston and Dorothy were the only three Irish doctors with practical experience of the vaccine.[7] Although Dorothy finally had her committee, she was faced with chairing yet another group with a diverse range of views with respect to how a national vaccination programme should proceed. The inaugural meeting of the National BCG Committee was held on 4 July 1949.[8] The functions of the new committee were defined: '...to direct and be responsible for the expansion of BCG vaccination in Ireland; to train, appoint and supervise vaccinators and be responsible for their work; to keep central records of vaccination in Ireland; to print and circulate leaflets and to direct propaganda in association with the Department of Health and to arrange for importation and storage of vaccine'.[9] All vaccinations were to be voluntary and were to be preceded by tuberculin testing. Only tuberculin-negative persons would be offered vaccinations. Following vaccination, a further tuberculin test would be carried out to ensure that the vaccination had 'took' and the person was now tuberculin positive (this latter practice was later discontinued as it was too time consuming).

The incidence of infectious diseases including tuberculosis had begun to decline in Ireland but there were still more than 3,000 deaths in Ireland from tuberculosis in the preceding year.[10] The Minister for Health publicly put his weight behind the new vaccination campaign.[11] Behind the scenes, the relationship between Noël Browne and Dorothy began to deteriorate. The committee was based in St Ultan's Hospital with a complex funding arrangement. The hospital was to pay the costs and the deficit was to be treated as part of the 'deficit on the annual accounts of the hospital'.[12] While the hospital and committee were intended to be separate enterprises, there was some overlap. At the same time as the committee started work, St Ultan's Hospital refused to admit patients to its newly 'opened' BCG unit.[13] There was also disagreement over the provision of office accommodation for the National BCG Committee. There was no room at St Ultan's and she fitted out a room as an office and meeting room in her home for the first few months. She was adamant that office space would not be provided out of St Ultan's Hospital's 'already cramped premises'.[14] Once Dorothy provided an assurance that the BCG unit would open, Browne promised office space.[15]

The Hospital Commission suggested that St Ultan's Hospital and the BCG committee would share a secretary, while Dorothy wanted a full-time secretary for the committee. Just one month after work had commenced, the Department of Health requested a progress report. Dorothy responded that they would get their report as soon as the committee got a full-time secretary.[16] A full-time secretary was duly appointed.

In addition to various disagreements with Noël Browne, Dorothy engaged in a series of battles with the committee's local health authority officials, Mairead Dunlevy and Morgan Crowe, and the Department of Health's tuberculosis inspector, Theo McWeeney, although she always remained a personal friend of his. At the outset, a leading article in the *Journal of the Medical Association of Éire* based on information supplied by Dorothy celebrated the establishment of the BCG committee and raised the hackles of officialdom.[17] The statement that 'the whole BCG development in this country came about through voluntary efforts' prompted Theo McWeeney to write a memo to James Deeny in which he noted the lack of any credit for the development of BCG vaccination by central or local authority 'except in its most recent aspects'.[18] There was much counting up and comparing of vaccinations completed by Mairead Dunlevy in Dublin Corporation and Dorothy and Pat Alston in St Ultan's Hospital and the Rotunda Hospital in an attempt to prove the department had been active with respect to BCG.[19] A response to the leading article was drafted stating Mairead Dunlevy had done 400 vaccinations by 30 June 1949 while Dorothy Price had done 400 to 500 in total, over a much longer time period. In the end, the typed draft was red pencilled 'did not issue' but the episode illustrated the bad feeling among the members of the committee.

The continuance of the Dublin Corporation BCG scheme alongside the National Committee's work also became a source of confusion and contention. For instance, when Dorothy approached Professor Joseph Warwick Bigger, Dean of Physic in Trinity College Dublin (TCD), to offer vaccinations to medical students, she found her fellow committee member, Mairead, had pre-empted her by offering the services of the Dublin Corporation BCG scheme.[20] Mairead Dunlevy's understanding or deliberate misunderstanding was that the national scheme, which was headquartered in Dublin, did not include Dublin.[21] Meanwhile, Dorothy and Pat Alston were vaccinating in St Ultan's Hospital, Dublin, while Dorothy seemed determined to vaccinate in as many other Dublin institutions as possible. There was even confusion among the local authority officials themselves with Morgan Crowe suggesting that the National BCG Committee instigate a campaign to vaccinate newborns in all hospitals, to prevent tubercular meningitis, only to be informed by Mairead Dunlevy that Dublin Corporation was considering a plan.[22] Dorothy privately dubbed the various officials 'those stupid fellows'.[23]

When Mairead Dunlevy suggested that County Medical Officers of Health (CMOHs) be allowed to vaccinate after two weeks' training, Dorothy vehemently disagreed.[24] After some work had been commenced by a committee-appointed vaccinator in Tipperary North, Mairead Dunlevy contended that there was no need for him to return to the county as the CMOH should be able to carry on with the work. Dorothy riposted by reading out extracts from a letter from the CMOH stating that he did not have time to do the testing.[25] Meanwhile, Theo McWeeney pointed out that the Department had quite recently sent a number of CMOHs to Copenhagen to be trained and that they could vaccinate as efficiently as anyone trained by the National BCG Committee. He suggested the committee's vaccinator would ask the CMOH after a first visit if he wished to carry on. The BCG committee would do the recording and distribute the vaccine.[26] Morgan Crowe asked, pertinently, why a local authority (Mairead Dunlevy and the Dublin Corporation scheme) could vaccinate in Dublin but not 'down the country'.[27] Dorothy and Harry Counihan remained opposed to vaccinations being carried out by anyone other than a committee trained vaccinator. Dorothy's need for control of the vaccination had become almost obsessive. She stated that she 'personally would not be responsible for the appointment of any doctor as a vaccinator unless I had with my own eyes seen him perform (with sterile saline) a BCG-type of intradermal injection on my own arm and on the arm of an infant.'[28] Her reasoning was that the 'right subject' had to be chosen for vaccination; accurate records had to be kept; a true intradermal injection was required and the vaccine was labile and had to be used within fourteen days of the time it was prepared in Sweden.[29] These would all seem to be reasonable precautions and systems that could be put in place by any trained doctor or nurse.

From being the radical advocate of BCG vaccination, who pushed it in the face of opposition, Dorothy was now seen as too conservative in her approach. She was aware of this irony. On 25 November 1949, she confided to Arvid Wallgren:

> There is at present a wave of enthusiasm for BCG; all doctors want to be doing it at once, but of course they will tire of the new craze in two years' time! I expect from today to be thrown out for being too old-fashioned. I am having an awful time, up in the skies one day, expecting immediate dissolution the next.[30]

In the end, Dorothy and Harry Counihan came up with a compromise. The BCG committee would control all vaccinations done with the Swedish vaccine imported by them. There would be no restriction on the importation of BCG vaccine from the State Serum Institute, Copenhagen, or the State Laboratory, Gothenburg, Sweden, by any other doctor. A vote of four to three carried Dorothy's motion on 5 December 1949.[31] If Dorothy had lost the vote about the vaccinators, she had prepared a motion that the committee should be wound down as it would cease, in her opinion, to have any useful function.[32]

In October 1949, while the various battles were being fought, the actual work of vaccination commenced.[33] Dorothy wanted a slow controlled rollout of the vaccine carried out by her personally-appointed vaccinators. Pat Alston was appointed as a part-time vaccinator while John Cowell was appointed to a full-time position. Dorothy's close working relationship with Pat did not make John feel excluded. In fact, Dorothy wrote to him: 'I can't imagine anyone more ideal to have come into our little BCG world and become one of us so quickly. I think we shall succeed and no small part of the success will be due to your personality and enthusiasm and skill.'[34] It was with evident glee that Dorothy informed Arvid Wallgren she was going to preach his doctrine to all CMOHs and TOs.[35] She ordered 1,000 reprints of his leaflet *Calmette Vaccination in Europe* for distribution. Dorothy wrote: 'We are anxious to teach our doctors the right and simple doctrines, especially in these days when publications on BCG tend to be numerous and confusing'.[36] The committee began to make plans to begin targeted vaccination – deans of medical schools, heads of sanatoria and general hospitals were to be approached in addition to local authorities.[37] Six voluntary hospitals sent their tuberculin-negative probationer nurses for vaccination.[38]

228

As vaccination began, local administrative and technical difficulties became evident. BCG was being given in an environment where tuberculosis was still endemic in the population so the process of pre-vaccinal testing, vaccination and post-vaccinal testing was lengthy and cumbersome, involving up to five procedures per patient.[39] This protocol, which was designed to ensure the prospective vaccine recipient was not incubating tuberculosis, was later modified.[40] An impressive overall conversion rate from tuberculin negative to tuberculin positive (indicating immunity had been established) of 95 per cent was achieved among the 18,693 individuals vaccinated in the first 18 months but there were occasional glitches – both with delivery of the vaccine and the need for refrigeration. In June 1950, the committee noted an unsatisfactory conversion rate for some groups vaccinated at 'the height of the sunny season'. These patients had to be revaccinated. To prevent a recurrence, the liquid vaccine was transported in iceboxes during the summer months. Overcrowded sessions, where doctors had to perform large numbers of vaccinations under time pressure, were found to result in poor conversion rates. An upper limit of 600 vaccinations per doctor per week was imposed. Another problem was the poor quality of equipment. Backward leakage between the syringe and barrel could lead to accidental under-dosage.[41] A letter to Dorothy from John Cowell who was in Nenagh in October 1949 provides a flavour of early obstacles to rolling out a mass vaccination campaign.[42] Single-use needles were still not available. The vaccine was fluid and perishable and refrigeration was not readily available. Telephones were not installed in most homes. John Cowell wrote:

> A hasty line whilst the needles are boiling up for to-day's tour. I arrived all in good time. They had called twenty-nine for the clinic session of which twenty-three turned up. Later we did seven cases in outlying areas and found one boy missing – he had taken refuge somewhere and couldn't be found! They have twenty-two for today in their homes and thirty-seven for tomorrow – a total of ninety which I honestly feel I won't manage. Unfortunately, they have written to all these cases to expect us at an approximate time. I propose to review the situation this evening after the full day's experience. If I feel I

can't fit them all in I'll get them to post another note. Some of the places are up mountain lands and take quite a time to reach...[43]

The following day, he told Dorothy that so far they had done fifty Mantoux tests, some in outlying areas. He had difficulties with the car sticking in the mud but his general sense was that people were very anxious to receive protection against tuberculosis.[44]

In addition to worrying about the pace of vaccination, Dorothy also had to contend with other difficulties. Her most serious clash with Noël Browne came about when she received a request from the World Health Organisation (WHO) to fill out a tuberculosis schedule for Ireland. The Minister felt this was 'properly a matter for the Department'.[45] Dorothy had not seen the WHO request as a matter of contention: she had previously replied blithely to the WHO that she was consulting officials in the Department of Health as she was on 'very good terms with the Minister and the Department'.[46] Browne's letter of 28 December 1949, expressing his displeasure, was therefore, something of a shock:

> As we know, your connection with BCG is twofold – as a technical expert of international reputation and as chairman of the national committee. Your selection as corresponding member of WHO arises from the fact that you are an acknowledged expert and is independent altogether of your connection with the national committee. Accordingly, in keeping with the established principle, the range which would normally be covered by you in your reports is the range in which you would cover if you had no connection with the committee. In due course, the report which will be made by the government to the WHO will cover the work of the national committee.[47]

Dorothy drafted a reply on 16 January 1950, and the following day, she suffered a stroke, with partial paralysis and temporary loss of speech. However, she felt the matter was urgent and she asked John Cowell, whom she trusted implicitly, to type up her reply to the Minister. Liam Price notes that Dorothy 'thought it strange' that Browne should raise such a matter by letter, instead of talking to her about it.[48] In her written response, Dorothy noted the 'paucity of scientific material' produced in Ireland. Unless she provided the WHO with material dealing with 'administrative and other aspects of tuberculosis work', she opined that there was little point in her being a corresponding member. In view of his letter, and as she now saw the situation, it would be difficult for her to carry out her obligations to the WHO without 'occasional conflicts' between her duties to them and her duties to the BCG committee. Dorothy then expressed her willingness to resign from the WHO as she would 'prefer to do so rather than allow a mere matter of this nature to interfere with the working of the BCG committee, or interrupt in any way the cordial relations between you and me'.[49] There is no record of Noël Browne's reply but Dorothy did not resign from the WHO until 1951.[50]

In January 1950, Dorothy was too ill to continue her work as chairman of the National BCG Committee. She proposed Professor R.A.Q. O'Meara as her successor while Noël Browne was not happy with this choice. The Minister reluctantly gave way to Dorothy's wishes: 'I am terribly encouraged indeed by the wonderful report of the work to date of the BCG committee and I heard that some of the very hardened and slightly cynical members of the Civil Service have been amazed at the progress which you have made...'[51] Browne further stated that he would deal with 'the point' she had raised as she had suggested, because he was anxious to repay, even in this 'very tiny way' some of the 'deep debt' which he owed to her. By April 1950, a triumphant Dorothy told Arvid Wallgren (who had sent her pink and red carnations to cheer her in her illness): 'I had the Minister here twice and finally persuaded him to do what I wanted. So after six weeks delay the right people were appointed. I think this battle kept me alive for the first month as it gave me something to live for.'[52] Despite the various clashes between Dorothy and Noël Browne, their working relationship is perhaps more remarkable for its long term cordiality and the continued respect with which they regarded each other. Noël Browne resigned from government soon afterwards, over the 'Mother and Child' controversy where the Catholic hierarchy and the Irish Medical Association famously opposed his plans to provide non-means-tested medical care to mothers and children up to the age of sixteen.[53] Dorothy was frankly delighted when he was subsequently re-elected as an independent candidate, with only '750 votes less than the prime minister who forced him to resign'.[54]

Dorothy's stroke left her with a weakness on her left side. She had to learn to walk again and used a stick. Limited movement returned to her left arm but she was stoic. 'My doctor Synge, Professor of Medicine in Trinity College & a Swedophile (his sons speak Swedish) says "What more do you want, you will have a good right arm & a brain & speech, don't grumble."' In the midst of her recovery, Dorothy also worried for Liam who had 'been wonderful' but had had a 'rotten time poor fellow'.[55] By April, Dorothy's arm movements were recovering somewhat and her face was straight. She could talk but not sing. The 'awful nightmare – three months of it' in a nursing home was over and she felt herself again. She was going home for Easter with the help of a day and a night nurse and Liam had a flat made on the ground floor so she could get into her study and the dining room. They moved soon afterwards from 10 Fitzwilliam Square to 8 Herbert Park, a more manageable house. Dorothy did not think she would work again but she pretended she was going back shortly to the National BCG Committee 'to keep the wicked ones in order'.[56] In 1950, Dorothy retired from St Ultan's due to ill health although she remained closely involved with the hospital. For instance, in 1952, she objected to a proposed playroom for the tuberculosis unit. While she acknowledged it was not her place to obstruct 'any plan for the improvement of T.B.' when she was no longer there, she was adamant that 'if you carry out your plan that you would call it "day room" rather than "play room". This latter term is not a term for a hospital but rather is employed in children's home type buildings.'[57]

R.A.Q. O'Meara found that it was 'impossible for him to play the same part as Dorothy in directing the medical programme of the committee' and he proposed the appointment of John Cowell as medical director.[58] John Cowell was appointed and Dorothy continued to receive the minutes of meetings from him.[59] The high opinion she had formed of him when he first joined the committee continued and, through him, she proffered advice and recommendations to the committee.[60] While John frequently consulted Dorothy, Harry Counihan pointed out that John Cowell was 'not a nonentity'. He was 'a meticulous fellow … at records and organisation and making sure the paperwork was in order. He was very, very good at it. He introduced systems. We were up and down the country vaccinating people'.[61]

Nonetheless, after one year in operation, the National BCG Committee was criticised for its continuing separation from the tuberculosis service and its failure to widen the network of vaccinators to include nurses and CMOHs. A United Nations WHO representative, Dr D.R. Thomson, who visited Ireland and looked at its tuberculosis services, came to the conclusion that while the committee had 'performed a useful function in initiating BCG in different counties', it would not seem advisable 'to keep BCG vaccination as a sort of monopoly, or at any rate as a programme divorced from other aspects of tuberculosis control'.[62] With respect to the Dublin Corporation BCG scheme, he pronounced it to be 'a very sound project, carefully planned and executed and functioning as an integral part of the tuberculosis programme in the city'. The role of the national committee, in Thomson's opinion, was to maintain technical standards, ensure a regular supply of tuberculin and vaccine and maintain and process statistical records. These were the very points raised by James Deeny and the Departmental and local authority officials on numerous occasions. Dr Thomson further stated that one standard BCG vaccine should be used throughout the country.[63] Dublin Corporation had, by this time, vaccinated some 2,000 people using Danish vaccine while the National BCG Committee, had tuberculin tested more than 17,000 people and vaccinated 6,594 using Swedish vaccine. Both vaccines were internationally recognised and the WHO representative did not recommend one over the other. John Cowell did not seem to take the visit very seriously and reported to Dorothy 'we had Dr Thomson in from WHO, an American, brought by Dr Daly on the Department of Health's latest grand tour … [he] enquired on looking at my flagged map of Ireland, what we intended to do when this small island was vaccinated'. Dorothy must have cheered when Noël Browne chose not to act on Dr Thomson's report and the *status quo* remained with two vaccination and tuberculin testing systems in place.[64]

In keeping with Dorothy's wishes, nurses continued to be excluded from vaccinating.[65] Noel Browne disagreed with the favourable assessment of Dublin Corporation's tuberculosis service.[66] Furthermore, the Minister stated, that from recent inspection at St Ultan's Hospital of the committee's activities, he was satisfied that the committee was doing excellent work and he felt that this work would not be as well done if undertaken by CMOHs and their staff. He indicated, therefore, that the committee should be allowed to carry on as at present but he agreed that where a CMOH was anxious to commence BCG vaccination, he or she should be given facilities to do so with the caveat that any new scheme should comply with the standards of the BCG Committee as regards records and type of vaccine. He stressed that there should be no friction between the CMOH and the National BCG Committee where a scheme was being carried out by local staff.[67]

By the end of 1950, the committee had expanded the number of vaccinators to include five full-time and one part-time doctors. Other personnel changes included the departure of Theo McWeeney from the committee – he left Ireland to join the WHO after he had felt compelled by Browne to resign his position as tuberculosis inspector.[68] James Deeny, who was also unable to get on with Browne, left the position of chief medical adviser to head up Ireland's first National Tuberculosis Survey.[69] The committee's approach to vaccination changed and local authorities were afforded the opportunity to begin their own schemes or to take over the scheme commenced by the committee.

— •••······•··•·  ••··•··•···• —

In October 1950, Dorothy wrote to Arvid asking for his help and advice with her illness. As a result of the left-sided hemiplegia, her arm was almost useless, due to 'an unusual atrophy of the deltoid, which means that the head of the humerus is dropping down and forwards'. In time, she feared that this could lead to other complications. For the present, she supported it with a pad in the axilla. Dr Synge suggested some form of light sling and wondered if Arvid could recommend a suitable orthopaedic doctor or surgeon in Sweden who would give an opinion and, also, if he knew of any really good instrument maker in Sweden who would make a light shoulder brace. Dorothy had been told that very light aluminium was being used in the United States but if it was being used in Sweden, it would be a shorter trip. She hoped all was going well for Arvid in 'the big world. My world is Liam and our new house and garden; it is strange to be looking at life through a window'.[70]

Arvid consulted his colleagues and recommended Mr Osmonde-Clarke in London. Dorothy noted: 'If you ever find a good man in London, he is sure to be a Trinity Irishman, like Mr Clarke'.[71] Meanwhile, Dorothy found that massage provided her with some relief. In 1951, Dorothy flew to London to see Mr Osmonde-Clarke and Mr Donal Brooks. The following year, she wrote to Arvid to thank him for offprints of his papers which kept her up to date with tuberculosis in Sweden. Sadly, she ended the letter: 'I lead a vegetable existence – not unpleasant when you get used to it – the highlight is Liam. It is not "living" in any sense, a sort of waiting and quite happy. Just had two months at Castleruddery with pleasant memories of four years ago with you and Gudrun.'[72]

Sandra, Dorothy's great niece, remembers happier times with Dorothy and her brother or sister playing patience on green baize boards which they balanced on their knees. Dorothy always had a cigarette in her mouth and the ash would grow longer and longer until it eventually fell on the board and she would brush it away.

— ........... .....•....... —

Although Dorothy never returned to work with the National BCG Committee, she remained in close contact with it. She also retained her general interest in tuberculosis and wrote book reviews for the *Irish Journal of Medical Science* (*IJMS*) as well as articles for other publications. In 1952, using data accumulated by the committee, she published the results of a survey of 10,000 tuberculin reactions including 'every age-group, from infancy to fifty years, and persons in every walk of life and all income groups'.[73] The overall results showed that, as might be expected, rates of exposure to tuberculosis, as demonstrated by a positive tuberculin reaction, increased with age. Only 6.9 per cent of children up to the age of 4 years demonstrated a positive reaction. Dorothy's paper provided important information about the epidemiology of tuberculosis in Ireland. Confirming what had been found in previous smaller-scale studies, it showed that urban areas had a greater percentage of positive reactions although there were exceptions.[74] There were no significant gender differences. The first major rises in tuberculin positivity coincided reasonably well with age of school entry (4–5 years), with the second rise occurring at school-leaving age (fourteen years). Vaccination prior to these ages was recommended while, for young adults, the best age to vaccinate was determined to be at seventeen years.

In addition to informing vaccination policies, Dorothy pointed out the usefulness of interrogating the details of the survey, which allowed micro-analysis of vectors of disease such as unpasteurised milk or contact with a sputum-positive case.[75] The field sheets, recording the tuberculin testing results for each local authority area, were given to the relevant CMOH, providing a 'veritable gold mine of information relevant to the spread of tuberculosis'. John Cowell noted that the vaccination campaign, as a 'side-line', was proving to be a 'fairly productive case-finding machine'.[76]

In 1954, five years into the campaign, two studies analysed the achievements and shortcomings of the national BCG campaign. The first of these was an analysis, by Dorothy, of 140,697 vaccinations.[77] This final paper, published posthumously, represented her personal views rather than those of the committee. R.A.Q. O'Meara, on behalf of the BCG committee, had requested that Dorothy did not publish this paper:

> Too often the results of BCG vaccination schemes have been presented in the past in a form from which no accurate and incontestable deductions as to its efficacy could be made. I have in mind, for this country, the collection of accurate comparative data for the incidence of tuberculosis in the vaccinated and unvaccinated living in comparable conditions and have already planned that when Cowell is freed from office work, he will undertake investigations of this type. Your paper cuts right across this endeavour and will I fear substitute for the best something which is much less effective and something which is not acceptable to me nor I think to the committee as a whole.[78]

Dorothy ignored the wishes of the committee and risked the possibility of bad publicity for her beloved vaccine by outlining twenty-one cases of tubercular disease which occurred among the 140,000 vaccinated persons. Eleven of the cases were already incubating infection. Seven members of this subgroup recovered and four died. Of the other ten patients who developed tuberculosis some time after being fully immunised, five recovered, three were still under treatment and recovering, one died and one could not be contacted. Dorothy never claimed the vaccine would afford complete protection and she attributed these cases to 'an attack of an unusually heavy dose of tubercle infection'. The occurrence of ten cases of disease among 140,000 artificially immunised persons in a country where tuberculosis was still endemic was an excellent result.[79] In addition, there were sixteen 'undesirable' reactions to the vaccine, a rate of 0.011. All of the reactions were mild and none of them required treatment. This compared very well with the results of the WHO programme where some post-vaccination ulcerations were observed.[80]

The second analysis of the BCG vaccination campaign was also published in 1954 and was written by Dorothy's *bête noire* James Deeny who correctly criticised the overall rate of vaccination achieved in the first five years. A leading article in *The Lancet* echoed these criticisms.[81] In the report on *The National Tuberculosis Survey*, James Deeny recommended vaccination on a 'greatly increased scale'. For instance, he pointed out that there were 850,000 children under 15 years of age, and approximately half of these might be expected to be tuberculin negative. In addition, there were about 65,000 births per year and these would all be tuberculin negative at birth. Together, this made up a target of half a million for vaccination with BCG with a continuing annual programme of 65,000 vaccinations of newborns. The report suggested that 'the present rate of vaccination is too slow and is not likely to provide mass protection within a reasonable time'.[82] Despite James Deeny's criticism, the rate of vaccination did not increase substantially. In the end, the Irish vaccination campaign did not reach a critical mass of the population sufficiently quickly to achieve 'herd immunity' prior to the end of the tuberculosis epidemic in the late 1950s. Vaccination was offered on a voluntary basis and, initially, there was some prejudice on the part of the Irish public against the BCG vaccine but this was quickly overcome.[83] Later, as tuberculosis rates declined, apathy rather than opposition had to be overcome. In the early years, however, one of the main determining factors in the low numbers vaccinated under the auspices of the National BCG Committee was probably Dorothy's view that quality and a slow controlled rollout of the campaign was more important than quantity. She did not believe both quality and quantity were simultaneously obtainable. The 'mere amassing of numbers' which she disdained was, however, the very point of any mass vaccination programme.[84]

While the criticisms were valid, the introduction of BCG vaccination did have an effect on the tuberculosis epidemic. In particular, the targeting of groups most at risk of contracting tuberculosis for vaccination was a strategy that paid off. The successful vaccination of contacts of the tubercular, such as family members, meant that the spread of the disease was greatly reduced. It has been suggested that the BCG campaign was largely responsible for ending tubercular meningitis (which, at this time, was usually fatal) in Irish children. BCG was particularly effective in these cases:

none of the Irish infants and children who were vaccinated with BCG in the first decade of the campaign contracted tubercular meningitis. However, only one quarter of all children under five years of age were vaccinated by 1957. A study of the records of the Registrar General shows that deaths from tubercular meningitis had begun to fall before significant numbers of neonates and young children were vaccinated. So, while BCG paid a part in eliminating tubercular meningitis and miliary tuberculosis, its potential was not fully realised.[85]

Moreover, the early campaigns were not as successful as they might have been in vaccinating other vulnerable groups including pre-school children, young emigrants and healthcare workers. Despite much propaganda and the opening of evening clinics, young adults were apathetic about taking up the vaccine. Perhaps the greatest anomaly was the committee's early concentration on the school-going population *in lieu* of vigorous targeting of neonates.

The first decade of the BCG campaigns coincided with the ending of the Irish tuberculosis epidemic. However, it also coincided with a number of other interventions, such as the development of effective antibiotic therapy, the provision of sufficient X-ray equipment in Ireland, the case finding work of James Deeny's National Tuberculosis Survey, the increased availability of hospital and sanatoria beds and better housing and nutrition. Dorothy, herself, was conscious of the role of confounding factors and, in 1950, wrote that she did not expect to live to see the results of the BCG campaign, which would take five to ten more years to become obvious. In contrast, she sniped: 'Dr Dunlevy of the Dublin Corporation thinks that after one year she has reduced the childhood TB mortality by BCG (I think it was mainly by streptomycin)'.[86]

Separating out the effect of the BCG campaign from other complementary and contemporaneous activities is not possible. In addition to providing direct protection to those vaccinated, BCG had an unquantifiable indirect effect in reducing the amount of infection in the environment, thereby reducing risk to the population. Although the campaign did not vaccinate sufficient numbers in the early years, the cumulative effect of increasing numbers of vaccinations played a role in the ending of the epidemic. In addition to the contribution made by BCG to the ending of the tuberculosis epidemic, Dorothy's tuberculin studies of the 1930s, 1940s and early 1950s were crucial to understanding the changing epidemiology of tuberculosis in

Ireland. These surveys showed that the Irish were not inherently tubercular and that many young rural adults had not been exposed to tuberculosis. The future of many of these adults lay in migration and they were at risk of contracting tuberculosis if they migrated to urban or healthcare settings where tuberculosis disease was commonplace. As well as its usefulness in tracking the epidemiology of tuberculosis, tuberculin was also of use for individual diagnosis of the disease. As pointed out by Dorothy, without the test, the consequences for individual patients were a lack of treatment for the tubercular whose diagnosis had been missed or inappropriate treatment and prolonged bed rest for the non-tubercular who had been mistakenly deemed tubercular.[87]

Dorothy's work on tuberculosis including her research and publications, her work on voluntary national committees and her continuous highlighting of the problem of tuberculosis in Ireland as well as her struggles to introduce tuberculin testing and BCG vaccination, place her among the most active of the Irish medical profession in the first half of the twentieth century, with respect to the disease. Much of the credit for the ending of Ireland's tuberculosis epidemic has been claimed by two of her contemporaries, Dr Noël Browne, Minister for Health (1948–51), and Dr James Deeny, chief medical adviser (1944–50) to the Department of Local Government and Public Health and its successor the Department of Health.[88] Each bitterly disputes the other's version of the genesis and implementation of national policy in the late 1940s and early 1950s. In fact, the ending of the tuberculosis epidemic owes much to the work of many hardworking doctors, including Dorothy Price, Noël Browne, James Deeny, Pat Alston, Robert Collis, Theo Dillon, John Duffy, Mairead Dunlevy, E.J.T. McWeeney, and others not included in this memoir.

———

Dorothy did not live to see the end of the tuberculosis epidemic in Ireland. She had a second stroke on 28 January 1954 and died two days later, without recovering consciousness.[89] Her funeral and the gathering afterwards at 8 Herbert Park were private, allowing the family and close friends to grieve together. Dorothy was buried in St Maelruain's Cemetery in Tallaght, County Dublin. Her life and work were publicly celebrated in obituaries in British and Irish medical journals as well as in national and local newspapers. Harry Counihan, who was first her student and then her colleague on the National BCG Committee, wrote in the *Journal of the Irish Medical Association*:

> Dr Dorothy Price, whose sudden end we all deplore, was a giant in present-day Irish medicine … Her brilliant intellect, matched by her nobility of character, made her remarkable. Travelling in pursuit of knowledge she became intimate with Wallgren, Heimbeck, Pagel and others, who were rapidly advancing knowledge of tuberculosis in the "thirties". As a member of this international aristocracy of talent, her work aimed to satisfy their critical judgement rather than to impress a local audience … Her honesty gave her the capacity to say 'no' in one word, which some found refreshing and others disconcerting. She was above all pettiness and prejudice.[90]

The obituary in *The Irish Times* described her as 'one of Ireland's outstanding authorities in the treatment of tuberculosis and a pioneer of BCG vaccination in these islands'.[91] It also incorrectly named her as one of the founders of St Ultan's Hospital. John Cowell wrote in the *British Medical Journal* that Dorothy's work as consultant physician at St Ultan's earned her an international reputation. He also noted that her book *Tuberculosis in Childhood* was 'a classic in its subject' and enjoyed a 'world-wide circulation'. Dorothy was nominated by the Irish Medical Association as a candidate for the award of the Leon Bernhard Foundation prize given by the WHO for practical achievement in social medicine.

Pathologist Walter Pagel wrote an appreciation in the *Lancet* and the *BMJ* which lauded her pathological achievements:

> She spent many hours in the post-mortem room selecting specimens for investigation. These specimens bespoke her rare gift for the detection of the essential behind the phenomena, and proved to be corner stones in our knowledge of, for example, epituberculosis, congenital tuberculosis, and the early histological changes in primary infection of the human lung (probably the earliest changes so far known).[92]

He added that her deep interest in her subject combined with a 'rare sense of humour' made her visits to London special occasions.

In response to a commemoration of Dorothy written by Mairead Dunlevy, which he felt was overly admiring, James Deeny wrote:

> In association with the national struggle for independence, there emerged a remarkable group of women. They had usually strong Republican sympathies, were generally upper class, well-educated, sometimes well-off, highly-political, knew everybody and were generally beloved. They were endowed with enormous compassion, were self-less, determined and nothing could stop them. They were wonderfully romantic at times, quite irresponsible and played parts in a great number of sectors [this word is partly crossed out] of our national life. The group included well-known people like Madame Maude Gonne McBride right across to devoted unknown women in trade unions, the civil service and religious orders. Dorothy Price was one of these.[93]

The early part of Dorothy's life and her involvement in the War of Independence was mentioned in some of the obituaries. According to the *Irish Press*: 'When the news of her death yesterday reached the scattered members of flying columns which she had once served, Mick Crowley, Florence Begley, the piper of Crossbarry, and Pete Kearney paid tribute to her great services.'[94] Although Dorothy left various short accounts of that time, she did not leave a full witness statement as so many of her compatriots did. In 1947, the Bureau of Military History was established with the ambitious remit to collect witness statements and contemporaneous documents and photographs from participants in the revolutionary period in Ireland from 1913 to 1921. The Bureau collected this material for ten years and was then closed to the public for almost forty-five years. Many of Dorothy's contemporaries and friends, as well as her sister Alice, deposited witness statements.

In the end, the only material in the collection that bears her name are a handful of photographs. These include a Cumann na mBan cyclist corp en route to Bodenstown, where Irish revolutionary, Theobald Wolfe Tone is commemorated. There is a picture which includes Mrs Eamonn

Ceannt, Madeline ffrench Mullen, and Madam Markievicz. A further group of photographs taken by Dorothy captures the aftermath of a raid on 21 Dawson Street by auxiliaries 'F' Coy, on 31 December 1920. Eileen McGrane, captain of the University Branch of Cumann na mBan was living there at the time.[95] A note on the envelope containing the photographs states that Dorothy had intended the photographs to be attached to her statement which she 'was resolved to give' but could not on account of her health.[96] Dorothy's sister, Alice, provided the Bureau with a statement in 1955. Many of Dorothy's friends – including Dorothy Macardle, Denis Lordan and Michael Crowley – also gave statements. Dorothy is mentioned, in a number of statements, as a member of Cumann na mBan or as tending to the wounded in Dublin and Cork.

A practical memorial to Dorothy was raised in 1955 in St Ultan's Hospital. Donations from her brother, Robert, and her sister, Alice, provided sun blinds for the BCG balcony. St Ultan's also put up a bronze plaque in her memory.[97] This is now stored in the St Ultan's Archive in the Heritage Centre of the Royal College of Physicians of Ireland. Dorothy's niece, Mary, continued Dorothy's interest in the Children's Sunshine Home, in Stillorgan, and served as a Board member there from the mid-1950s through to the early 1970s. The family connections continued when Mary's daughter, Sandra, took her son, David, to St Ultan's in 1975 for vaccination by Pat Alston.

After Dorothy died, Liam remained close to her family. According to Sandra Lefroy, 'many people remember Liam as austere but after Dorothy died he used to come to us for Sunday lunch and always brought ice cream (which would often have melted en route)'. Liam continued to fight Dorothy's battles, championing the work of the National BCG Committee when its existence was threatened.[98] He also wrote to her many correspondents asking for copies of her letters in order to document her life's work. He compiled a comprehensive, and sometimes charmingly biased, memoir which was published in 1957 by Oxford University Press for private circulation only. The first ten pages were written by Dorothy so she clearly intended to write an autobiography. The response to the book was poignant. Walter Pagel wrote to Liam 'under the fresh impression – or rather impact of the memoir which we received this morning'. He continued: 'And what a wealth of personal remembrances! Could we ever forget the stately room at 10, Fitzwilliam Place and the gathering there of your and her friends;

this wonderful atmosphere of friendship and understanding – so different from the usual cold professional meetings.'[99] He also joked about when Dorothy patiently bore with his eternal search for lost luggage. Walter regretted that the book was for private consumption as Dorothy's struggle was insufficiently documented in medical history. However, he understood that it might re-animate old feuds.

Norah Lawrence, a cousin of Dorothy's, wrote to Liam that it still 'came as a revelation' to her what an important person Dorothy was and what great work she did. 'She was always so very modest about herself. Took her work seriously but never herself!' She remembered that Dorothy, even as a young girl:

> shewed [sic] great character, and the quality of going through with anything she believed to be right, at whatever cost to herself. I can so well remember her standing up for Mrs Green [Aunt Alice] to my grandmother, who had been running her down, one day at Formosa [Berkshire, home of the Young family], forgetting I think that Dorothy was there. As grandmother was a person to whom few dared to stand up, it took real courage in a niece of 17.

Norah added that she was filled with mingled admiration and fear of the consequence, 'being far too much of a coward to back Dodo up! To grandmothers' credit it must be said, though I think she was annoyed, she did underneath respect Dorothy all the more for it'.[100]

A long-standing family friend, Kathleen (Katz) Brabazon, who had spent four months in Alice's house looking after Penny and Sandra when 'Granny Alice' was ill (allowing Mary to return to her husband Jim in Nigeria), wrote to Liam: 'I think the most wonderful thing about her was her lack of bitterness. She faced all her disability with such courage. I am so glad I had those months living opposite you.'[101] Robert Barton told Liam that the book was a

> living tribute to you both. Not only does it put on record the sacrifice of self that Dorothy made for her ideal, her ability, initiative and application but the whole story is enshrined in the atmosphere of affection that you had for her and she for

you. It is obvious that you consulted together or you could not have written so intimately of her struggle, disappointments and final success ... you are wise however to limit circulation for it might arouse controversy.[102]

In 2008, Harry Counihan, by this time a retired luminary of the Irish medical world and former chairman of the Richmond Hospital, Dublin,[103] was anxious that Dorothy's work should not be forgotten. His summation of the Prices is a fitting end to a shared journey: 'Liam was 'a scholar as well as a judge and a great husband', while Dorothy 'was a marvellous person and a great fighter'.[104]

He told the author:

As a doctor, she was very good, with a very analytical turn of mind. Her greatest characteristic was her single-mindedness. She was a very strong character. If she had any objective, she pursued it and tried to get her way one way or another ... Dorothy Price was a great person – for her day she was really outstanding among the women doctors in her single-mindedness and her determination to get the job done and to understand what was going on. Her book was quite good for its time. She was very, very particular about patients. She knew every detail of her personal patients. She was very thorough. She was a revelation to me. Most of the people I knew practicing medicine hadn't the same fire about it or the determination either. I feel Dorothy Price was exceptional. She was not really trained to be a researcher and academic. She did it all on her own.[105]

━ ·······.·······.·······━

This biography has attempted to knit together some of the rich material that made up Dorothy Stopford Price's life. The collections of letters and papers in archives and libraries as well as the memories of those who knew her have provided the stuff of an extraordinary story. However, many unanswered questions remain. There are teasing gaps in correspondence and diaries and the chronology is sometimes unclear as letters were often dated by the day and month with no year provided. It has been an absorbing pursuit: some stitches may have been dropped and some patches of material inserted incorrectly. Nonetheless, it is hoped that the reader will excuse any errors – which are solely the responsibility of the author! – and focus, instead, on the determination that brought Dorothy from her Victorian childhood into the heart of Ireland's struggle for independence and, thence, to her medical career where she became a childhood tuberculosis expert and one of the key figures in the ending of Ireland's tuberculosis epidemic.

## NOTES

1. L. Price, *Dorothy Price. An Account of Twenty Years' Fight against Tuberculosis in Ireland* (Oxford: Oxford University Press, 1957), p.116. For private circulation only.

2. J. Robins, *Custom House People* (Dublin: Institute of Public Administration, 1993), p.137; Internal memos, 15 March 1949 to 22 April 1949 (NAI, Dept. Health, D113/19); Kathleen Lynn diaries, 25 April 1949 (RCPI, KL/1/3).

3. D. Price to A. Wallgren, draft letter, 18 May 1949 (TCD, Price papers, MS 7538(269)).

4. D. Price to A. Wallgren, 18 May 1949 (NLI, MS 15341(11)).

5. Review and digest of selected publications by Price (TCD, Price papers, MS 7537(263)).

6. D. Price to A. Wallgren, 18 May 1949 (NLI MS 15341 (11)).

7. Browne to Price, 10 June 1949 (TCD, Price papers, MS 7538(282)); Draft memo of agreement between St Ultan's Hospital and members of the National BCG Committee (TCD, Price papers, MS 7538(345)); *National BCG Committee Report for the Year ended 31 December 1974* (RCPI, SU/2/25), p.4; Interview with H.E. Counihan, 9 June 2008; Price to Browne, 13 May 1949 (TCD, Price papers, MS 7538 (261)). Price suggested that the committee should comprise Kathleen Lynn 'to sign cheques', Morgan Crowe, E.J.T. McWeeney, Henry E. Counihan and Professor Robert A.Q. O'Meara. Browne added the following doctors to Price's proposed committee: Joseph Logan, medical superintendent at Peamount Sanatorium, Mairead Dunlevy, assistant City MOH of Dublin County Borough and Edmond T. Freeman, visiting physician to the Mater Hospital, Dublin.

8. Minutes of National BCG Committee meeting, 4 July 1949 (TCD, Price papers, MS 7539(121)).

9. D. Price, *BCG scheme for St Ultan's* (TCD, Price papers, MS 7538(252)).

10. Dáil Debates, vol. 116, 11, col. 1796-7, 1 July 1949. The number of deaths from all forms of tuberculosis was 3,017, a decrease of 683 on the preceding year. There were 1,233 deaths from diarrhoea and enteritis in infants under two in 1943. This had fallen to 1,092 in 1945

and 340 in 1948. The numbers of deaths from diphtheria, whooping cough and measles had also declined significantly. For the fourth successive year, no death from typhus occurred.

11. Dr Noël Browne's speech, copy, 20 June 1949 (NLI Accession 6436, Cowell papers, MS 41653).

12. Department of Health to An Runaí (secretary), Teach Ultain (St Ultan's Hospital), D.O.H. Ref P.H.35/213D, 24 June 1949 (TCD, Price papers, MS 7538(296)).

13. Letter on Browne's behalf to the secretary, Teach Ultain (St. Ultan's Hospital), Ref P.H. 35/312D, 16 May 1949 (NAI, Dept. Health, D series); Price, notes, 16 July 1949 (TCD, Price papers, MS 7538(300)).

14. Price, notes, 16 July 1949 (TCD, Price papers, MS 7538(300)).

15. Price, notes, TCD, Price papers, MS 7538(308)).

16. D. Price to H.P. Coll, Department of Health, 12 August 1949 (TCD, Price papers, MS 7538(318)).

17. W. Doolin, 'Editorial', *JMAÉ*, 25, 145 (1949), pp.1–2; Price, *Dorothy Price*, p.122.

18. E.J.T. McWeeney to the Chief Medical adviser, memo, 1 September 1949 (NAI, Dept. Health, D113/6).

19. Deeny and Mc Weeney, series of memos and notes, July 1949, as well as a draft response to the *JMAÉ* (NAI, Dept. Health, D113/6).

20. Price and Bigger correspondence with respect to BCG for medical students in TCD (TCD, Price papers, MS 7538(333-8)).

21. M. Dunlevy, 'Vagaries of BCG-Induced Tuberculin Allergy', *Postgraduate Medical Journal* 40 (1964), pp.81–3.

22. Minutes, National BCG Committee meeting, 3 November 1949 (TCD, Price papers, MS 7539(137)).

23. D. Price to A. Wallgren, draft letter, 12 December 1950 (TCD, Price papers, MS 7539(101)).

24. Minutes, National BCG Committee meeting, 15 September 1949 (TCD, Price papers, MS 7539(130)); Price, notes (TCD, Price papers, MS 7538(385)).

25. Minutes, National BCG Committee meeting, 10 November 1949 (TCD, Price papers, MS 7539(139)).

26. Price, notes, 28 November 1949 (TCD, Price papers, MS 7538(428)).

27. Minutes, National BCG Committee meeting, 10 November 1949 (TCD, Price papers, MS 7539(139)).

28. L. Price, *Dorothy Price. An Account of Twenty Years' Fight against Tuberculosis in Ireland* (Oxford: Oxford University Press, 1957), p.116. For private circulation only.

29.  Price, *Dorothy Price*, p.126.

30.  D. Price to A. Wallgren, draft letter, 25 November 1949 (TCD, Price papers, MS 7538(397)).

31.  Minutes, National BCG Committee meeting, 15 December1949 (TCD, Price papers, MS 7538(141)).

32.  D. Price, notes (TCD, Price papers, MS 7538(426)); Price, strategy notes (TCD, Price papers, MS 7538(427)).

33.  *National BCG Committee Report July 1949 – December 1950* (RCPI, SU/2/1), p.2.

34.  D. Price to J. Cowell, 24 December 1949 (TCD, Price papers, MS 7538(417)).

35.  D. Price to A. Wallgren, 2 September 1949 (TCD, Price papers, MS 7538(323)).

36.  D. Price to A. Wallgren, 2 September 1949 (TCD, Price papers, MS 7538(323)).

37.  Draft programme for National BCG Committee (TCD, Price papers, MS 7538(346)).

38.  Minutes, National BCG Committee meeting, 1 September 1949 (TCD, Price papers, MS 7539(128)).

39.  *National BCG Committee Report July 1949 – December 1950* (RCPI, SU/2/1), p.4.

40.  Ibid.

41.  Ibid.

42.  G. [Signature indecipherable ?Blennerhasset] to Price, 11 February1951 (TCD, Price papers, MS7539(238)).

43.  J. Cowell to D. Price, 19 October 1949 (TCD, Price papers, MS 7538(381)); Price, *Dorothy Price*, pp.130–1.

44.  J. Cowell to D. Price, 19 October 1949 (TCD, Price papers, MS 7538(382)).

45.  B. Chisholm, director general, WHO, Geneva, to Price, 20 February 1949 (TCD, Price papers, MS 7539(2/7)).

46.  D. Price to J.B. McDougall, tuberculosis section, WHO, 17 September 1949 (TCD, Price papers, MS 7539(14)).

47.  N. Browne to D. Price, 28 December 1949 (TCD, Price papers, MS 7539(21)).

48.  Price, *Dorothy Price*, p.137.

49.  D. Price to N. Browne, 20 January 1950 (TCD, Price papers, MS 7539(41/1/2)).

50.  D. Price to J.B. McDougall, WHO, 6 February 1951 (TCD, Price papers, MS 7539(236)).

51.  N. Browne to D. Price, 10 February 1950 (TCD, Price papers, MS 7539(33)); Minutes, National BCG Committee Meeting, 2 March 1950 (TCD, Price papers, MS 7539(144)).

52.  D. Price to A. Wallgren, 2 April 1950 (NLI, MS 15341(11)).

53. J. Horgan, *Noël Browne: Passionate Outsider* (Dublin: Gill & Macmillan, 2000), pp.110–43.

54. N. Browne to D. Price, May 1950 (TCD, Price papers, MS 7539(52)); Price to Wallgren, draft letter, June 1951 (TCD, Price papers, MS 7539(252)).

55. D. Price to A. Wallgren, 2 March 1950 (NLI MS 15341 (11)).

56. D. Price to A. Wallgren, 2 April 1950 (NLI MS 15341 (11)).

57. St Ultan's Hospital to D. Price, letter (TCD, Price papers, MS 7539 (299)); D. Price to St Ultan's Hospital, draft letter, 30 April 1952 (TCD, Price papers, MS 7539(300)).'

58. Minutes, National BCG Committee meeting, 2 March 1950 (TCD, Price papers, MS 7539(144)).

59. Draft appointment letter, 9 August 1949 (TCD, Price papers, MS 7538(316)); Correspondence D. Price and J. Cowell (TCD, Price papers, MS 7539(53/67/71/72/74/75/103)).

60. D. Price to J. Cowell, 24 December 1949 (TCD, Price papers, MS 7538(417)).

61. Interview with H.E. Counihan, 9 June 2008.

62. Thomson was assistant director of the International Tuberculosis Campaign in Copenhagen.

63. Minutes, National BCG Committee meeting, 20 October 1949 (TCD, Price papers, MS 7539(135)).

64. Thomson report, July 1950 (NAI, Dept. Health, D113/21).

65. H. B. M. Murphy, 'BCG Vaccination', Correspondence, *BMJ* 2, 4566 (1948), p.106.

66. N. Browne to K. Winge, 12 December 1950 (NAI, Dept. Health, D34A/108); Reports of Department of Health Conferences, 4 and 6 April 1951 (NAI, Dept. Health, D34A/108).

67. Memo, August 1950 (NAI, Dept. Health, D113/21).

68. J. Deeny, *To Cure and to Care: Memoirs of a Chief Medical Officer* (Dun Laoghaire: Glendale Press, 1989), pp.171–3; Interview with M. McWeeney (E.J.T. McWeeney's daughter), 2008; T.W.T. McWeeney to D. Price, 10 June 1950 (TCD, Price papers, MS 7538(54)).

69. Robins, *Custom House People*, p.167.

70. D. Price to A. Wallgren, 22 October 1950 (NLI MS 15341 (11)).

71. D. Price to A. Wallgren, 12 December 1950 (NLI MS 15341 (11)).

72. D. Price to A. Wallgren, 24 July 1952 (NLI MS 15341 (11)).

73. D. Price, 'A Tuberculin Survey in Ireland', *IJMS* 6, 314 (1952), p.85.

74. B.F. Scallan, 'Tuberculin Allergy', *JIMA*, 28, 165 (1951), pp.49–50; M.P. Flynn, 'A Tuberculin Survey in County Offaly', *JIMA*, 31, 185 (1952), pp.312–20.

75. Price, 'A Tuberculin Survey', p.89.

76.  J.St.P. Cowell, 'Experiences in the National BCG Scheme', *IJMS*, 6, 320 (1952), p.362.

77.  D. Price, 'Analysis of 140,697 BCG Vaccinations', *IJMS*, 6, 338 (1954), pp.56–64.

78.  R.A.Q. O'Meara to Price, 2 December 1953 (TCD, Price papers, MS 7539(374)).

79.  HPSC, *Tuberculosis Guidelines 2010* (Dublin: HPSC, 2010), p.88; WHO, *Tuberculosis* (Geneva: WHO, 1993), appendix 2, p.3.

80.  Murphy, 'BCG Vaccination', p.106.

81.  Leading article, *The Lancet* 264, 6844 (1954), pp.903–4.

82.  J. Deeny, *Report of the National Tuberculosis Survey, 1950–53* (Dublin: Medical Research Council, 1954), p.254.

83.  Vaccination was not compulsory under the Health Act 1947 which came into operation on 1 April 1948.

84.  Minutes, National BCG Committee meeting, 10 April 1951 (TCD, Price papers, MS 7539(172)).

85.  See A. Mac Lellan, That 'Preventable and Curable Disease': Dr Dorothy Price and the Eradication of Tuberculosis in Ireland, 1930-1960 (UCD, 2011, unpublished thesis).

86.  Price to Heaf, copy of letter, 22 June 1950 (TCD, Price papers, MS 7539(58)).

87.  D. Price, *Tuberculosis in Childhood* (Bristol: Wrights, 1948, 2nd ed.), p.v.

88.  See, for instance, N. Browne, *Against the Tide* (Dublin: Gill & Macmillan, 1986); Noël Browne, 'Church and State in Modern Ireland', *Queen's Politics Occasional Paper*, 4 (Belfast, 1991); Deeny, *To Cure and to Care*; J. Deeny, 'Towards Balancing a Distorted Record', *IMJ* 80, no. 8 (1987), pp.22–5; J. Deeny, *The End of an Epidemic. Essays in Irish Public Health 1935–65* (Dublin, 1995); 'Medics, Mitres and Ministers', Radharc documentary, 18 December 1991, Ref. 312.

89.  Price, *Dorothy Price*, p.149.

90.  H.E. Counihan, 'Dr Dorothy Stopford Price', *JIMA*. 34, 201 (1954), pp.72, 84.

91.  *The Irish Times*, 1 February 1954.

92.  W. Pagel, Dr Dorothy Stopford Price, *BMJ* 1, 4866 (1954), p.882.

93.  J. Deeny, undated notes (RCSI, Deeny papers); also cited in G. Jones, *'Captain of all these Men of Death': The History of Tuberculosis in Nineteenth- and Twentieth-Century Ireland* (Amsterdam and New York: Editions Rodopi, 2001), p.145.

94.  *Irish Press*, 2 February 1954.

95.  E. McCarville, witness statement (Bureau of Military History (BMH), witness statement 1752).

96.  J. Kissane collection (BMH, Contemporary Documents 266/7/1-2).

97.  M.Gilmartin, secretary, St Ultan's Hospital to L. Price, 11 January 1955 (NLI, MS 15342).

98.  L. Price to J. Costello [Taoiseach], copy of letter, 9 June 1954 (NLI, MS 15342). He asked that the work of the National BCG Committee should not be curtailed with vaccinations done by the local authorities. He reiterated Dorothy's belief that 'the work of vaccination would be very quickly reduced to very small proportions on account of the great number of other duties which medical officers of health and their assistants have to perform: she considered that there might be a risk of undesirable reactions which would bring this work into disrepute if persons not specially trained carried it out; she thought it unlikely that any but a central authority would keep the records which she considered an essential part of the work.'

99.  W. Pagel to L. Price, 11 February 1957 (NLI, MS 15342).

100.  N. Lawrence to L. Price, 22 March 1957 (NLI, MS 15342).

101.  K. Brabazon to L. Price, 3 April 1957 (NLI, MS 15342).

102.  R. Barton to L. Price, 22 April 1957 (NLI, MS 15342).

103.  *Irish Independent*, 2 August 2009. An appreciation of Harry Counihan, who died aged 91 years.

104.  H.E. Counihan to A. Mac Lellan, letter, 19 May 2008.

105.  Interview, H.E. Counihan, 2008.

# DOROTHY PRICE PUBLICATIONS

## BOOKS

Price, D. *Tuberculosis in Childhood* (Bristol, 1942). 1st edition.

Price, D. *Tuberculosis in Childhood* (Bristol, 1948). 2nd edition.

## MEDICAL JOURNALS

Price, D. 'Autogenous Vaccines in Intestinal Infections of Infants', *IJMS*, 6, 2 (1930), pp.59–64.

Stopford Price, D. 'The Feeding of Young Infants in Gastro-Enteritis', *Medical Press and Circular*, 183, 27 (1931), pp.512–4.

Price, Dorothy. 'Report of a Case of Amyoplasia Congenital with Pathological Report', *Archives of Diseases of Children*, 8 (1933), pp.343–54.

Price, Dorothy. 'A Report on Tuberculin Skin tests in Children', *IJMS*, 6, 103 (1934), pp.302–4.

Price, Dorothy. 'Primary Tuberculosis of the Lungs in Children', *IJMS*, 6, 110 (1935), pp.54–75.

Price, Dorothy. 'Mediastinal Gland Tuberculosis in Young Children', *IJMS*, 6, 125 (1936), pp.200–9.

Price, Dorothy. 'A Case of Congenital Tuberculosis', *British Journal of Tuberculosis*, 31, 4 (1937), pp.264–70.

Price, Dorothy. 'Hospital Treatment for Tuberculous Children', *JIF-SMU*, 3, 14 (1938), p.23.

Price, Dorothy. 'Tuberculosis in Infants', *BMJ*, 1, 4022 (1938), pp.275–7.

Price, Dorothy. 'Tuberculosis in Adolescents', *IJMS*, 6, 159 (1939), pp.124–9.

Price, Dorothy. 'Note on the Tuberculous Phlycten', *IJMS*, 6, 175 (1940), pp.327–30.

Price, Dorothy. 'Report of a Tuberculin Survey amongst Children in Dublin Hospitals made by the Irish Paediatric Association', *IJMS*, 6, 187 (1941), pp.241–55.

Price, Dorothy, 'The Prevention of Tuberculosis in Infancy', *IJMS*, 6, 199 (1942), pp.252–5.

Price, Dorothy, and McManus, Adeline. 'A Report on the Investigation into Phylctenular Opthalmia', *IJMS*, 6, 215 (1943), pp.603–12.

Pagel, W., and Price, D.S. 'An Early Primary Tuberculous Pulmonary Focus about Four to Eight Weeks Old', *American Review of Tuberculosis*, 6, 47 (1943), p.614.

Price, Dorothy. 'The Role of B.C.G. Vaccination in the Prevention of Tuberculosis', *IJMS*, 6, 221 (1944), pp.147–56.

Price, Dorothy. 'Precautions taken against Tuberculosis in an Irish School', *IJMS*, 6, 232 (1945), pp.128–30.

Price, Dorothy. 'Tuberculosis in Infancy', *Irish Medical Directory and Hospital Yearbook*, no. 8 (1945), pp.43–7.

Price, Dorothy. 'Erythema Nodosum', *JMAÉ*, 17, 101 (1945), pp.150–1.

Price, D., Alston P., and Murphy K. 'The Dublin Moro Tuberculin Test', *JMAÉ*, 18, 105 (1946), pp.40–1.

Price, Dorothy. 'Is B.C.G. Vaccination a Practical Proposition in Éire?', *IJMS*, 6, 252 (1946), pp.779–86.

Price Stopford, Dorothy. 'The prognosis of Primary Tuberculosis of the Lung', *Tubercle*, 28, 2 (1947), pp.27–31.

Price Stopford D. and Alston, Patricia. 'Method of B.C.G. Vaccination Employed in St Ultan's Hospital', *IJMS*, 6, 264 (1947), pp.711–6.

Price Stopford, Dorothy. 'The Need for B.C.G. Vaccination in Infants', *Tubercle*, 30, 1 (1949), pp.11–13.

Price, Dorothy, and Alston, Patricia. 'Report on B.C.G. Vaccination in St Ultan's Hospital', *IJMS*, 6, 283 (1952), pp.330–1.

Price, Dorothy. 'A Tuberculin Survey in Ireland', *IJMS*, 6, 314 (1952), pp.85–91.

Price, Dorothy, 'Analysis of 140,697 B.C.G. Vaccinations', *IJMS*, 6, 338 (1954), pp.56–64.

## NEWSPAPER ARTICLE
Price, Dorothy, 'Tuberculosis and B.C.G. Vaccination', *The Irish Times*, 8 July 1952.

## CLINICAL POSTS
Physician, St Ultan's Hospital, Dublin.
Clinical assistant (children), Royal City of Dublin Hospital.
Consultant physician, National Hospital for Consumption, Ireland.
Consultant physician, Sunshine Home, Stillorgan.
Medical officer, Coláiste Moibhí, Dublin.

## DOROTHY PRICE OBITUARIES
*IJMS*, 6, 338 (1954), p.95.
*JIMA*, 34, 201 (1954), p.72, p.84.
*BMJ*, 1, 4861 (1954), pp.589-90.
Pagel, Walter. 'Appreciation', *BMJ*, 1, 4866 (1954), p.882.
*The Lancet*, 263, 6811 (1954), pp.578–9.
*The Irish Times*, 1 Feb. 1954.
*Irish Press*, 2 Feb. 1954.
*Irish Independent*, 1 Feb. 1954.

## COMMEMORATION
The Dorothy Price medal, awarded annually by NUI Maynooth for post-graduate achievement in immunology.

Dorothy Stopford Price seminar room, TCD medical centre, St James's Hospital, Dublin.

Voted fifth in 'greatest Irish scientist poll', 2010, Science.ie.

Winner of Ireland's Greatest Woman Inventor Competition, 2013 (Voting open to 12–18-year-olds in the Republic of Ireland). http://www.siliconrepublic.com/innovation/item/34187--wit2013/

Dorothy Price plaque, Commissioned 2011, to be placed at Charlemont Clinic (formerly St Ultan's Hospital), Dublin, by the National Science and Engineering Plaques Committee.

# Archival Sources

**Dublin Diocesan Archives**
McQuaid papers
Lea Wilson papers

**Trinity College Dublin Manuscripts**
Elinor Dorothy Price neé Stopford papers

**National Library of Ireland**
Dorothy Price papers
John Cowell papers
Crowley family papers
Rosamond Jacob diaries (Dorothy Price references collated by Dr Clara Cullen, UCD)
Edie Stopford papers
Robert Stopford papers
Liam Price photograph albums

**National Archives of Ireland**
Department of the Taoiseach, S series
Department of Health, D series
Correspondence files of Department of Local Government and Health 1920–1953 including treatment of T.B.
T.B. Section Dublin Corporation 1945–55

**Royal College of Physicians of Ireland, Heritage Centre**
St Ultan's Hospital papers

Kirkpatrick collection
BCG Committee annual reports

**Royal College of Surgeons of Ireland**
James Deeny papers

**Wellcome Trust Archives, London**
The Ring Irish College Case, 1931–1939

**Irish Red Cross Archives, Dublin**
Minute Books of the Anti-Tuberculosis section, 1943–56
Minute Books of the Sub-Committee on selection (for Ballyroan), 1943–56
Minute Books of the Survey Sub-Committee, 1943–56

**Irish Military Archives**
Bureau of Military History: Contemporary Document Collection (1913–1920)
Bureau of Military History: Witness Statements
Bureau of Military History: Prisoner Table

**Bodleian Library, Oxford**
Sir Matthew Nathan papers

## JOURNALS AND NEWSPAPERS
*American Review of Tuberculosis*
*Annals of Surgery*
*Archives of Diseases of Children*
*Boston Medical and Surgical Journal*
*British Journal of Tuberculosis*
*British Medical Journal (BMJ)*
*Canadian Journal of Comparative Medicine*
*Cork Examiner*
*Dublin Journal of Medical Science (DJMS)*
*Irish Hospital Yearbook and Medical Directory*
*Irish Journal of Medical Science (IJMS)*
*Journal of the Irish Free State Medical Union (JIFSMU)*
*Journal of the Medical Association of Éire (JMAÉ )*

*Journal of the Irish Medical Association (JIMA)*
*Irish Independent*
*Irish Medical Journal (IMJ)*
*Irish Press*
*Irish Nursing World*
*Irish Red Cross Monthly Bulletin*
*The Irish Times*
*Journal of the Statistical and Social Inquiry Society of Ireland*
*Journal of the Royal Sanitary Institute*
*Journal of the Royal Institute of Public Health*
*The International Journal of Tuberculosis and Lung Disease*
*The Lancet*
*The Medical Press and Circular*
*Studies: An Irish Quarterly Review*
*Tubercle*
*Transactions of British National Association for the Prevention of Tuberculosis (NAPT)*
*Ulster Medical Journal (UMJ)*

## INTERVIEWS

Dr H.E. Counihan, Dublin. June 2008 (now deceased). Former member, National Consultative Council on Tuberculosis and National BCG Committee.

Sandra Lefroy, Killaloe, County Clare. September 2008 – June 2009–2013; ongoing communication. Great-niece of Dorothy Price.

Dr Barbara Stokes, Dublin. May 2008 (now deceased). Former member of staff, St. Ultan's Hospital.

Gillian Leonard, Dublin. November 2008. Daughter of a friend of Dorothy Price.

Dr Pauline O'Connor, Dublin. October 2009. Former member of staff, St. Ultan's Hospital.

## UNPUBLISHED THESES

Alston, Patricia., 'Primary Tuberculosis of the Lung in Childhood', MD thesis. UCD, 1944.

Fanning, P.R., 'Dissertation on the Diagnosis of Early Pulmonary Tuberculosis', MD thesis. UCD, 1936.

Price, Dorothy., 'The Diagnosis of Primary Tuberculosis of the Lungs in

Children', MD thesis. TCD, 1934.

Mac Lellan, A., 'That "Preventable and Curable Disease": Dr Dorothy Price and the Eradication of Tuberculosis in Ireland, 1930–1960'. Ph.D thesis. UCD, 2011.


## SECONDARY SOURCES

Atkins, P.J., 'Lobbying and Resistance with regard to Policy on Bovine Tuberculosis in Britain, 1900–39: an Inside/Outside Model', in L. Bryder, F. Condrau and M. Worboys (eds), *Tuberculosis Then and Now. Perspectives on the History of an Infectious Disease* (Montreal: McGill-Queen's University Press, 2010), pp.189–212.

Barrington, B., 'Introduction', in J. Deeny (ed.), *The End of an Epidemic: Essays in Irish Public Health 1935–65* (Dublin: Farmar, 1995), pp.1–7.

Barrington, R., *Health, Medicine and Politics in Ireland 1900–1970* (Dublin: Institute of Public Administration, 1987).

Barry, T., *Guerilla Days in Ireland* (Dublin: Irish Press, 1949).

Beiner, G., Marsh, P. and Milne, I., 'Greatest Killer of the Twentieth Century: the Great Flu in 1918-19', *History Ireland* (March-April 2009), pp.40–3.

Brock, T.D., *Robert Koch. A Life in Medicine and Bacteriology* (Washington: ASM Press, 1999).

Browne, N., *Against the Tide* (Dublin: Gill & Macmillan, 1986).

Browne, O'D., *The Rotunda Hospital 1745–1945* (Edinburgh: E. & S. Livingstone, 1947).

Bryder, L., *Below the Magic Mountain. A Social History of Tuberculosis in Twentieth-Century Britain* (Oxford: Oxford University Press, 1988).

Bryder, L., Condrau F. and Worboys, M., 'Tuberculosis and its Histories: Then and Now', in F. Condrau and M. Worboys (eds), *Tuberculosis Then and Now. Perspectives on the History of an Infectious Disease* (Montreal, Kingston, London and Ithica: MacGill-Queen's University Press, 2010), pp.3–23.

Ceannt, A., *The Story of the Irish White Cross 1920–1947* (Dublin: At the Sign of the Three Candles, 1948).

Clear, C., *Women of the House. Women's Household Work in Ireland 1926–1961* (Dublin: Irish Academic Press, 2000).

Coakley, D., *Baggot Street: a Short History of the Royal City of Dublin Hospital* (Dublin: Board of Governors, Royal City of Dublin Hospital, 1995).

Coleman, M., *The Irish Sweep: A History of the Irish Hospital Sweepstake*

*1930–87* (Dublin: UCD Press, 2009).

Collis, R., *Marrowbone Lane* (Dublin: Runa Press, 1943).

Collis, W.R.F., *The State of Medicine in Ireland* (Dublin: Parkside Press, 1943).

Cooney, J., *John Charles McQuaid: Ruler of Catholic Ireland* (Dublin: O'Brien Press, 1999).

Corlett, C. and Weaver, M. (eds), *The Price Notebooks* (Dublin: Dúchas, 2002).

Cox, C. and Marland, H. (eds), *Migration, Health and Ethnicity in the Modern World* (Houndmills: Palgrave Macmillan, forthcoming 2014).

Cullen, C. (ed.), *The World Upturning: Elsie Henry's Irish Wartime Diaries, 1913–1919* (Dublin: Irish Academic Press, 2013).

Cullen, C. and Ó hÓgarthaigh, M. (eds), *His Grace is Displeased: Selected Correspondence of John Charles McQuaid* (Dublin: Irish Academic Press, 2012).

Daly, M.E., *Industrial Development and the Irish National Identity 1922–1939* (Syracuse: Syracuse University Press, 1992).

Daly, M.E., '"An Atmosphere of Sturdy Independence". The State and Dublin Hospitals in the 1930s', in G. Jones and E. Malcolm (eds), *Medicine, Disease and the State in Ireland, 1650–1940* (Cork: Cork University Press, 1999), pp.234–52.

Deeny, J., *Report of the National Tuberculosis Survey, 1950–53* (Dublin: Medical Research Council, 1954).

Deeny, J., *To Cure and to Care: Memoirs of a Chief Medical Officer* (Dun Laoghaire: Glendale Press, 1989).

Dormandy, T., *The White Death: A History of Tuberculosis* (London: the Hambledon Press, 1999).

Dubos J. and Dubos, R., *The White Plague: Tuberculosis, Man and Society* (Boston: Little, Brown, 1952).

Earner-Byrne, L., 'Managing Motherhood. Negotiating a Maternity Service for Catholic Mothers in Dublin 1930–1954', *Social History of Medicine*, 19, 2 (2006), pp.261–77.

Feeney, T., *Seán MacEntee. A Political Life* (Dublin: Irish Academic Press, 2009).

Feldberg, G.D., *Disease and Class. Tuberculosis and the Shaping of Modern North American Society* (New Brunswick: Rutgers University Press, 1995).

Ferriter, D., *The Transformation of Ireland 1900–2000* (Dublin: Profile Books, 2004).

Ferriter, D., *Occasions of Sin: Sex & Society in Modern Ireland* (London: Profile Books, 2009).

Ferriter, D., 'Sex and the Archbishop: John Charles McQuaid and Social Change in 1960s Ireland', in T. E. Hachey (ed.), *Turning Points in Twentieth-Century Irish History* (Dublin: Irish Academic Press, 2011).

Figgis, D., *AE (George W. Russell): a Study of a Man and a Nation* (New York: Dodd, Meade and Company, 1916).

Fleetwood, J.F., *The History of Medicine in Ireland* (Dublin: Skellig Press, 1983).

Foley C., *The Last Irish Plague: the Great Flu Epidemic in Ireland 1918–1919* (Dublin: Irish Academic Press, 2011).

Garvin, T., *Preventing the Future. Why was Ireland so Poor for so Long?* (Dublin: Gill & Macmillan, 2004).

Gatenby, P., *The School of Physic, Trinity College Dublin: A Retrospective View* (Dublin: Trinity College, 1994).

Girvin, B., *The Emergency: Neutral Ireland 1939–45* (London: Pan Macmillan, 2006).

Gray, T., *The Lost Years. The Emergency in Ireland 1939–45* (London: Warner Futura, 1997).

Hart, P., *The IRA & its Enemies: Violence and Community in Cork 1916–1923* (Oxford: Oxford University Press: 1999).

Hedgecoe, A., 'A Form of Practical Machinery: the Origins of Research Ethics Committees in the U.K., 1967-1972', *Medical History*, 53, 3 (2009), pp.331–50.

Hopkinson, M., *The Irish War of Independence* (Dublin: Gill & Macmillan, 2004).

Horgan, J., *Noël Browne: Passionate Outsider* (Dublin: Gill & Macmillan, 2000), pp.35–7.

Huntford, R., *Shackleton* (London: Hodder & Stoughton, 1996).

Jackson, A., *Ireland: 1798–1998: Politics and War* (Oxford: Blackwell, 1999).

Jones, G., *'Captain of all these Men of Death'. The History of Tuberculosis in Nineteenth- and Twentieth-Century Ireland* (Amsterdam and New York: Editions Rodopi, 2001).

Jones, G., 'The Rockefeller Foundation and Medical Education in Ireland in the 1920s', *IHS*, 30, 120 (1997), pp.564–80.

Jones, V., *A Gaelic Experiment: the Preparatory System 1926–1961 and Coláiste*

*Moíbhí* (Dublin: Woodfield Press, 2006).

Kannel, W.B. and Levy, D., 'Commentary: Medical Aspects of the Framingham Community Health and Tuberculosis Demonstration', *International Journal of Epidemiology*, 34, 6 (2005), pp.1187–8.

Kayne, G., Pagel, W. and O'Shaughnessy, L. (eds), *Pulmonary Tuberculosis: Pathology, Diagnosis, Management and Prevention* (Oxford: Oxford University Press, 1939).

Keane, M., *Ishbel. Lady Aberdeen in Ireland* (Newtownards: Colourpoint Books, 1999).

Kelly, L., 'Rickets and Irish Children: Dr Ella Webb and the Early Work of the Children's Sunshine Home, 1925–1946', in A. Mac Lellan and A. Mauger (eds), *Growing Pains: Childhood Illness in Ireland, 1750–1950* (Dublin: Irish Academic Press, 2013).

Kelly, L., *Irish Women in Medicine, c.1880s–1920s: Origins, Education and Careers* (Manchester: Manchester University Press, 2013).

Kennedy, F., 'The Suppression of the Carrigan Report: a Historical Perspective on Child Abuse', *Studies*, 89, 356 (Winter 2000), pp.354–63.

Keogh, D., *Jews in Twentieth-Century Ireland: Refugees, Anti-Semitism and the Holocaust* (Cork: Cork University Press, 1998).

Kirkpatrick, T.P.C. and Jellet, H., *The Book of the Rotunda Hospital: an Illustrated History of the Dublin Lying In Hospital* (London: Adlard and Son, Bartholomew Press, 1913).

Lee, J.J., *Ireland 1912–1985: Politics and Society* (Cambridge: Cambridge University Press, 1990).

Mac Lellan, A., 'The Penny Test: Tuberculin Testing and Paediatric Practice in Ireland, 1900–1960', in A. Mac Lellan and A. Mauger (eds), *Growing Pains: Childhood Illness in Ireland 1750–1950* (Dublin: Irish Academic Press, 2013), pp.123–41.

Mac Lellan, A., 'Victim or Vector: Tubercular Irish Nurses in England 1930–1960', in C. Cox and H. Marland (eds), *Migration, Health and Ethnicity in the Modern World* (Houndmills: Palgrave Macmillan, 2013).

Mac Lellan, A. and Mauger, A. (eds), *Growing Pains: Childhood Illness in Ireland, 1750–1950* (Dublin: Irish Academic Press, 2013).

Macardle, D., *Irish Republic* (Dublin: Irish Press, 1937).

Macardle, D., *The Unforeseen* (London: Peter Davies, 1945).

Martin, F.X., *The Howth Gun-Running and the Kilcoole Gun-Running 1914: Recollection and Documents* (Dublin: Browne and Nolan, 1964).

McCarthy, C., *Cumann na mBan and the Irish Revolution* (Cork: The Collins Press, 2005).

McDowell, R.B., *Alice Stopford Green: A Passionate Historian* (Dublin: Allen Figgis, 1967).

McKee, E., 'Church-State Relations and the Development of Irish Health Policy. The Mother-and-Child Scheme, 1944-53', *Irish Historical Studies*, 25, 98 (1986), pp.159–94.

Milne I., 'Through the Eyes of a Child: Spanish Influenza remembered by Survivors', in A. Mac Lellan and A. Mauger (eds), *Growing Pains: Childhood Illness in Ireland, 1750–1950* (Dublin: Irish Academic Press, 2013).

Mitchell, D., *A 'Peculiar' Place: the Adelaide Hospital, Dublin: Its Times, Places and Personalities, 1839–1989* (Dublin: Blackwater Press, 1989).

Molidor, J., 'Dying for Ireland: Violence, Silence and Sacrifice in Dorothy Macardle's Earth-Bound: Nine Stories of Ireland, 1924', *New Hibernia Review*, 12, 4 (Winter 2008), pp.1–2.

Niemi, M., *Public Health and Municipal Policy Making: Britain and Sweden, 1900–1940* (Aldershott and Burlington: Ashgate Publishing, 2007).

Ó Broin, L., *Dublin Castle and the 1916 Rising: the Story of Sir Matthew Nathan* (Dublin: Helicon, 1966).

Ó Broin, L., *Protestant Nationalists in Revolutionary Ireland: The Stopford Connection* (Dublin: Gill & Macmillan, 1985).

Ó hÓgartaigh, M., 'Dorothy Stopford-Price and the Elimination of Childhood Tuberculosis', in M. Ó hÓgartaigh (ed.), *Quiet Revolutionaries. Irish Women in Education, Medicine and Sport, 1861–1964* (Dublin: The History Press Ireland, 2011).

Ó hÓgartaigh, M., *Kathleen Lynn. Irishwoman, Patriot, Doctor* (Dublin and Portland: Irish Academic Press, 2006).

Parkes, S.M., 'Higher Education, 1793–1908', in W.E. Vaughan (ed.), *A New History of Ireland VI: Ireland under the Union 1870–1921* (Oxford: Oxford University Press, 2010).

Parkes, S.M., 'The "Steamboat Ladies", the First World War and After', in S.M. Parkes (ed.), *A Danger to the Men? A History of Women in Trinity College Dublin 1904–2004* (Dublin: The Lilliput Press, 2004).

Pihl, L. (ed.), *Signe Toksvig's Irish Diaries 1926–1937* (Dublin: The Lilliput Press, 1994).

Piper, L., *The Tragedy of Erskine Childers: Dangerous Waters* (London: Hambledon and London, 2003).

Porter, R., *The Greatest Benefit to Mankind: A Medical History of Humanity from Antiquity to the Present* (London: HarperCollins, 1999).

Price, D., *Tuberculosis in Childhood* (Bristol: Wrights, 1942, 1948).

Price, L., *Dorothy Price. An Account of Twenty Years' Fight against Tuberculosis in Ireland* (Oxford: Oxford University Press, 1957). For private circulation only.

Ramert, L., 'Lessons from the Land: Shaw's *John Bull's Other Island*', *New Hibernia Review*, 16, 3 (Autumn 2012), pp.43–59.

Robins, J., *Custom House People* (Dublin: Institute of Public Administration, 1993).

Rosenthal, S.R., 'Tuberculin Sensitivity and BCG Vaccination', in S.R. Rosenthal (ed.), *BCG Vaccine: Tuberculosis, Cancer* (Boston and New York: Little, Brown, 1980), pp.183–4.

Shuster, E., 'Fifty Years Later: the Significance of the Nuremburg Code', *New England Journal of Medicine*, 337, 220 (1997), pp.1437–40.

Smith, J.J., 'The Politics of Sexual Knowledge: The Origins of Ireland's Containment Culture and the Carrigan Report (1931)', *Journal of the History of Sexuality*, 13, 2 (April 2004), pp.208–33.

Smith, F.B., *The Retreat of Tuberculosis, 1850–1950* (London, New York and Sydney: Croom Helm, 1988).

Smith, N.C., *Dorothy Macardle: A Life* (Dublin: Woodfield Press, 2007).

Stephens, J., *Insurrection in Dublin* (Dublin and London: Maunsell, 1916).

Townshend, C., *Easter 1916: The Irish Rebellion* (London: Allen Lane, 2005).

Townshend, C., *The Republic: The Fight for Irish Independence* (London: Allen Lane, 2013).

Wagner, R., *Clemens von Pirquet: His Life and Work* (Baltimore: John Hopkins Press, 1968).

Wallgren, A. and Dahlstrom, G., 'The Intradermal Method', in S.R. Rosenthal (ed.), *BCG Vaccine: Tuberculosis, Cancer* (Littleton: PSG Publishing, 1980), pp.146–8.

Whyte, J., *Church & State in Modern Ireland 1923–1979* (Dublin: Gill & Macmillan, 1980).

Wills, C., *That Neutral Island: A Cultural History of Ireland during World War Two* (London: Faber and Faber, 2007).

## ELECTRONIC SOURCES

Dictionary of Irish Biography (http://dib.cambridge.org).

Dictionary of Australian Biography (http://adb.anu.edu.au).

The full text of the Carrigan Report (http://the-knitter.blogspot. ie/2005/06/full-carrigan-report_24.html).

Sidney Street Siege (http://content.met.police.uk/Article/The-Siege-of-Sidney-Street/1400015482933/historicalcases).

# INDEX